Strengthening Experiential Education: A New Era

Garry Hesser, General Editor
Augsburg College, MN

National Society for Experiential Education
Mt Royal, New Jersey
2014

Strengthening Experiential Education: A New Era

Garry Hesser, General Editor
Augsburg College, MN

TABLE OF CONTENTS

Strengthening Experiential Education: A New Era

INTRODUCTION

Garry Hesser, General Editor
Augsburg College, MN

In preparation for a sabbatical leave in 2010, I began to think about the upcoming 25th Anniversary of the publication of **_Strengthening Experiential Education Within Your Institution_** and just how formative and transformative that the book, its authors, and the FIPSE initiative had been, not only for experiential education, but for higher education overall. As the leadership of the National Society for Experiential Education [NSEE] prepared to celebrate its 40th Anniversary in 2011, they encouraged me to undertake a revision and recruit colleagues for this important task. Our charge was to update the original as a gift to our members and a resource for the wider K-16 educational community. I am deeply grateful for Augsburg College's support for this project, and for me personally and professionally, both through its sabbatical leave program and its long term support for experiential education which is at the heart of our mission and curriculum.

The NSEE Board made a very generous decision in the gift-giving spirit that has marked NSEE since its beginning. They gave the original as a "40th birthday gift" to our members and any others who wanted access to some of the best thinking about experiential education. A pdf copy of the original is posted on NSEE's website. This celebration of the 25th Anniversary of _Strengthening_ also initiated a year of celebrating NSEE's 40th year of existence in 2011.

As for the original, my colleagues and I, along with the Board, continue to believe that _Strengthening Experiential Education Within Your Institution_ (Kendall, 1986) stands the test of time as a classic. It remains both valuable and fundamentally valid to this day. We trust that you and others have found this gift useful, along with John Duley's essay that has become a Prologue to this revised 2nd edition. John was one of the original FIPSE consultants and authors of the 1st Edition, as was Sharon Rubin. Both John and Sharon continue to inspire, support, and challenge us in both personal and provocative ways as they add continuity to this updating. Their involvement in this revised edition helps to "bookend" the past with the present.

Our revision captures, we trust, most of the major developments in the field of experiential education and K-16 education over the past 25 plus years. It also includes a new chapter on Assessment by our longtime colleague and former NSEE Board member, Rob Shumer. Our insightful and generous authors include longstanding members, as well as

1

newcomers. We represent a wide range of professional experience, institutions and areas of expertise. David Moore, our NYU colleague, wrote an original chapter entitled "Theoretical Foundations for Experiential Education", but it became a central chapter in his new book, *Engaged Learning in the Academy: Challenges and Possibilities*, published by Palgrave Macmillan (2013). Unfortunately, that prevented it from being included in this revised edition. However, David's major thesis is found in the Epilogue where he underscores the critical importance of making experience educative through the sound practices advanced by NSEE and spelled out in this book, as well as in the original version. I recommend David's book and its theory chapter as a complement to this volume. His book also offers further augmentation of the claim that Jane Kendall, Jane Permaul, Sharon Rubin, Tom Little, John Duley and John Dewey were quite correct about the importance of experience in learning *when done effectively.*

This new edition embraces the original format. Each chapter title identifies a critical aspect of organization development and institution building. Hence, this revision can be seen as a "second edition." On the other hand, most of the chapters are major revisions, with each building upon ideas from the original. Another basic difference distinguishes these two editions. The original was an ongoing collaboration and the product of many meetings and exchanges among the five authors, with Jane Kendall drafting and integrating the various pieces that her colleagues produced. In this revision, each chapter was written by a separate author(s) who was selected based on a judgment about their expertise and experience in the field. Consequently, the final version of each chapter is the product of a dialogue between the author and editor. As a result each chapter can be used as a "stand-alone" resource if you are addressing any particular issue. However, like the original, this revision also provides you with a collage that systemically and comprehensively addresses institutionalization and strengthening experiential education.

Mary King's ongoing monitoring of sources and her leadership of NSEE's Experiential

Education Academy has helped me to be even more aware of the never ending stream of new organizations and collaborations. This current abundance further underscores that the National Society for Internships and Experiential Education [NSIEE], as NSEE was once known, and the authors of the original *Strengthening* were both prophets and contributors to a "sea change" in education. Each of the authors noted above has endeavored to retain and emphasize the strengths of the original chapter that they were charged to rewrite and update. In addition, we have also done our best to introduce you, our readers, to new developments, resources and allies. Each of the authors of this revision has devoted themselves to researching the landscape and sharing their own knowledge and experience with all of us. I trust that you will agree with me that we have been blessed by an insightful and exceptionally gracious collection of NSEE members who have given of their time and deep insights to craft and share their knowledge and wisdom as lifelong experiential learners and educators.

Dewey and NSIEE were right

The connection between learning and active engagement in society and community was fundamental to John Dewey and the founders of the National Society for Internships and Experiential Education [NSIEE], just as it was to Jefferson, Madison, Washington, Locke, Socrates, et al. Consequently, I think that all would be quite intrigued with the emerging consensus in K-16 education that stresses the interdependence between education and democracy. Dewey's stress on experience was grounded in the dialectic between one's previous experiences and the situation in which the learner finds herself or himself. This "continuity" and "interaction" underscores the bedrock and centrality of experience in the entire learning process.

NSEE, AAHE, AAC& U, Campus Compact, David Kolb, Peter Ewell, George Kuh, et al have led K-16 education to another Deweyian shift in our thinking about pedagogy, one that changes the emphasis from a teaching focus to learning itself, e.g., the "learning paradigm" (Tagg, 2003). Indeed, it appears that most educational theory and research now affirms John Dewey's focus on the critical importance of designing experiences that are "educative", i.e., result in learning. As early as 1916 Dewey insisted that

"we never educate directly, but only indirectly by means of the environment. Whether we permit chance environments to do the work, or whether we design environments for the purpose, makes a great difference".

Dewey laid the groundwork for the paradigm shift from teaching to learning, often referred to as "backward design". Dewey contended that we can call what we do "educative" only when there is evidence that the designed experiences, techniques, programs, or "projects", as he called them, lead to substantive learning. This involves the integration of past and present experiences which enables the learner to contribute to society and grow as a person. To put it another way, Dewey framed the issue well in *How We Think,* when he insisted that these "projects", namely, educational techniques and pedagogy, are *educative* when they generate interest, are worthwhile intrinsically, present problems that awaken new curiosity, create a demand for more information, and foster growth and development over time (1933). Similarly, the assessment movement, at its best, asks what John Duley, Urban Whitaker, and our other experiential education pioneers insisted upon when they, too, said: "show me the evidence for the learning if there is to be academic credit". You will find this discussed in greater detail in the new chapter 8 by Rob Shumer and Mary King's chapter 4 on quality.

NSIEE's Seminal and Collaborative Role

David Kolb, Dwight Giles, and Jane Kendall, along with other NSEE leaders and staff, played a seminal role in bringing educators back into a dialogue with Dewey. They, along with NSIEE's founders, contributed to the fundamental changes that have marked the educational enterprise since the early 1970's. *Strengthening Experiential Education* was a critical punctuation mark in the higher education enterprise when it appeared in 1986. As you read the original and this revised edition, try to envision just how far we have come. Experiential education and community-based pedagogy have moved from the margins into the very center of how the educational enterprise and pedagogy are framed today. Perhaps the most obvious evidence for that "movement to the center" is illustrated by the prominence that "high impact practices" and "backward design" have assumed in higher education overall. They have, indeed, taken center stage at AAC&U. NSEE's 2011 and 2012 keynote speakers, George Kuh on "high impact practices" and Peggy Maki on "backward design and assessment", underscored this shift and punctuated NSEE's role in the dominant discourse on effective teaching and learning.

Back in 1986, when *Strengthening Experiential Education* was published, Russ Edgerton and the American Association for Higher Education [AAHE] were the lead catalysts, colleagues and receptive contributors to the new and renewed focus on "effective educational practice" and "rethinking scholarship". Ernest Boyer, Donald Schoen, Helen and Alexander Astin, Parker Palmer, Lee Shulman, and Zee Gamson were other prominent voices and allies. The National Society for Internships and Experiential Education [NSIEE] also became an influential player, thanks to Jane Kendall and the FIPSE Consultants: John Duley, Jane Permaul, Sharon Rubin, and Tom Little. Joan Macala and Robert Sigmon led a very strong Board at that time. It included: William Burke, Barbara Baker, Richard Couto, Nadinne Cruz, Mary Gawlik, Keats Jarmon, Anne Kaplan, Marlyn Lawrentz, Marilynne Moyers, Rob Shumer, Pamela Smith, Louise Stone, and Urban Whitaker. Past Presidents and officers included James Case, John Duley, Tim Stanton, Jane Permaul, Steve Brooks, and David Moore, with Richard Ungerer, Sally Migliore and Michael Goldstein serving as staff and legal counsel for Jane Kendall and the Board. These colleagues and their supportive institutions are the "shoulders" on which all of us associated with NSEE and much of K-16 educational reform stand today.

AAC&U's LEAP Initiative and Kuh's "High Impact Practices"

More recently, the Association of American Colleges and Universities [AAC&U] has assumed AAHE's torch of pedagogical and educational reform. In January 2005, AAC&U undertook the Liberal Education and America's Promise initiative [LEAP; www.aacu.org/leap] with the aim of making the "aims and intended outcomes of liberal education the preferred framework for all students' college learning, whatever their background, career aspirations, or life circumstances". LEAP's emphasis on "essential learning outcomes", gained through "engagement, practice, active involvement, and demonstrated application*", are in close alignment with Dewey and our founders, again underscoring the claims of experiential educators that "Dewey was right" [see chapters 2 and 3 for greater elaboration].

As asserted earlier, the original 1986 edition of *Strengthening* was a forerunner, collaborator, and "seed planter" for this sea change in higher education which also has engaged the entire K-16 educational enterprise. AAC&U's promotion of Kuh's "High Impact Practices"

<www.aacu.org/leap/hip.cfm> is further evidence of the wide embrace of experiential education. Two other initiatives illustrate this shift: 1) "Bringing Theory to Practice" and its offspring [BTtoP; <http://aacu.org/bringing_theory>]; and 2) the "Symposium on Effective Practice". The latter was led by Richard Freeland and Clark University. Its proceedings and papers appear in the Fall, 2009, edition of *Liberal Education* and document how fundamental this change has become <http://www.aacu.org/liberaleducation/le-fa09/le-fa09_index.cfm>. Again, these developments closely correspond to the themes outlined in the 1986 edition of *Strengthening* and the experiential pedagogies which NSEE has supported and advocated from the beginning.

An Explosion of Attention to Citizenship, Civic Engagement, and Social Responsibility
In addition to the trends noted previously, Campus Compact has also played a seminal role since its founding in 1985 by the presidents of Brown, Georgetown and Stanford Universities and the president of the Education Commission of the States. Compact now has 1100 university and college presidents as members and 34 state Compact affiliates with a long history of collaboration with NSEE. The *Michigan Journal of Community Service Learning,* under the direction of founding editor, Jeff Howard, approaches its 20th year of publication [www.umich.edu/~mjcsl], as does the *Journal of Higher Education Outreach and Engagement* [www.jheoe.uga.edu]. Along with current NSEE professional development through the Experiential Education Academy (EEA; www.nsee.org) and Campus Compact endeavors (www.campuscompact.org), the experiential education net spreads ever more widely to embrace what our founding mothers and fathers seeded and tilled.

A few other examples illustrate this shift. In 2012 Merrimack College's Center for Engaged Democracy, led by Dan Butin, hosted its 3rd Annual Research Institute on Community Engagement. Tufts University, an early beneficiary of NSEE-FIPSE consulting 20 years ago, hosted a 2012 Summer Institute of Civic Studies, and these two institutions will co-host a 2013 conference on "The Future of Community Engagement". These endeavors, along with AAC&U's "Bringing Theory to Practice", further illustrate the current major emphases on civic engagement and community-based learning. As is elaborated in Chapter 3, BTtoP's mission underscores most of the central visions embraced and emphasized by our NSIEE founders:

> The mission of the BTtoP Project has, for the last decade, been to examine, understand, and encourage the interdependent relationships among engaged forms of higher learning, student well-being, civic development, and the initiating and sustaining of transformational changes in higher education (BTtoP website).

One final example reveals the "sea change" that NSIEE/NSEE helped to create, offering resources we can and should capitalize upon. On January 10, 2012, the White House hosted a major event focused on civic learning and democratic engagement. It highlighted the American Commonwealth Partnership [ACP], which is hosted by my own institution, Augsburg College, where the Center for Democracy and Citizenship is now located. Similar to NSEE's founders and the authors of *Strengthening,* ACP's focus is on the civic purpose of higher education [see chapter 3 and www.facebook.com/democracyu]. AAC&U and BTtoP took the lead in producing the *Crucible Moment* document, which was introduced at the White House and is also available on line. AAC&U, BTtoP, and most higher education associations are major players in this American Commonwealth Partnership. All of this activity underscores higher education's emphasis on "Civic Learning: Personal and Social Responsibility". This reality was highlighted in a May 1, 2012, report to AAC&U Presidents and members on civic learning developments:

> On January 10, 2012, at a White House gathering, the National Task Force on Civic Learning and Democratic Engagement (CLDE) released *A Crucible Moment*: *College Learning and Democracy's Future*, representing recommendations by educators and civic leaders across many constituencies…..
>
> In brief, *Crucible Moment* call[s] on higher education to reclaim its civic mission and to make civic learning at the college level expected rather than optional in both general education and college majors. (AAC&U website)

Conclusion

In summary, as is elaborated upon in chapters 1 and 3, the thesis and assumption underlying this revised edition is quite simple and straightforward. *There has been a "sea change" in higher education since the 1986 edition was published. NSEE contributed to and has benefitted immensely from those changes. And one corollary or consequence of this profound change is that experiential education professionals will be more effective in institutionalizing experiential education in their respective institutions and K-16 education overall <u>if we exploit the resources and legitimating</u> entities that currently exist and are emerging every day. Very few of us in 1986 were bold enough to predict the prominent place that experiential education would assume throughout the K-16 enterprise. Put simply, high impact learning practices, civic engagement, community-based learning and research, and classroom engagement are the new mantras in K-16 education. <u>**Experiential education has, indeed, moved to center stage. We are certainly in a new era, one requiring competent experiential education professionals "now more than ever".**</u>*

The good news is that everyone seems to be in 'our' game now, and we celebrate that reality, along with the involvement of NSEE in these changes. But, *equally important*, this new recognition and emphasis on "high impact", experiential pedagogy requires curricular design and ongoing formative assessment that consistently makes experience "educative" as Dewey underscored. High impact practices, without grounding in the solid practices long affirmed by NSEE, can be ineffective, if not miseducative. In that spirit we offer the reissue of the original and this updated and revised 2nd edition. My co-authors and I hope that this revised edition adds significantly to the many other NSEE resources you will consult and find useful in your growing collaborations in which you introduce and/or deepen the quality of learning that derives from the sound practices that NSEE has developed and espoused since its beginning.

References & Resources

Association of American Colleges and Universities. (2012). *A crucible moment*: *College learning and democracy's future*. Washington DC: AAC&U.

Association of American Colleges and Universities. (2007). *College learning for the new global century* (pdf). Washington, DC: AAC&U.

Bok, D. (1986). *Higher learning.* Cambridge, MA: Harvard University Press.

Boyer, E. (1996). The scholarship of engagement. *Journal of Public Outreach* 1,1, 11-20.

Boyer, E. (1990). *Scholarship reconsidered: Priorities of the professoriate.* Carnegie.

Boyer, E. (1987). *College: The undergraduate experience.* NY: Harper

Brooks, S., & Althof, J. (1979). *Enriching the liberal arts through experiential learning.* SF: Jossey-Bass.

Butin, D. (2010). *Service-learning in theory and practice: The future of community engagement in higher education.* Palgrave Macmillan.

Cross, K.P. & Steadman, H. (1996). *Classroom research: Implementing the scholarship of teaching.* SF: Jossey-Bass

Dewey, J. (1916). *Democracy and education.* NY: Macmillan.

Dewey, J. (1933 & 1910). *How we think.* Boston: Heath.

Edgerton, R. (1997). *Education White Paper.* Wash DC: Pew Forum on Undergraduate Learning

Eyler, J. (2009). The power of experiential education. *Liberal Education*, 95 (4), 22-26.

Eyler, J. & Giles, D. (1999). *Where's the learning in service-learning?* SF: Jossey-Bass.

Fitzgerald, H., Burack, C., & Seifer, S. (2010). *Handbook of engaged scholarship: Contemporary landscapes, future directions, institutional change, Vol 1. (Transformation in higher education).* East Lansing: Michigan State University Press.

Fitzgerald, H., Burack, C., & Seifer, S. (2010). *Handbook of engaged scholarship: Community-campus partnership, Vol 2. (Transformation in higher education).* East Lansing: Michigan State University Press.

Freeland, R. M. (2009). The Clark/AAC&U conference on liberal education and effective practice. *Liberal Education*, 95 (4), 3-7.

Freeland, R.M. (2009). Liberal education and effective practice: The Necessary Revolution in Undergraduate Education. *Liberal Education*, 95 (1), 4-8.

Harward, D.W. (2007). Engaged learning and the core purposes of liberal education: Bringing theory to practice. *Liberal Education*, 93 (1), 3-8.

Horton, M. & Freire, P. (1990). *We make the road by walking.* Philadelphia: Temple University Press.

7

Howard, J. (1994-present). *Michigan Journal of Community Service Learning.* Univ of MI.

Hutchings, P., Huber, M.T. & Ciccone, A. (2011). *The Scholarship of Teaching and Learning Reconsidered: Institutional Integration and Impact.* SF: Jossey-Bass [Wiley].

Hutchings, P. & Wutzdorff, A. (1988). *Knowing and doing: Learning through experience.* J-B.

Jacoby, B. (2009). (Ed). *Civic engagement in higher education: Concepts and practices.* San Francisco: Jossey-Bass.

Keeton, M. (1980). *Defining and assuring quality in experiential learning.* SF: Jossey-Bass.

Kendall, J., et al (1986). *Strengthening experiential education within your institution.* Raleigh: National Society for Internships and Experiential Education.

Kolb, D. (1984). *Experiential learning: Experience as the source of learning and development.* NJ: Prentice-Hall.

Kuh, G. (2008). *High-Impact Educational Practices: What They Are, Who Has Access to Them, and Why They Matter.* Washington, DC: AAC&U.

Levine, P. (2011). What do we know about civic engagement? *Liberal Education* 87, (2).

McKeachie, W. J. *Teaching Tips.* (8th Ed.) (1986) Lexington, Mass.: Heath.

McKinney, K. (2007). *Enhancing learning through the scholarship of teaching and learning: The challenges and joys of juggling.* SF: Jossey-Bass/Anker.

National Task Force on Civic Learning and Democratic Engagement. (2012). *A crucible moment: College learning and democracy's future.* Washington, DC: AAC&U.

Palmer, P. (1987). Community, conflict and ways of knowing. *Change Magazine,* 19 (5), 20-25.

Palmer, P., et al. (2010). *The heart of higher education: A call for renewal.* SF: Jossey-Bass.

Saltmarsh, J. & E. Zlotkowski (2011). *Higher education and democracy: Essays on service-learning and civic engagement.* Philadelphia: Temple University Press.

Saltmarsh, J. & Hartley, M. (2011). (Eds). *"To serve a larger purpose": Engagement for democracy and the transformation of higher education.* Philadelphia: Temple University Press.

Schneider, C.G. (2009). The Clark/AAC&U challenge: Connecting liberal education with real-world practice. *Liberal Education,* 95 (4), 2-3.

Shulman, L. (2002). *Making differences: A table of learning.* Palo Alto, CA: The Carnegie Foundation for the Advancement of Teaching.

Sigmon, R. (1996). *Journey to service-learning: Experiences from independent liberal arts colleges and universities.* Washington DC: Council of Independent Colleges.

Stanton, T. (1987). *Integrating public service with academic study: The faculty role.* A Report of Campus Compact: The Project for Public and Community Service. Providence, RI

Stoecker, R. (2012). *Research methods for community change: A project-based approach. (2nd Ed).* Sage.

Strand, K. (2003). Principles of best practice for community-based research. *Michigan Journal of Community Service Learning.* 9 (3), 5-15.

Tagg, J. (2003). *The Learning Paradigm College.* Bolton, MA: Anker

Thomas, D. & Brown, J. (2011). *A new culture of learning: Cultivating the imagination for a world of constant change.* Self-published.

Zlotkowski, E. (1996). *Successful service-learning programs: New models of excellence in higher education.* Bolton, MA: Anker.

Zlotkowski, E. (1996-2000) Service-Learning in the Disciplines Series [21 volumes]: AAHE.

Zlotkowski, E. (1996). Linking service-learning and the academy: A new voice at the table. *Change* (Jan-Feb)—see entire Disciplinary series edited by Zlotkowski, AAHE-Campus Compact

Author

GARRY HESSER is the Sabo Professor of Citizenship and Learning at Augsburg College in Minneapolis, MN where he teaches courses on Sociology, Community, Urban Sociology, Urban Planning, Religion and Society, Leadership, and Community-Based Research. He chaired the Metro-Urban Studies program for thirty years and was a Visiting Professor in Planning and Public Policy at the University of Minnesota [Humphrey School of Public Affairs]. In 2004, he was named the Carnegie-CASE Professor of the Year [Minnesota] and in 2002 was named the Distinguished Sociologist of Minnesota by the Sociologists of Minnesota. Garry received Campus Compact's Thomas Ehrlich Award in 1998 and was named a Pioneer by NSEE in 2001. Garry's Ph.D. is from the University of Notre Dame, following a B.A. from Phillips University and a M.Div. from Union Theological Seminary (NYC). He was president of the National Society for Experiential Education (NSEE) and the Higher Education Consortium for Urban Affairs (HECUA). As a member of the NSEE-Campus Compact-AAHE Consulting Corps, he has led workshops on experiential education and service-learning on over sixty campuses and at professional meetings. He is the author of *Experiential Education as a Liberating Art*; "Principles of Good Practice in Service-Learning"; "Examining Communities and Urban Change"; "Benefits and Educational Outcomes of Internships"; and co-editor of *Cultivating the Sociological Imagination: Concepts and Models for Service-Learning in Sociology.*

PROLOGUE

On the Occasion of the 40th Anniversary of the Founding of NSEE

REFLECTIONS ON THE PAST IN PREPARATION FOR THE FUTURE

John S. Duley
Emeritus Professor, Michigan State University

In 1967, the time of our birth as a movement, Marshall McLuhan wrote *The Medium is the Massage* (2001). He was not only a sage but a prophet. What he wrote then is as true today as the day he wrote it. He wrote,

> The young today live mythically and in depth. But (in the classroom) they encounter instruction in (which knowledge is) organized by means of classified information— subjects are un-related, they are visually conceived in terms of a blueprint....The student finds no means of involvement for himself and cannot discover how the educational scheme relates to his mythic world of electronically processed data and experience that his clear and direct responses report.

Many of our institutions suppress all the natural direct experience of youth, who respond with untaught delight on their iPods to the poetry and the beauty of the new technological environment, the environment of popular culture. It could be their door to all past achievement as an active (and not necessarily benign) force.

It is a matter of greatest importance that our educational institutions realize that we now have civil war among these environments created by media other than the printed word. The classroom is now in a vital struggle for survival with the immensely persuasive 'outside' world created by new informational media. <u>Education must shift from instruction, from imposing of stencils, to discovery</u>—to probing and exploration and to the recognition of the language of forms." (Emphasis mine.)

Experiential Education is learning by discovery: This is our legacy and our privileged position in education!

This is the challenge we face: to be faithful to our legacy and our privileged position in education. For this challenge we have two gifts: One from Bob Sigmon in his "Principles for Service," and the other from Lee Shulman in his paper, "Making a Difference; A Table of Learning" in which he introduces us to the "Pedagogies of Engagement." First to the gift of Bob Sigmon.

Bob Sigmon contributed his gift to us early in the history of our movement. His deep sensitivity to the nature of the learning that ought to take place on the part of all participants in any Service/Learning-Civic Engagement activity led him to describe principles which have become a central part of the developing Scholarship of Engagement Movement (see Frank Fear, 2006). This is a parallel movement to our own, and we need to be fully engaged with it. Its participants have come to the understanding that they and we, if we wish to be effective, cannot seek to do our service **for** others but **with** them, in dialogue and vulnerability. Those we seek to serve are not meant to be recipients of our services but invite us to join them as partners, to learn from them and with them in seeking to meet the needs that they and their organizations have identified. The purpose of Bob's principles is to help us understand and serve in this way.

Sigmon's Principles for Service.

In his instructive article, Robert Sigmon (1979) proposes three fundamental principles of service-learning projects. Elemental to these principles is Sigmon's position that learning grows from the service task(s), and that mutuality is an important dimension of learning. He instructs the reader about the importance of having an understanding of Robert Greenleaf's (*Servant Leader*) concept of *service* as it informs Sigmon's way of thinking about service: Serve in a way that care is taken to ensure that other people's highest priority needs are being served. Additionally, Sigmon's thinking is rooted in the belief that all persons are of unique worth, have gifts for sharing with others, have the right to understand and act on their own situations, and are dependent on each other for survival, e.g.., the more able and the less able being able to serve each other (p.62).

Sigmon differentiates between *acquirers* and *recipients* of services, *acquirers* being actively involved in the request for and control of service, self-analysis of the situation, and the selection of type of service and service provider (p.59). *Recipients* is an inappropriate word. It is too passive, implying a situation in which the persons are not involved in any way in determining what services will be provided, when, or by whom. Importantly, he notes that *acquirers* of services could also be those who provide services; those who oversee, manage, direct, or otherwise ensure that service is mobilized and brought to fruition; and, those who provide resources, e.g., policy makers. Such distinctions inform the foundations of these fundamental principles and, in turn, should determine how service-learning should be conducted and taught in academic institutions (7).

1. *Principle One:* **Those being served control the services(s) provided.**
   Does the service being provided make any sense to those expected to benefit from the services delivered?
   Who is being served by this activity?
   How are those to be served involved in stating the issue and carrying out the project?
   Who are the individuals who fill the roles in any service delivery activity? How do they relate to each other?

2. *Principle Two:* **Those being served become better able to serve and be served by their own actions.**
   Do those served grow as persons?
   Will they be better able to serve themselves and others because of it?
   Do they become healthier, wiser, freer, more autonomous, more likely themselves to become servants?
   What is the effect on the least privileged in society?
   Will they benefit? Will they not be further deprived?

3. *Principle Three:* **Those who serve also are learners and have significant control over what is expected to be learned.**

All the active partners in a service-learning experience are learners: those being served, the student, faculty, campus program coordinator, the community supervisor, those being served, policy makers, tech staff. Who in a given instance:
  Initiates the tasks?
  Defines the tasks?
  Approves the methods used in the tasks?
  Monitors the task activities?
  Determines when the task is completed satisfactorily?
  Benefits from the task being done?
  Decides that a server doing a task should be withdrawn from the work?
  Is the server responsible to in the community?
  Who owns the final product when the service is completed?

Now back to the challenge: "How to break through the educational lock-step system in which students learn to become professional students seeking credentials and not learning; psyching out what the professor wants from them in order to be granted an A or a 4.0 grade?" For McLuhan professionalism is environmental. Amateurism is anti-environmental. Student professionalism merges the individual into patterns of the institutional academic environment. Amateurism seeks the development of the total awareness of the individual and the critical awareness of the ground rules of society. The amateur can afford to lose. The professional student cannot. The professional tends to classify and specialize, to accept uncritically the ground rules of the environment. The ground rules provided by the mass response of his student colleagues, the academic system, and reinforced by some parents serve as a pervasive environment of which he or she is contentedly unaware. To become an amateur student is to become critically aware of the ground rules of the educational environment, live with them but not be controlled by them, and find the freedom to assume responsibility for one's own engaged learning.

Lee Shulman's taxonomy, "A Table of Learning"

For an answer to our challenge, I turn our attention to a more contemporary writer, **Lee Shulman,** who recently retired after productive tenure as President of the Carnegie Endowment for Teaching. In his article, "Making a Difference: A Table of Learning" (2002), he provides us with a valuable taxonomy for experiential learning to become a process of discovery. Shulman's discussion of this taxonomy begins with references to the work of Russ Edgerton, a former Education Officer of the Pew Charitable Trust and President of AAHE when *Strengthening Experiential Education* first appeared. Edgerton wrote a paper which has propelled, according to Shulman, many of the most interesting initiatives in higher education today. In this paper Dr. Edgerton coined the phrase "pedagogies of engagement" by which he meant "approaches that have within them the capacity to engage students actively with learning in new ways." Dr. Edgerton was writing about service/learning, but also about an array of approaches, from problem-based and project-based learning to varieties of collaborative work, and field based instruction. Edgerton used the rubric "pedagogies of engagement" to describe them all. In engagement the student taps into an interest, concern, idea, or social need which arouses his or her curiosity and leads to ownership. That is, it becomes his or her concern, need, interest, idea or recognized social need that he or she wants to do something about and not something the professor has imposed through a syllabus.

In Lee Shulman's taxonomy the point is that for effective learning to take place the student must be engaged. We need to learn how to work with students so their learning grows out of who they are and what they value. The taxonomy Dr. Shulman provides looks something like David Kolb's learning cycle, but I think it is significantly different.

Commitment	Engagement
Judgment	Understanding
Reflection	Action

In his learning model David Kolb used the flat, sterile language of objectivity, in keeping with the academic context: Concrete Experience, Observation and Reflection, Abstract Conceptualization, and Active Exploration, and thereby excluded the affective domain. Shulman incorporates the affective domain of learning by using words freighted with affective nuances:

Engagement is not just exposure to concrete experience, but *involvement* of a personal nature that involves the whole person in a way that may challenge one's values, which leads to,

Understanding is not just the acquiring of more data or information to be processed into abstract concepts, but something much broader—the student needs to do what she can to understand the context in which she is going to serve. She needs to go on the organization's website and learn what its purpose and mission is, to visit the agency, if possible, before showing up to serve, meet some of the people, and seek to understand their socio-economic situation. The faculty member needs to help her understand the context in which she will be serving.

Action involves a mutuality of collaboration based on the student's *understanding* of the needs of the agency and its participants following Bob Sigmon's principles of service.

Reflection is the kind of deep reflections that are called "soul searching"—what does this say about my life? About who I am? What I value? My world view? Which leads to

Judgment relates to our values and the direction in which we want our lives to go, what is important to us, and to what we want to commit ourselves and moves us to

Commitment is an act of the whole person, the giving of one's life to activities consistent with one's life experience.

An example of a service/learning experience that was an embodiment of Shulman's taxonomy is the 1965-68 Michigan State University and Rust College Student Tutorial Education Project (STEP), in Holly Springs, Mississippi. In 2007, 40 years after the project, a reunion was held of the MSU student and faculty volunteers. During that conference twelve of the students were interviewed about the impact of this experience on their lives and careers. Kay Snyder who participated in the project in 1965, is a professor of Sociology and Women's Studies at Indiana

State University in Indiana, Pennsylvania. The following excerpt from her interview indicates the extent of engagement she and the other students had coming into the project.

> "I was a participant in the 1965 STEP. I was very involved in the organizing and the fund raising that occurred before we went the first year. I was the social science coordinator that first year. There was a core group of students who knew director John Duley and the faculty members who were setting up the program. They involved us from the very early stages of the planning, so when I think how it was that this program had such an impact on my life, it was because we were working alongside of faculty who were committed to civil rights and for whom this was a very serious operation. You have to realize that the first year wasn't just fund raising; it was figuring out what we were going to teach, how we were going to teach it, how we were going to organize these students. None of us had done this before; none of us had been teachers. So it was working with faculty and being listened to that made us realize that we could do all of those things."

The interviews also indicated that the learning process for these students followed Lee Shulman's taxonomy: engagement, understanding, action, reflection, judgment and commitment. All ended up serving the common good—five as change agents, five as people who made the quality of life better for those they related with, and two who served the common good through their profession (Duley, 2011).

In the early days of the Service-Learning Movement we provided for this process of engagement (without consciously knowing that was what we were doing) through requiring students to find and secure their own field placements using CAHED (Creative Alternatives in Higher Education), a comprehensive resource of volunteer opportunities, national and international, provided by the Campus Ministry at Michigan State University. (Today this would not be needed, since we have Google.)   Once we approved their selection and they secured the placement, they participated in a preparation seminar which included being individually dropped off in small towns of 500 to 5,000 people and told to learn as much about that community as they could in six hours. When we picked them up for a debriefing they could not tell us what they had learned or how because they had a story to tell—about their survival. At the seminar meeting the next week we listed, on a flip chart, all of the methods they used to learn about their village. Then we gave them a list of the techniques used by sociologist and anthropologists in such studies. This process helped them realize they could take charge of their own education.

We also introduced them to the work of Harrison and Hopkins (1967) on the skills needed for successful Peace Corps performance and the work of George Klemp on "Skills Necessary for Superior Performance in the World of Work" (1977), which are not skills learned in the classroom. We instructed them to practice some of these skills during their placements, and provided them with a mechanism for reporting their use of them, indicating that these would become the basis of a final paper on what they learned through this experience. Through this and other processes they became "engaged"--the field study became theirs and not ours.

14

CONCLUSION

The point of this paper is that we are not simply dealing with concrete experiences from a limited, flat, cognitive perspective. Such a perspective leads only to new data which we turn into abstract concepts and then go actively looking for new concrete experiences. No! We are dealing with "Discovery" learning which is life transforming. It doesn't just add new data to our data base. If you do not believe this, learn it from some of the newly "engaged" scholars whose lives have been transformed by the use of the principles Bob Sigmon recommends. Read the book *Coming to Critical Engagement,* edited by Frank Fear (2006), which describes in detail the life-transforming experiences he and his three faculty colleagues had while they were doing what Experiential Learning is all about.

We need to reclaim our heritage!

References

Duley, J. (2011). Service learning and civic engagement as preparation for a life committed to working for the common good. Unpublished paper. Service Learning Archives, Michigan State University. East Lansing, MI, Web: http://servicelearning.msu.edu

Fear, F. (Ed.) (2006). *Coming to Critical Engagement.* Lanham, MD: University Press of America, Inc.

Harrison, R. and Hopkins, R. (1967). An alternative to the university model. *Journal of Applied Behavior Science,* 4.

Klemp, G. (1977). Three factors of success in the world of work: Implication for curricular development in higher education. A paper presented at Group 4 on "Are the Skills Related to Job Success Taught? Some research evidence." 32nd National Conference on Higher Education, AAHE, Chicago, Illinois, March 21.

Kolb, D. and Fry, R. (1975). Toward an applied theory of experiential learning. In Cary Cooper (Ed.). *Theories of group process.* London/New York: John Wiley & Sons.

McLuhan, M. and Fiore, Q. (2001) *The medium is the massage: An inventory of effects,* 1967, by Jerome Agel, 2001, Gingko Press Inc., Berkeley, CA, pp 92-93, 100

Shulman, L. (2002). Making a difference: A table of learning. *Change,* 34. 36-44.

Sigmon, R. (1979). Service learning: Three principles," *Synergist,* National Center for Service Learning.(Spring).

Author

JOHN DULEY is an Associate Professor Emeritus, Instructional Development Consultant, Office of Learning and Evaluation Services, Michigan State University.(MSU) He began his work as a Campus Minister, 1948-68, served as the Director of the MSU-Rust College Student Tutorial Education Project in Holly Springs, Mississippi, 1965-68, Assistant Professor, Director of Off-Campus Cross-Cultural Learning Program, Justin Morrill College, MSU, 1968-76. He was a member of the Founding Conference of the Society for Field Experience Education 1971 (SFEE), served as the Membership Chairman on the SFEE Steering Committee 1972-75, chaired and hosted the 2nd SFEE National Conference 1973 at MSU, and edited the Conference papers in the Jossey-Bass Journal, *New Directions in Higher Education*), "Implementing Field Experience Education" (Vol 2 No 2 Summer 1974). From 1979-85 he served on the Board of Trustees, National Society of Internships and Experiential Education (NSIEE), was President 1982-83. In 1978-82 he was Director of the CAEL-W.K.Kellogg Project LEARN in Michigan. John is the recipient of the 2001 MSU Outstanding Leadership in Community and Economic Development Award, the 2008 MSU Center for Service Learning and Civic Engagement "Outstanding Service-Learning Pioneer Award," the State of Michigan, Governor George Romney "Life Time Achievement Award for Volunteer Service," and in 2010 was named the NSEE Experiential Education Pioneer Award. Since 1982 he has been a Community Organizer.

Chapter 1

BUILDING EXPERIENTIAL EDUCATION INTO THE MISSION AND VALUES OF YOUR INSTITUTION: NEW CONTEXTS

Garry Hesser
Augsburg College
with assistance from Peter Gotlieb,
Saint Peter's University

Abstract

In addition to building your institution's experiential education into and upon the unique and often changing mission and values of your institution, this chapter urges readers to take full advantage of the wider and diverse cultural context of K-16 education, much of which has embraced engagement and experiential education. Experiential educators will be more effective if we also build upon the contributions of AAHE, Wingspread, AAC&U, Carnegie Foundation, Campus Compact, NERCHE, NSEE, et al. In addition, disciplinary associations increasingly are lending support to teaching experientially, embracing high-impact practices and engaged department strategies to further complement the "engaged institution" approaches brought into focus by Campus Compact and the American Commonwealth Project. The times and culture are indeed changing.

Outline
Taking Inventory of Your Institution
The Times They Are A'Changing
Context, Context: Building Experiential Education Upon and Within the Mission and
    Values Consensus That Now Exists
    -The K-16 "Consensus"
    - Disciplines and Professions
Integrating and Building EE into Your Institution's Values and Mission
Conclusion

Taking Inventory of Your Institution

In its original form, Jane Kendall and her colleagues designed this chapter to assist "faculty and administrators involved in experiential education to analyze the present status of experiential learning within their institutions as well as to assess their own roles. Several diagnostic instruments [were] presented [to assist you in assessing the] "value" [of experiential education] to the institution in different ways." (Kendall, 1986, p. 7)

When Peter Gotlieb and I initially reviewed the original chapter, we both concurred that its content and resources were still quite valuable for today. The examples and suggestions offered were based on a wide variety of different types of educational institutions where the original FIPSE consulting had taken place. The inventory forms and suggestions provided in the original are still very useful. The full text is available on the NSEE website. We recommend that you make use of the chapter and the inventory forms in your current work. An outline of the original chapter is found in Appendix A.

As you will note, the original chapter focused primarily on discerning the compatibility and congruence between experiential education, in its many forms, with the unique values and mission of a particular educational institution. Jane Kendall and her colleagues put it this way in the original chapter:

> When you can understand the cultural values of your own institution, you can understand not only how to help experiential learning become better institutionalized, but also how to express your own values about experiential learning more effectively.
>
> The issue of values is a complex one. In an article on "Values as the Core of Institutional Commitment: Finding a Common Ground," Jane Kendall [in an earlier article] points out that in addition to historic and administrative values, the institutional culture also incorporates the particular values of the faculty, the students, and in the case of experiential learning, the values of the field site supervisors as well. Although there are a number of ways in which these interested parties may seek a working balance among their values, there is no magic administrative structure, no magic model that will solve the problems of match between the values of experiential learning programs and the institution.
>
> Even when some consensus is reached, it does not necessarily hold. Organizations evolve through times as conditions change, and so must our values. A new president, a change in student demographics, a new business environment in the state, [a Presidential election or 9/11]…can all result in a change of direction for a campus. Experiential learning, if it is to stay vital and responsive to institutional needs and priorities, must always be seen in this complex cultural context….
>
> Despite the notion of a cultural context specific to each institution, we can generalize somewhat about the values that colleges and universities typically hold. The three-legged stool of teaching, research and community service is a familiar metaphor in higher education, although the varying lengths of the legs may make sitting on such a stool extremely precarious! A fourth and often unspoken value for any school is institutional stability and status. Any organization aims to maintain its own existence, and most colleges and universities are also aware of how they are perceived by the general public and by peer institutions in terms of their quality and overall prestige. The four priorities of teaching, research, community service and institutional stability and status vary, of course, from institution to institution. Yet there are ways in which experiential learning relates quite rapidly to each of these values. (Kendall, 1986, pp. 8-9)

The Times They Are A'Changing

Back in the 1980s, our colleague, John Duley, convinced many of us that "marginality was advantageous." In addition, Frank Newman, the President of the Education Commission of the States and former President of the University of Rhode Island, underscored the "marginality" of experiential education in a quote setting the tone of the original chapter in the 1986 edition:

> The faculty has been extremely negative. Not all faculty, of course, but the general reaction has been, 'This isn't any of our business. Students aren't here to get into these frivolous things like learning citizenship and becoming able to function in American society. Students are here to learn mathematics or sociology. That's why they come to my class.'...We have a major task on our hands to convince the faculties of this country that they've got to change their ways on this issue. I think it's absolutely at the core of our problems (quoted in original edition of *Strengthening*; Kendall, 1986, p. 49).

Few, if any, of us in 1986, were bold enough to predict the cultural and value shifts that have transpired in K-16 education, particularly the prominent place that experiential education has come to play as highlighted in the Introduction and chapter 3. High impact pedagogies, community-based learning and research, civic engagement and classroom engagement are now in vogue. As discussed throughout this new edition, there has, indeed, been a "sea change" in higher education since the 1986 edition was published. *And NSEE contributed to and has benefitted immensely from that change.*

A central claim of this revised chapter is captured in the subtitle: "new contexts". One corollary or consequence of this profound change is that you and I, as experiential education professionals, will be even more effective in increasing the quantity and quality of experiential education in our institutions if we acknowledge and affirm these wider cultural and value contexts in which our institutions function. In other words, it is essential and strategic for us to exploit these resources and legitimating entities that currently exist and are emerging with every day that passes.

I have not done a "content analysis" of current college catalogues, as K. Patricia Cross used to do. However, I have yet to see a catalogue or website of any college or university that does not highlight and promote its community engagement, service-learning, internships, international study and community-based learning. This is true for community colleges and premier research institutions, as well as every other institution in between, something you will find documented in every chapter in this revision. Our challenge, of course, is to operationalize these claims with experiential education of quality and substance, a theme that our colleagues advocate throughout this revision. And, fortunately for us, as we "walk this talk", *we have a very different context* and *consensus about mission and values* than existed for earlier professionals in the field.

Context, Context: Building Experiential Education Upon and Within the Mission and Values Consensus That Now Exists

The major point I wish to make is this. Your success in building experiential education into the mission and values of <u>your institution</u> requires you to be very mindful of <u>both</u> the uniqueness of your institution <u>and</u> the larger cultural and value contexts that now exist. You will find this reality elaborated in chapter 3 and throughout this new edition. On the one hand, there is certainly much to critique. The glass is certainly "half empty" when it comes to how fully this consensus is accepted and put into practice. Certainly there is a major amount of work and "walking the talk" that is needed in order to make the "mission and values" consensus a fuller reality in our own institutions and throughout K-16. On the other hand, as one whose teaching career began in the early 1970's, I daily celebrate that the glass is definitely half full. In other words, compared to the mid-1980s when *Strengthening* was first written, you and I have a very different cultural and values context and base in which we and our institutions operate. It is definitely a "new era".

Consequently, as you and I make use of the excellent strategies, suggestions and inventories available in the original chapter regarding the values and mission of our institutions, I suggest that we also broaden our horizons and scope to consider the larger systemic and institutional contexts within which K-16 education now functions. George Kuh, Dwight Giles, Patti Clayton and Peggy Maki did this for us convincingly in recent Annual NSEE Conference keynotes. Figure 1 is one way to visualize these new contexts:

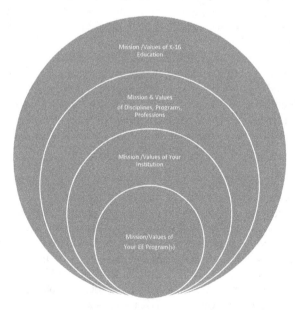

Figure 1: Mission, Values and Vision of Your EE Program in Context

The K-16 "Consensus". In chapter 3, "Increasing Faculty Involvement", you will find a much more detailed overview of the changes in the K-16 "Cultural and Values Context". There you will also find a discussion concerning many of the scholars and educators who were instrumental in bringing about these fundamental changes. Researchers and theorists like James Coleman, David Kolb, K. Patricia Cross, Zelda Gamson, Alexander and Helen Astin, Bill McKeachie, Richard Light, Howard Gardner, Robert Kegan, Steve Brookfield, Peter Ewell, Ernest Boyer, Lee Shulman, Gene Rice, Parker Palmer et al laid the groundwork. They, along with our own NSEE pioneers like Jane Kendall, John Duley, Bob Sigmon, Jane Permaul, Sharon Rubin, Tim Stanton, Dwight Giles, Dick Couto, David Moore, et al have provided us with a very different context for our work.

In addition to these individuals, many organizational entities have embraced theories and practices related to experiential learning. These include the American Association for Higher Education [AAHE], led by Russ Edgerton, the Carnegie Foundation for the Advancement of Teaching, Campus Compact [both national and state expressions], the Association of American Colleges and Universities [AAC&U], the Corporation for National and Community Service and NSEE, along with many others. They have literally and fundamentally reshaped the culture and values of K-16 education regarding the legitimacy and necessity of active learning, engagement and experiential education. Every chapter in this revision underscores and illustrates this reality, especially chapters 2, 3 and 4, each with further documentation in their Appendices.

As noted frequently throughout this revision of *Strengthening*, two examples illustrate this basic shift in the culture and values of K-16 and higher education overall. The Carnegie Foundation, led by Ernest Boyer and Gene Rice, coined the phrase and provided support and legitimacy for the "Scholarship of Engagement" (Boyer, 1996). In addition, under the leadership of Lee Shulman, the Carnegie Foundation created the "Engaged Campus Elective Classification" which has been sought and earned by over three hundred colleges and universities to date. Endeavors of substance like this have furthered the legitimation and institutionalization of experiential education and furthered the vision of NSEE's founders.

Parallel to, and in concert with the Carnegie Foundation, the American Association of Colleges and Universities [AAC&U], led by Carol Geary Schneider, has committed itself fully to four major initiatives: 1) Liberal Education and America's Promise [LEAP]; 2) Bringing Theory to Practice [BTtoP]; 3) Effective Practice; and 4) the American Commonwealth Partnership [ACP]. All of these are spelled out in the Introduction and chapter 3, with website access provided. Put simply, the current cultural and values milieu that exists today is a quantum leap from the context that fed Frank Newman's 1980's pessimism. Times were definitely different when our founders and Jane Kendall put together the FIPSE proposal that initially supported twenty campus consultations that led to the publication of *Strengthening* in 1986.

This "new era" in which we work is very much the result of NSEE's role as a significant player and collaborator over the years. Just how successful we will continue to be at building experiential education more deeply into the mission, values, and practices of K-

16 education is closely linked to two responses on our part: 1) our ability to see and activate the synergy among the supportive, overlapping, and changing cultural contexts, as is illustrated in Figure 1; and 2) our effectiveness in assisting our faculty colleagues in deepening student learning by means of the sound experiential pedagogical practices that are, and have been, espoused by NSEE and throughout the two editions of *Strengthening*. **In other words, this "new" emphasis on community-based pedagogies, engaged learning and high-impact practices provides experiential education both with greater legitimacy in the academy and underscores the need for competent experiential education professionals "now more than ever".**

As stressed in the Introduction, the good news is that the wider cultural milieu, including our own institutions, embraces "high impact", experiential pedagogy. But, *equally important*, this cultural shift that embraces experiential education calls for and requires curricular design and ongoing formative assessment that consistently makes experience "educative" as Dewey underscored. High impact practices, without being grounded in the solid practices long affirmed by NSEE, can be ineffective, if not miseducative. *Yes, skilled experiential education professionals are all the more essential if learning is to be derived from the high impact practices now being identified and recommended.*

My co-authors and I hope that this revised edition, along with the Experiential Educational Academy [EEA] and our many other NSEE resources, will be of value in your work and growth as a professional. We trust they will assist you in your expanding collaborations in which you introduce and/or deepen the quality of learning that derives from the effective practices that NSEE has developed and espoused since its beginning.

Disciplines and Professions. Almost every observer of higher education emphasizes the influence and power of disciplinary thinking and the associations that advance each particular discipline and profession. Their purview includes not only what is studied, but how they socialize, support and integrate members into that disciplinary and professional community, Over the last few decades, the Faculty Development network [POD] and Carnegie's support of the Scholarship of Teaching and Learning [SoTL] have emerged. Together, they have played major roles in shifting the emphasis to "learning outcomes", including how experiential pedagogies offer "high impacts", regardless of which discipline. In addition, Lee Shulman and the Carnegie Foundation have also stressed the importance of developing competence related to the teaching of specific subjects and disciplines (Shulman, 2003). For greater elaboration peruse the Introduction and chapters 2, 3 & 4 and strategize on additional ways that you can collaborate with and support these endeavors in your own institution.

In that context, and with the significance of academic disciplines fully in focus, Ed Zlotkowski, a former NSEE Board member, undertook to address and change the "values and mission" of the disciplinary context within which you and I do our work. With the full support of Russ Edgerton and AAHE, Ed set out to impact all of higher education through and with disciplinary collaboration. Ed embraced and took full advantage of the overall changes in thinking about teaching and learning and the role of "engagement", active learning, service-learning and community-based learning. With a prophetic vision and great persistence, he drew the disciplines into the mix, working closely with many disciplinary associations, resulting in a major contribution that persists to this day (Zlotkowski, 1996b).

Operating on two levels, Ed recruited scholars from within a wide range of disciplines. He and his disciplinary sources identified respected scholars and teachers who had solid standing and respect in their respective disciplines. In addition, he went further, actively courting and convincing the professional associations of each discipline to collaborate and co-sponsor the specific volume related to their respective discipline. The result was twenty-one volumes of *Service-Learning in the Disciplines,* published and widely promoted by AAHE during the late 1990s and early 2000s. They are still in print and would enhance any library collection or resource library (Zlotkowski, 1996-2000).

Each monograph in this 21 volume series was built upon co-sponsorship and collaboration with each respective disciplinary association. This further linked disciplinary norms and values to the work of scholars and teachers from within that discipine. To accomplish this, Zlotkowski recruited both individual scholars and the disciplinary professional associations in order to further influence the shift to effective teaching and learning particular to each discipline. For example, the Sociology monograph that I was privileged to author and edit with James Ostrow and Sandra Enos, *Cultivating the Sociological Imagination: Concepts and Models for Service-Learning in Sociology,* proclaims conspicuously on its front cover: "Published in cooperation with American Sociological Association" (Ostrow, Hesser, Enos, 1999).

Similarly, Kerrissa Heffernan and Campus Compact identified quality syllabi and courses that incorporate experiential education. Virtually every discipline is represented, and they are available on Campus Compact's website. Note that the syllabi are arranged by discipline and futher reinforce Shulman's emphasis on pedagogy that is also discipline specific (Heffernan, 2001). Campus Compact has also developed Engaged Department workshops and materials that expand disciplinary thinking and practice, as is described in Appendix B (Battistoni. 2003). The engaged department approach builds upon and complements the rich collection of course syllabi and work that Zlotkowski, AAHE and NSEE initiated and have supported (www.campuscompact.org).

In addition, John Saltmarsh and Dwight Giles at the New England Resource Center for Higher Education [NERCHE], which is housed at the University of Massachusets Boston, continue collaborations begun under the leadership of Zelda Gamson. Zelda was the co-author of the *Wingspread Principles* and a NSEE Board member in the 1990's. And Dwight has served NSEE in leadership roles for three decades. Another recent illustration is seen in the prominent headlines and disciplinary support that 19 different academic departments at the University Minnesota received for designing and carrying out graduate level community-based reseach to serve the interests and address the questions and needs of communities in the Twin Cities [Minnesota].

Further examples illustrating these trends can be found in Dan Butin and Merrimack College's 4th Annual summer institute on commmunity engagement. In 2012 it was offered in collaboration with Tufts University's Tisch College of Citizenship and Public Service in 2012. In addition, chapter three elaborates on Carnegie and Boyer's *Scholarship Reconsidered,* which spawned the Scholarship of Teaching and Learning [SoTL] and Faculty Development/Professional and Organizational Development [POD]. Yes, "the times they are a'changin", within the disciplines and throughout the academy.

Integrating and Building EE into Your Institution's Values and Mission

Ed Zlotkowski and the leadership of NSEE, AAHE, AAC&U, Compact, et al, knew full well that the work of turning rhetoric and the "stated values and mission" into reality is easier said than done. The original authors of *Strengthening Experiential Education Within Your Institution* knew that as well. Consequently, Ed complemented his 21 volume series with another book which consists of a dozen case studies, published under the title, *Successful Service-Learning Programs: New Models of Excellence in Higher Education* (1996). Each chapter is a case study that explicitly illustrates how each specific college or university has created and built successful, and fully integrated, experiential education programs upon and into their unique mission and values. I also recommend Ed's book to you as you do your own work utilizing this new edition of *Strengthening* as well as the original.

In addition to the trends noted previously, the *Michigan Journal of Community Service Learning,* under the direction of founding editor, Jeff Howard, approaches its 20th year of publication [www.umich.edu/~mjcsl], as does the *Journal of Higher Education Outreach and Engagement* [www.jheoe.uga.edu]. Every issue of these journals further illustrates and contributes to the new era in which we operate.

Finally, note that the first edition of *Strengthening* was punctuated with examples and case studies of institutions that successfully built their varied forms of experiential education into and upon their respective espoused mission and values. As an updating complement, this new edition also provides you with additional case studies of institutions like Metro State, Purdue University Calumet, Lesley, St. Cloud State, Elon, Ramapo and others.

Conclusion

To conclude this brief expansion and update of chapter 1, I invite you to revisit the original chapter and think of your work along the lines of Figure 2 below, seeing the work that you and your colleagues are doing as at the center of the Venn diagram. At any given moment in time, your ecological realities are embedded in at least three sets of cultural and value contexts. Each domain or "circle" can validate, challenge, or be neutral for your efforts to create or maintain quality experiential education endeavors. It is also very helpful to remember Jane Kendall's sage advice quoted above:

> Organizations evolve through times as conditions change, and so must our values. A new president, a change in student demographics, a new business environment in the state [an election]...can all result in a change of direction for a campus.

Experiential learning, if it is to stay vital and responsive to institutional needs and priorities, must always be seen in this complex cultural context.... (Kendall, 1986, p. 8).

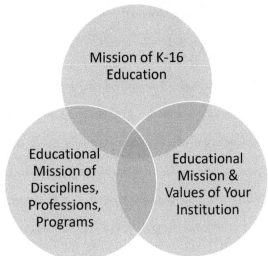

Figure 2: Interrelatedness of Dimensions/Levels of Mission and Vision

As you pursue your institutionalization objectives, I trust and hope that you will find these ideas helpful, along with the original chapter and its inventories. All of the chapters that follow, including their case studies, should further expand and complement your efforts. I encourage you to take advantage of all that NSEE, AAHE, AAC&U, Carnegie, Compact and others have created and now offer as resources and validation for your work in your own educational setting. And remember, much of this change and these new values and cultural contexts are due in many ways to NSEE and our colleagues over the years, including those who have contributed to this new edition. Experiential education professionals are needed now, more than ever, if K-16 education is going to take learning to the next promising level. So, let us all exercise our agency and creativity as we educate and are educated by those with whom we engage. Best wishes.

References & Resources

Association of American Colleges and Universities. (2012). *A crucible moment: College learning and democracy's future.* Washington DC: AAC&U.

Association of American Colleges and Universities. (2007). *College learning for the new global century* (pdf). Washington, DC: AAC&U.

Battistoni, R. et al. (2003). *The engaged department toolkit.* Providence, RI: Campus Compact.

Bok, D. (1986). *Higher learning.* Cambridge, MA: Harvard University Press.

Boyer, E. (1996). The scholarship of engagement. *Journal of Public Outreach* 1,1,11-20.

Boyer, E. (1990). *Scholarship reconsidered: Priorities of the professoriate.* Carnegie.

Boyer, E. (1987). *College: The undergraduate experience.* NY: Harper.

Brooks, S., & Althof, J. (1979). *Enriching the liberal arts through experiential learning.* SF: Jossey-Bass.

Butin, D. (2010). *Service-learning in theory and practice: The future of community engagement in higher education.* Palgrave Macmillan.

Cross, K.P. & Steadman, H. (1996). *Classroom research: Implementing the scholarship of teaching.* SF: Jossey-Bass.

Dewey, J. (1916). *Democracy and education.* NY: Macmillan.

Dewey, J. (1933 & 1910). *How we think.* Boston: Heath.

Edgerton, R. (1997). *Education White Paper.* Washington DC: Pew Forum on Learning.

Eyler, J. (2009). The power of experiential education. *Liberal Education,* 95 (4), 22-26.

Eyler, J. & Giles, D. (1999). *Where's the learning in service-learning?* SF: Jossey-Bass.

Fitzgerald, H., Burack, C., & Seifer, S. (2010). *Handbook of engaged scholarship: Contemporary landscapes, future directions, institutional change, Vol 1. (Transformation in higher education).* East Lansing: Michigan State University Press.

Fitzgerald, H., Burack, C., & Seifer, S. (2010). *Handbook of engaged scholarship: Community-campus partnership, Vol 2. (Transformation in higher education).* East Lansing: Michigan State University Press.

Freeland, R. M. (2009). The Clark/AAC&U conference on liberal education and effective practice. *Liberal Education*, 95 (4), 3-7.

Freeland, R.M. (2009). Liberal education and effective practice: The Necessary Revolution in Undergraduate Education. *Liberal Education*, 95 (1), 4-8.

Harward, D.W. (2007). Engaged learning and the core purposes of liberal education: Bringing theory to practice. *Liberal Education*, 93 (1), 3-8.

Heffernan, K. (2001). *Fundamentals of service-learning course construction.* Campus Compact

Horton, M. & Freire, P. (1990). *We make the road by walking.* Philadelphia: Temple University Press.

Howard, J. (1994-present). *Michigan Journal of Community Service Learning.* University of Michigan.

Hutchings, P., Huber, M.T. & Ciccone, A. (2011). *The Scholarship of Teaching and Learning Reconsidered: Institutional Integration and Impact.* SF: Jossey-Bass [Wiley].

Hutchings, P., & Wutzdorff, A., (1988). *Knowing and doing.* San Francisco: Jossey-Bass.

Jacoby, B. (2009). (Ed). *Civic engagement in higher education: Concepts and practices.* San Francisco: Jossey-Bass.

Keeton, M. (1980). *Defining and assuring quality in experiential learning.* SF: Jossey-Bass.

Kendall, J., et al (1986). *Strengthening experiential education within your institution.* Raleigh: National Society for Internships and Experiential Education.

Kolb, D. (1984). *Experiential learning: Experience as the source of learning and development.* NJ: Prentice-Hall.

Kuh, G. (2008). *High-Impact Educational Practices: What They Are, Who Has Access to Them, and Why They Matter.* Washington, DC: AAC&U.

Levine, P. (2011). What do we know about civic engagement? *Liberal Education* 87, (2).

McKeachie, W. J. *Teaching Tips.* (8th Ed.) (1986) Lexington, Mass.: Heath.

McKinney, K. (2007). *Enhancing learning through the scholarship of teaching and learning: The challenges and joys of juggling.* SF: Jossey-Bass/Anker.

National Task Force on Civic Learning and Democratic Engagement. (2012). *A crucible moment: College learning and democracy's future.* Washington, DC: AAC&U.

Ostrow, J., Hesser, G., Enos, S. (1999). *Cultivating the sociological imagination.* Wash DC: AAHE.

Palmer, P. (1987). Community, conflict and ways of knowing. *Change Magazine,* 19 (5), 20-25.

Palmer, P., et al. (2010). *The heart of higher education: A call for renewal.* SF: Jossey-Bass.

Saltmarsh, J. & E. Zlotkowski (2011). *Higher education and democracy: Essays on service-learning and civic engagement.* Philadelphia: Temple University Press.

Saltmarsh, J. & Hartley, M. (2011). (Eds). *"To serve a larger purpose": Engagement for democracy and the transformation of higher education.* Philadelphia: Temple University Press.

Schneider, C.G. (2009). The Clark/AAC&U challenge: Connecting liberal education with real-world practice. *Liberal Education,* 95 (4), 2-3.

Senge, P. et al. (2004). *Presence: Human purpose and field of the future.* NY: Crown

Shulman, L. (2002). *Making differences: A table of learning.* Palo Alto, CA: The Carnegie Foundation for the Advancement of Teaching.

Sigmon, R. (1996). *Journey to service-learning: Experiences from independent liberal arts colleges and universities.* Washington DC: Council of Independent Colleges.

Stanton, T. (1987). *Integrating public service with academic study: The faculty role.* A Report of Campus Compact: The Project for Public and Community Service. Providence, RI

Stoecker, R. (2012). *Research methods for community change: A project-based approach.* (2nd Ed). Sage.

Strand, K. (2003). Principles of best practice for community-based research. *Michigan Journal of Community Service Learning.* 9 (3), 5-15.

Tagg, J. (2003). *The Learning Paradigm College.* Bolton, MA: Anker

Thomas, D. & Brown, J. (2011). *A new culture of learning: Cultivating the imagination for a world of constant change.* Publisher unknown

Zlotkowski, E. (1996a). *Successful Service-Learning Programs: New Models of Excellence in Higher Education.* Bolton, MA: Anker.

Zlotkowski, E. (1996-2000) Service-Learning in the Disciplines Series. 21 volumes, AAHE-Campus Compact

Zlotkowski, E. (1996b). Linking service-learning and the academy: A new voice at the table. *Change* (Jan-Feb)—see entire Disciplinary series edited by Zlotkowski, AAHE-Campus Compact

Appendix A

Building Experiential Education into the Mission and Values of Your Institution, 1st Edition

Why Is It Important for Experiential Education to Be Connected to the Values and Mission of Your Institution?
What Are the Most Common Values and Missions of Colleges and Universities, and What Does Experiential Education Contribute to Them?
1. Teaching
2. Research
3. Public/Community Service & Citizenship
4. Institutional Stability and Status

Why Experiential Education?
Analyzing the Values of Your Institution
Is Experiential Education Consistent with the Values of Your Institution?
Teaching and Experiential Learning Values
Identifying Student-Centeredness in Learning
Is Experiential Education Valued and Recognized at Your Institution?
How Much is Experiential Learning Used at Your Institution?
Is the Role of the Experiential Educator Valued Within Your Institution?
Assessing the Value of the Experiential Educator to the Department or Institution
Articulating the Contribution of Experiential Education to the Mission and Values of Your Institution

Appendix B

ENGAGED DEPARTMENTS & THE SCHOLARSHIP OF ENGAGEMENT
"How can service-learning [civic engagement] enhance subject matter learning?"

(Eyler & Giles, 1999)

Description/definition/assumptions:

-*Academic departments* approach civic engagement and community-based learning with their academic department as a unit of engagement and change.

-Subject matter learning is still largely the province of disciplines.

-Disciplines function largely through academic departments.

-Effective teaching and learning makes extensive use of application and experience, and applying established concepts to new situations (Ewell, 1997).

-Boyer-Rice's expansion of scholarship embraces and legitimizes the "scholarship of engagement" (2003).

Engaged academic departments (Battistoni, et al, 2003):

(1) assess their full curriculum developmentally, epistemologically and pedagogically;

(2) develop strategies to include community-based work in both their teaching and their scholarship;

(3) analyze various models for integrating service-learning, community-based research, and other kinds of civic engagement into undergraduate and graduate curricula;

(4) develop a level of unit coherence that will allow them to model civic engagement and progressive change at the department level; and

(5) develop and maintain strategies and infrastructure for deepening or expanding partnerships and integrating civic engagement more coherently throughout their academic programs.

ENGAGED DEPARTMENTS focus upon:

1) Unit/departmental responsibility for engagement-related initiatives;

2) Departmental agreement on the concepts and terminology that allow faculty to explore the dimensions of engaged work most effectively;

3) Departmental agreement on how best to document, evaluate, and communicate the significance of engaged work; and

4) Strategies for deepening the department's community partnerships.

(Battistoni, et al, *The Engaged Department Toolkit,* 2003, Campus Compact)

5) Integrating a range of service-learning/community-based learning and research throughout the curriculum and overall requirements for the major. (Heffernan, 2001, Campus Compact; (www.campuscompact.org).

Authors

GARRY HESSER is the Sabo Professor of Citizenship and Learning at Augsburg College in Minneapolis, MN where he teaches courses on Community, Urban Sociology, Urban Planning, Religion and Society, Creativity, and Community-Based Research. He chaired the Metro-Urban Studies program for thirty years and was a Visiting Professor in Planning and Public Policy at the University of Minnesota [Humphrey School]. In 2004, he was named the Carnegie-CASE Professor of the Year [Minnesota] and in 2002 was named the Distinguished Sociologist of Minnesota by the Sociologists of Minnesota. Garry received Campus Compact's Thomas Ehrlich Award in 1998 and was named a Pioneer by NSEE in 2001. Garry's Ph.D. is from the University of Notre Dame, following a B.A. from Phillips University and a M.Div. from Union Theological Seminary (NYC). He was president of the National Society for Experiential Education (NSEE) and the Higher Education Consortium for Urban Affairs (HECUA). As a member of the NSEE-Campus Compact-AAHE Consulting Corps, he has led workshops on service-learning and experiential education on over sixty campuses and at professional meetings. He is the author of *Experiential Education as a Liberating Art*; "Principles of Good Practice in Service-Learning"; "Examining Communities and Urban Change"; "Benefits and Educational Outcomes of Internships"; and co-editor of *Cultivating the Sociological Imagination: Concepts and Models for Service-Learning in Sociology.*

PETER M. GOTLIEB is Associate Dean for Experiential Learning & Career Services and founding Director of the Cooperative Education & Internship Program at Saint Peter's University and has over 35 years of experience in the field of Experiential Education. He has served on the Boards of both the National Society for Experiential Education and the Cooperative Education & Internship Association and worked as a consultant for more than 30 colleges and universities, helping them establish and/or strengthen their Experiential Education programs. A regular workshop presenter, Peter has published articles in field of Experiential Education, and served as a member of the Editorials Boards of both the NASPA Journal and the Journal of Cooperative Education. In 2007 he was named the NSEE's Pioneer of the Year Award recipient for his contributions to the field, over the course of his long career. Peter has served also as an Evaluator for the Middle States Commission on Higher Education. He has participated as a member of the visiting team at several post-secondary institutions seeking reaccreditation. Peter earned an Ed.D. from Teachers College, Columbia University in the field of Higher & Adult Education with a concentration in Student Personnel Administration, following a Master's in Slavic Languages and Literatures from UCLA and an A.B. in Russian from the University of Pennsylvania.

Chapter 2
INTEGRATING EXPERIENTIAL EDUCATION INTO THE CURRICULUM

Roseanna Ross
St. Cloud State University, Minnesota
Beth J. Sheehan
Southern New Hampshire University

Abstract
Nothing is more critical to the legitimization of experiential education than curriculum integration. However, despite a rather strong consensus among educators and researchers about the need for experiential education in effective teaching and learning, integration remains a challenge. In the last decade and currently, the American Association for Colleges and Universities LEAP initiative and outreach have clearly identified "Essential Learning Outcomes" and "High Impact Practices" (2010), concluding that educational approaches that emphasize application and experience are most effective. Likewise, insights from research in cognitive science reveal pedagogical approaches that support active learning--learning in which students actively and uniquely create their learning--are the most effective (Ewell, 1997). This chapter provides insight into the issues and important questions that must be addressed to make integration possible at your institution. Expanding the timely and timeless conversation first introduced by the authors of the original "Strengthening," Ross and Sheehan retain critical pieces from the original, explore developments in this arena, offer personal insights and practical strategies, examples and worksheets that will help the reader successfully engage in the process of integration.

32

Introduction: A Personal Perspective

Developing a Program: Communication Studies Department at St. Cloud State University, St. Cloud, MN.

In 1984 when I was given the title "Internship Director" and was asked to develop an internship program for the Communication Studies department, I had no idea of where to look for guidance. I had always been engaged in active and applied learning activities, so I had a 'gut' response that there was a 'fit,' but even I was a little surprised that credited internships took place in areas other than medicine and law. St. Cloud State (SCSU) had a decentralized approach to experiential learning; every department/academic program handled its internships, study abroad, service-learning differently—and practices were all over the map. No such thing as 'best practice' had hit experiential learning at SCSU. Prior to this assignment, our department had created a course number and basic description; the department chairperson assisted the handful of students who interned. Not all faculty were supportive of internships, and among those who did agree to their practical value, there were those who questioned their academic value. I still recall the faculty discussion following my advocating for the credits to be counted to meet major requirements. One colleague responded that internships "do not belong at a 4-year university and are best suited for the technical college." Others supported having the course in the program but noted that we couldn't have students potentially substituting internship credits for one of our 'real' courses in their program. In addition, unlike disciplines like accounting or counseling, my own discipline has a broad range of possible internship activities, e.g. management, sales, training, government lobbying, public relations, human resources. I was simply quite confused, frustrated and befuddled as to how one could fairly assess what students were learning.

My continuing search for resources brought me to the National Society for Experiential Education (NSEE) and the original edition of "Strengthening." Again, my 'gut' thoughts and intuitive-based strategies were substantiated, supported by research, and expanded. Everything I needed to know to build a strong foundation for our internship program was there. And the arguments and rationale for supporting the validity of credited internships within an undergraduate program were clearly articulated for me to use in support.

Thirteen years later I found myself using the same arguments and same theoretical foundations to build the seminar for my study abroad program. A learning agreement prior to an education abroad experience? Whoever heard of such a thing! When I identified that education abroad was experiential learning, then it became evident that education abroad needed to be structured around best practice for student-directed learning. Soon after, I was involved with service-learning, and the process began again. And later, as the Director of our Faculty Center for Teaching Excellence, I was again advocating for, and supporting faculty in their efforts to integrate experiential learning into their programs. My copy of "Strengthening" is well worn.

The credibility of these experiences as 'learning experiences' was, and still is, built on a strong foundation of best practice for experiential learning. Each of these diverse experiential learning opportunities that I was and am engaged with at SCSU is designed such that: 1. The activity is integrated into the curriculum as part of/or accompanied by a credited course which is part of the teaching faculty's teaching load and which counts toward a major or minor program; 2. Students are required to create clearly articulated learning goals for the experience; 3. Reflection activities are structured to accompany the experience; 4. Final projects/presentations/portfolios are graded as evidence of the student's achievement of their learning goals. I invite you to consider these and other strategies of integration as you read through this and other chapters.

I felt honored to be asked to contribute to this chapter of the revised edition. But what struck me most as I leafed through those yellowed and torn pages of my copy of "Strengthening" was how much of what was in the original edition still spoke to the challenges of experiential educators today. Yes, there have been continuing developments in the field, but the foundation for those developments is strongly built on the work of these early pioneers.

My coauthor, Beth Sheehan, and I have retained the best of what was in this original chapter, knowing that it is sound and effective. What we have endeavored to do is engage the original with the parts of the ongoing conversation about experiential education that have unfolded since "Strengthening" was first written, many of which we have been privileged to be a part of (Inkster and Ross, 1998, 1995; Ross, 2000; Ross, 2000; Ross and Montrose, 2001, Sheehan, McDonald, and Spence, 2009; Sheehan and McDonald, 2011; Spence, Hess, McDonald & Sheehan, 2009). This is not only an updating/revision of the book but also a celebration of a seminal work.

--Roseanna

Working with Experiential Learning at Southern New Hampshire University.

I began my tenure at Southern New Hampshire University (SNHU) in 2005 knowing that the institution embraced experiential learning. As a result, I initiated conversations around my research and knowledge of experiential learning not only with faculty in my own department, but also faculty on the general education committee on which I served, and with administration in academic affairs. Through these conversations I learned that most shared a belief that students at our institution are "hands-on" learners and that we need to integrate more experiential learning opportunities. What integration means and how best to accomplish this however was not clear. Therefore, collaborating with Roseanna on this chapter was not just an honor but also a tremendous value as I work toward influencing the integration of experiential learning on the campus of SNHU.

--Beth

Why Is Integration Important?

Perhaps the single most compelling reason why experiential education should be integrated into the curriculum is simply that a rather strong consensus about effective teaching and learning among educators and researchers now exists that supports the need for experiential education. Dewey (1938), Kolb (1984), Chickering and Gamson (1987), Kendall (1986), Cross (1998) and Ewell (1997) were among many who laid the foundation. In the last decade and currently, the American Association for Colleges and Universities LEAP initiative and outreach have clearly identified "Essential Learning Outcomes" and the "High Impact Practices" (2010), concluding that teaching approaches that emphasize application and experience are most effective. Likewise, insights from research in cognitive science reveal pedagogical approaches that support active learning--learning in which students actively and uniquely create their learning--are the most effective (Ewell, 1997). In other words, the research related to effective teaching and learning that has appeared since 1986 underscores that experiential education is a "necessary though not sufficient" pedagogy for all levels of education. The research is clear—namely, that experiential education provides a structure and pedagogy that offers "high impact" leading to the deeper and integrated outcomes that we identify as worthy of academic credit. Therefore, integration is important because experiential education provides a structure to facilitate the best practices in teaching and learning that we know are impactful.

Despite such overwhelming consensus in the literature, experiential education at many institutions still remains on the periphery of the curriculum and on the periphery of what is meant by learning and education. On many campuses students do engage in experiential education but as a free elective. Although many faculty increasingly incorporate experiential education into their majors, it is not the norm. All too rarely is experiential education clearly integrated and articulated as integral to the curriculum in the way that AAC&U are proposing in the LEAP initiative. In general, experiential education is still perceived as less valuable and disconnected from traditional forms of learning and the practices on most campuses. For example, consider some of the comments by students that mirror these perceptions:

- Teachers are paid to teach us what they know, why am I spending 10 hours of my time working at a horse farm?
- I wanted to complete an internship but I couldn't make it fit into my program.
- I just wanted to go to Europe to experience a new culture, why do I have to take all of these classes too?
- I learned more in my internship than in any of my traditional courses!
- I wanted to take that consumer behavior course but the department store research project and presentation sounds like a lot of unnecessary work.

These comments arise when students are left on their own without a structure to help them understand the connections between classroom knowledge and experiential education. According to Ewell (1997) making connections is vital to what we know about teaching and learning. Ewell's survey of the literature related to cognitive psychology concludes that learning "is about making meaning for each individual learner by establishing and reworking patterns, relationships and connections" (1997, p. 4). When students are able to rework patterns, relationships and connections through intentionally structured experiential education practices, college curriculum becomes relevant and powerful.

Polanyi, Chemist/Philosopher, refers to these connections as tacit knowledge (1966). Polanyi demonstrated that everything we know is known in terms of something else (tacit knowledge). Tacit knowledge is used to probe and explore new experiences. For learning and growth to occur, students must use tacit knowledge from coursework ("what we know") to probe and explore a particular experiential education context ("in terms of something else"). In service-learning, education abroad, internships, role plays and other forms of experiential learning, such learning and growth can occur if and when students are invited to identify and use tacit knowledge from their traditional educational classes ("what we know") to probe and make meaning "in terms of something else" (Inkster & Ross, 1995).

Probing and exploration alone, however, do not necessarily translate into the deep, rich learning that transforms the way students think, behave, or view the world. As Dewey (1938) purported, experience can transform learning but not all experience is transformative. It is the responsibility of faculty and program directors to provide a structure for students to reflect on and process this probing and exploration. Integration of experiential education into the curriculum thus becomes an important step to establish a formalized approach to helping students transform their experiences and make deeper connections.

Integration is equally important to garner commitment among faculty, perhaps the constituency most invested in curriculum and student learning. For those faculty who already incorporate experiential approaches in the classroom, integration legitimizes the work that they are doing. For those not yet engaging in experiential education, integration sends an important message that engaging in experiential pedagogy is not only valued, but it is also integral to what it means to educate students at your institution. Integration is thus not only critical to student transformation, but to faculty transformation as well.

Lastly, integration ensures that experiential education initiatives will remain a reality at an institution long after any particular program director or administrator retires or moves on. For example, consider the opposite scenario: A particular academic administrator (e.g. Provost or Vice President for Academic Affairs) decides to acknowledge and dedicate resources to faculty incorporating service-learning initiatives in the classroom without creating strong support among the faculty or academic department. When that administrator leaves, it is quite feasible that experiential education will not receive the same support and that may then lead to a decrease in faculty participation. On the other hand, if experiential education, and in this example service-learning, is integrated into the curriculum with strong faculty consensus and support, it will remain embedded in the institution regardless of changes in administrative personnel. Essentially, the curriculum is the primary expression of an institution's vision for education. In summary, and it cannot be stated strongly enough, explicit acknowledgement of experiential education as an integral part of the institution's curriculum and teaching philosophy establishes legitimacy among students, faculty and administration.

What Does "Integration into the Curriculum" Mean?

Before one can discuss benefits of and strategies for integration, it is important to address what is meant by integration. Fundamentally, to 'integrate' means to incorporate or to assimilate or combine. In other words, experiential education programs and strategies that are clearly incorporated into a student's primary educational plan would be seen as 'integrated' (rather than an 'addition' or 'on top of'). Similarly, when faculty are rewarded and encouraged to engage in experiential programs or learning strategies and their efforts are clearly respected, then this would be further evidence of "integration" into the curriculum.

Or to come at this from the opposite perspective, the following scenarios could be evidence that experiential education should be better integrated into the curriculum: experiential education is seen as an 'add on' or as a separate entity apart from the student's primary education; or a student feels burdened to engage in experiential learning; or a faculty person feels disadvantaged for engaging in experiential education programs/strategies rather than supported and rewarded by the institution.

Integration can be looked at from a variety of perspectives. The three perspectives to be addressed here are: inclusion through availability/accessibility; inclusion as a "legitimate" and valuable component of the educational program; and inclusion as a legitimate and valued aspect of classroom pedagogy.

First, availability and accessibility of experiential education is fundamental to integration within our academic institutions. There must exist on our campuses opportunities for students to engage in experiential programs, and occasions for them to participate in experiential approaches to learning course content. At its most basic level, then, there must be **an awareness of the value** of experiential learning, **programs** for experiential opportunities such as internships, education abroad and service-learning, and **professional development** opportunities for faculty to learn about and utilize experiential approaches in their classes.

Examples of institutions making experiential education available and accessible to their students include: explicit mission statements acknowledging the importance of experiential education; the presence of offices and staff to support internships and service-learning; a departmentally designated internship coordinator for each academic unit. Other illustrations of integration include: a university-wide course number for internships; advising and orientation that encourage students to participate in a range of experiential programs, i.e., internships, education abroad, co-ops, and service-learning; availability of scholarships or financial support to encourage student participation. Perhaps the most important example of all is when institutions provide **faculty training** in the value of and strategies for experiential education that further enhance faculty utilization of experiential pedagogy in and outside the classroom.

Although access to and opportunities for experiential learning programs, activities and pedagogy is a fundamental first consideration in curricular integration, it is a far cry from integration that honors the educational value of an experiential approach. In short, availability is not enough.

The degree to which the experiential approach is valued within the student's program of study demonstrates the extent of its integration into the curriculum. Since academic 'credit' is the currency of value in our institutions, the experiential program must be credit generating (see chapter 6 as well). And those credits must be integral to the degree that the student is pursuing. Even if not a specific requirement within the student's program of study, credits have to be legitimized as satisfying requirements within the major rather than as general or university electives. That legitimacy is facilitated when the programs are clearly tied to the academic content that the student is studying through clearly stated learning objectives grounded in the field of study.

Examples of integration that demonstrate the value and legitimacy of experiential programs can be found in departments that require department seminars to accompany credited internships or service projects. Programs and/or seminars requiring students to develop learning objectives as part of the experience, and to report on their accomplishment of those objectives as part of the assessment of their learning and the successful earning of those credits, are programs that demonstrate integration. In addition, universities and colleges that have an experiential education graduation requirement and/or first year experiences that engage students in experiences and applications elevate the profile of curricular commitment from the departmental level to university level commitment.

Universities or colleges that purport to believe that participation in experiential programs are important to a student's education, but do not give credit for the activity, or do not recognize those credits within the degree requirements undermine the legitimacy of the educational activity. In short, they fail to fully integrate the program into the curriculum.

Finally, the experiential approach to classroom teaching must be honored as a legitimate and valued aspect of classroom pedagogy. Across the campus, faculty must be encouraged to explore experiential approaches to course content (Ewell 1997; Cross 1998; AAC&U 2006). The expectation that faculty include experiential approaches in their classes has to be clearly stated and then rewarded in faculty evaluations. The experiential activities/strategies that are utilized in the classroom have to be clearly tied to course content and stated learning objectives. And the products/activities of that experiential approach require evaluation as a component of the student's final grade for the class rather than as mere activity for activity's sake. Faculty who choose to include experiential approaches to their teaching, should be supported in their efforts to develop/design those activities, and recognized for the value that these activities bring to student learning. All of this is consistent with what has transpired in faculty and professional development since the first edition of this work. Readers are asked to review the work of a growing number of teaching and learning centers on campuses and publications of the national POD organization—Professional and Organizational Development in Higher Education (www.podnetwork.org/). The shift from a teaching paradigm to a learning paradigm and more engaging forms of pedagogy add support and impetus to classrooms embracing experiential learning.

The Most Critical Issue:
Does the Experience Have Academic Acceptability and Validity?

In order for experiential education to be integrated into the curriculum, it must be academically valid and acceptable to the faculty and administration. There are a number of issues and concerns that must be addressed around validity and credibility, but before moving forward there is one overarching point that is important to consider. A primary reason why administrators, and more so faculty, do not generally accept or view experiential approaches as valid is because, fundamentally, many believe learning takes place only within the classroom where the faculty person has control of all of the elements of the learning process.

When moving from a teaching-centered to a learning-centered focus, there is the perception that faculty and administrators cannot control the outcome. That can be discomforting. In general, there is the perception that every "experience" is subjective, according to an individual's interpretation. That becomes problematic when a faculty member or administrator is trying to ensure that students all leave with the same knowledge that has been identified as important. Some may believe that learning within the context of experiential education is left to chance rather than by design and that raises concerns when faculty are responsible for demonstrating academic rigor of an activity, course, or program. Additionally, since experiential learning contributes not only to students' cognitive development (or "hard skills") but also their social and emotional development ("soft skills"), faculty who do not see themselves as experts in psychology or those who do not know how to test or evaluate soft skills are left feeling like they have little control or are not qualified to lead experiential courses. And yet another "uncontrollable" component of experiential education is that students do not always develop "soft skills" as quickly as other competencies nor is the development of soft-skills always readily apparent.

To an extent this sense of a loss of control is a valid perception. But faculty often stop there. Without an understanding of the associated experiential education principles and practices (methods, structures, and evaluation tools), faculty and administrators often delegitimize experiential education and let their doubts and concerns dominate with questions like these: Is learning really taking place through experiential activities? Can you assess the learning? Is it college level learning? Is such learning really worthy of academic credit? How might this affect our accreditation? The acceptability of experiential education is dependent upon alleviating these concerns as well as designing an institutional process that will assure faculty that college-level learning worthy of academic credit is taking place.

Since the publication of the first edition of "Strengthening," the assessment movement and demands of accrediting bodies have increasingly asked the same questions of traditional forms of education, often noting that the burden of proof for "learning outcomes" worthy of credit in traditional courses must also be documented. (See below and the Appendix on Assessment by Shumer.) The chapter of this sourcebook entitled "Ensuring Quality in Experiential Education" provides a thorough discussion of the issue of quality controls. In the following section, however, we briefly review some of the academic acceptability concerns.

Is learning really taking place?

Reassuring faculty that learning is taking place starts at the institutional level. Establishing college-wide guidelines for the approval, monitoring and evaluation of program and course development helps reassure faculty that learning is taking place in experiential settings. Perhaps the greatest challenge facing any educator is that of assessing the quality and quantity of the learning that has actually taken place. Too often, however, faculty rely only on traditional methods to evaluate learning.

The **course proposal process,** which includes a university-wide endorsed course description, and the **course syllabus** are two strategies departments and faculty traditionally utilize to outline course content and learning outcomes. At the most fundamental level it is important that these both address the experiential components and learning expectations.

In the course proposal process, the crafting of the **course description**, although brief, can be one strategy a university department utilizes for designing and communicating the intellectual rigor required in a particular course. It may refer specifically to the experiential components and learning goals. Although an important part of the institutionalizing of the experiential

40

components of a course, the officially approved course description that appears in university catalogs most likely does not communicate the depth of the learning outcomes that the students will be expected to demonstrate.

A **course syllabus** is one of the most common strategies a faculty person utilizes to articulate for a 'public' the course objectives and student expectations (i.e. readings and assignments/activities) to fulfill the learning objectives associated with an experiential activity or assignment. Additionally, the syllabus typically outlines the basis for which grades will be given. Many faculty/departments consider the course syllabus to be a type of informal 'contract' with the student. The purpose of a well-designed syllabus is to articulate the connection between the experiential activity/assignment, classroom rigor and scholarship in the field, outlining the structured learning opportunities while describing how the student will be held accountable for fulfilling learning objectives.

Design of both the course description and the course syllabus are familiar strategies useful for faculty to gain control of the educational experience in designing and communicating the learning focus of a course, and providing a structure for assuring that learning is taking place. Unfortunately, these attempts to control the learning outcomes of the course too often focus on the faculty member (what the faculty member can provide). This, in some ways, reverts back to the "teacher-centered" approach, ignoring the unique and distinctive learning opportunities associated with experiential contexts and learning milieus.

As noted earlier, a critical method for assuring that learning occurs is to clearly **identify learning outcomes** that the student must demonstrate to receive credit or attain a grade. **Learning outcomes** clearly define the skills or knowledge that the student will be able to demonstrate and the conditions under which that demonstration will take place (i.e. exams, papers, presentations, interviews). This kind of documentation is more reliable than a generic syllabus or course description because it requires that the student provide evidence of learning, thus demonstrating their overall development. Learning outcomes are student centered and learning focused (cf. Tagg 2003, and others).

In the past such an approach has not been widely accepted among faculty as a valid representation of the intellectual rigor associated with a course. There has been a recent push in higher education toward outcomes-based learning and assessment by accreditors. Similarly, the Association of American Colleges and Universities (AAC&U) is pressing for a change in the way institutions measure the value of the education they provide students. Faculty and institutions are being challenged with the question: How do you know the students are learning what you/we said they would learn? Many institutions are now requiring faculty and program directors to use **learning outcomes and associated assessment tools** to assure that learning is taking place. The AAC&U has in fact created assessment rubrics (available for download on their website: http://www.aacu.org/value/rubrics) that faculty can put to use immediately to evaluate student learning outcomes connected to experiential initiatives (i.e. creative and critical thinking, personal and social responsibility, knowledge, intellectual and practical skills). Demonstrating the legitimacy and value of experiential courses should become less daunting as faculty become more educated and comfortable with outcomes-based approaches.

41

Is it college/university-level learning?

Similar to the first question (is learning taking place?), university/college-wide program and course guidelines can and should set the standard for what "college-level" learning means for the experiential education programs at your institution. College/university-level learning for all programs, including experiential education programs, should be defined according to the institution's mission and the nature of the students served. However, there is one general criterion that is helpful. College/university-level learning should be **more self-directed rather than teacher-directed** (Knowles, 1975), **and it should be about learning rather than instruction** (Barr & Tagg, 1995). Teacher directed approaches assume the student is dependent upon the teacher for what and how the learner should be taught, thus reinforcing college-level learning as the accumulation of knowledge through the delivery of information by an expert academic in the field. Conversely, self-directed learning acknowledges the student as essential to the learning and growth process. Malcolm Knowles' (1975) work in adult education revealed that self-directed approaches result in deeper and lasting learning while developing individuals who are more likely to take initiative and become lifelong learners. Students need to become self-directed learners if they are to leave college prepared for the rapidly changing world that they will enter upon graduation. Experiential education in all forms can and should incorporate Knowles' philosophy of self-directed learning (cf. Dewey, Kolb, Cross, Ewell, Barr and Tagg and others). See chapter 4 of this book entitled "Ensuring Quality in Experiential Education" for a more detailed discussion of "college level" learning.

Is the learning acquired worthy of the amount of credit being granted?

This question has permeated experiential education for years because of a historically agreed to assumption in much of K-16 formal education that credit is best awarded based on the number of hours a student spends in the classroom. The number of hours and thus credits is then correspondingly tied to an assumption that the most/best learning takes place in the classroom. In other words, faculty and administrators seem to believe that learning can be controlled in the classroom so it stands to reason then that "seat time" is where many administrators and faculty feel most comfortable awarding credit. Credit-by-hours, or "seat time," is inadequate for legitimizing the amount of credit earned for experiential learning, especially field experiences that can amount to a 40-hour workweek for students. In a traditional course it is assumed that for one-credit students spend 3-4 hours (includes in and out of classroom time) a week for a term. How can this be translated into an internship that ranges from 10-12 plus hours a week each week of a term? The shift towards outcomes-based assessment indicates that an hour spent in a classroom, or "seat time," is not an adequate measure of the learning taking place in the classroom. However, this system remains common practice.

Learning outcomes provide an easier and more effective way to compare the learning acquired through traditional courses with experiential education. The learning outcomes established by the institution, school or program could be directly identified and integrated into experiential education courses to establish common ground. Simply listing common outcomes is not enough to earn acceptance and credibility for academic credit. Documenting the learning and sharing assessments of learning outcomes is critical to demonstrate the validity and to assure faculty and administrator acceptance. If students engaged in experiential education demonstrate comparable learning outcomes desired for students in traditional courses, clearly the learning is just as worthy of college level credit.

Another concern related to credit is the awarding of grades for experiential learning. Some faculty are concerned that grade inflation occurs for students engaged in experiential education. For example, a faculty member teaching a traditional section of sociology might assume that the high grades given to students enrolled in their colleague's service-learning section must be a result of softer grading of student achievement (i.e. number of service hours completed). Interestingly, the faculty member would less likely assume that the students' stronger performance might be because students are more engaged and learn more effectively as a result of actively participating and experimenting in the service-learning course. If the institution has established learning outcomes and assessment rubrics, and the evidence collected reveals that learning is taking place, there should be no reason for faculty or others to be surprised by the grades granted in experiential education. In addition, it might shed light on the ill-advised assertion that grade inflation, not deeper learning, is the reason students "do better" when they engage in experiential pedagogies.

What Are the Challenges to Integrating Experiential Education into the Curriculum?

The challenges begin to be revealed as one considers the meaning and importance of integration. Ultimately, experiential education must gain equal status with other approaches to the teaching/learning process if it is to be successfully integrated into the curriculum. Experiential education must be seen as more than 'career education' or 'active learning.' Faculty and administration must recognize that college/university-level learning is taking place and that it is worthy of the credit being granted. Ironically, experiences that are "active" but not grounded in content knowledge may engage the student and may result in learning at some level, but most likely will not result in complete learning as defined by Kolb. These types of experiences will fail to inform the classroom knowledge as is fully possible.

As mentioned earlier (Polanyi, 1966), a well-structured, academically sound experiential approach gives students opportunities to manipulate their classroom/course knowledge to explore a complex and challenging set of experiences with that knowledge. Then in turn, this gives the student opportunities to utilize those experiences in the classroom to further explore the theories and concepts of the class (see chapters 3 and 4 for further elaboration and evidence).

For this to happen there must be a clear connection to the academic and learning outcomes identified as salient to each institution. The earlier edition of "Strengthening" built upon the work of Keeton (1980), Duley (1977), Little (1983), Kolb (1984) and other pioneers in the field. Kendall *et al* reflected in that treatise the best thinking of the time, suggesting that institutions must address five challenges in order to successfully integrate experiential education into the curriculum. These same challenges persist today.

The five challenges our institutions must address in order to be successful in this integration are:

43

1. The learning objectives of any and all experiential education must be clearly articulated--whether a classroom pedagogical strategy, a course, or an experiential program. The objectives must interface with/support the mission of the institution and must contribute in a qualitative way to the goals of the curriculum and/or learning objectives of the class.
2. Faculty and academic administrators need opportunities to know more about the value of experiential education and how it can be utilized as a teaching tool within each of the disciplines.
3. The use of experiential education by faculty must be a positive experience. The experience must at least be as meaningful and rewarding as teaching via more traditional means. Such programs and courses must provide faculty with incentives and rewards that are comparable to those gained through teaching utilizing traditional strategies.
4. The credit earned for learning that is achieved experientially must have equal status to credit earned through lecture and seminar formats.
5. Faculty must be fully consulted and involved in the integration effort and have full control over its use as they would over any other course or program in the curriculum.

Where Does Experiential Education Stand in Your Curriculum?

Before embarking on a campaign for further integration of experiential education in the curriculum, it is imperative to ascertain what experiential education is currently in place. Interestingly enough, there is likely more experiential education happening on most campuses than is evident, possibly as the result of the contributions of NSEE pioneers (including the first edition of *Strengthening*). Despite what has transpired since that 1986 publication, faculty are often practicing experiential education without identifying it as such. Furthermore, experiential education comes in so many forms and types and with a variety of possible purposes that it is frequently scattered across campus in a variety of forms (**see Appendix A**). Therefore, when assessing the status of experiential education within a department, division or the campus as a whole, it is important to establish a baseline of current practice:

1. **Begin by making a simple list of all the experiential education activities offered.** We suggest that you engage other colleagues in helping you to generate your initial list or as reviewers of what you create alone, as noted below. We are frequently surprised by others involvement in experiential education—either that we have forgotten or were not aware of. **Appendix A** lists the most common types and forms (most recently updated by NSEE). Review this to help identify areas where experiential education is in place. **Appendix B** lists examples of the goals of experiential education courses and programs (revised for this edition). This may also help in identifying what is already in place.
2. **For each course or program that uses experiential learning, ask the faculty and administrators involved in these activities to complete the Inventory of Experiential Programs and Courses (Appendix C), or to review your responses.** Appendix C and D have been adapted for this new edition to reflect the varied approaches to experiential learning. Therefore, parts of the Appendix C inventory are more relevant to experiential programs than to courses, so adapt based on the focus of the inventory. For each class that uses an experiential component, technique or process, ask the faculty person to

complete the Inventory of Experiential Components, Techniques or Processes **(Appendix D).**

3. **Tally the responses** from the inventory to determine the use of experiential education, the objectives being fulfilled, and the status of these activities. Questions following the inventory will help with analysis.
4. **Consider the strengths and weaknesses of the current offerings.** Questions following the inventory will help with this assessment.

The following questions will be helpful in interpreting the data from the inventory:

1. The extent to which experiential education is used on campus (or in the department) and by whom:
   - Is it mostly faculty or staff who are involved in delivering the courses or program?
   - What percentage of academic departments (or departmental faculty) list internships, practica, cooperative education, education abroad, field experience or other experiential learning activities?
2. The types of objectives which are being fulfilled, or which are perceived as being fulfilled by experiential education:
   - Which types are most frequently identified?
   - Which types are least valued?
   - Are they mostly academic or nonacademic?
3. The status that the programs, courses, components or techniques have in relationship to the curriculum and faculty/coordinator recognition/reward:
   - Does the 'currency' encourage student involvement?
   - Does the 'currency' encourage faculty involvement?
4. The consistency of policies and practices across the department or the campus:
   - Are there patterns that emerge about the way experiential learning is regarded?
   - Are there patterns that emerge about the way the department/university uses experiential learning?
5. The strengths and weaknesses of curricular integration:
   - What is the distribution of courses and programs among the three categories identified in Appendix A?
   - What departments and faculty are currently involved in experiential education? (These are the foundation/network for future efforts at integration.)
   - Is there a noticeable absence of faculty involvement or a disproportionate involvement by non-faculty in courses and programs?
   - Are the goals and objectives of current courses and programs academically situated or primarily in career and personal development?
   - Are there courses designated for field experience or internships in every department?
6. The status of the existing courses, programs, components or techniques:
   - Are there some that have achieved significant status as part of a curriculum in a department or a major? If so, what were the contributing factors to this success? Could they be used as examples for other departments?

- How could others that have been successful be strengthened? Would additional faculty involvement help, or better quality control, or more clearly identified values and goals?

This assessment exercise is intended to not only provide a status report, but to also assist in the discovery of the factors that have influenced the current status of experiential education on your campus, and to identify critical issues that require further consideration.

The identification of the specific issues important to your particular institution or department is the first step in formulating a strategy for integrating experiential education more fully into the curriculum.

What Are the Key Strategies for Making Integration Happen?

To this point, a lot of groundwork has been covered: why integration is important, identifying the associated challenges, demonstrating validity and acceptability, recognizing the possible goals and objectives, and taking inventory of existing experiential activities. If integration is to become a reality at your institution however, there's still more to do. The question now becomes, how can integration actually happen?

Throughout the process it is important to keep in mind that integration is not necessarily about dominating a curriculum or excluding other methods of teaching and learning. You have to determine the degree to which experiential education opportunities can help your institution, faculty and students accomplish its mission and meet the identified learning goals. When viewed this way, the process for integration becomes less threatening to those who may be more cautious about integration. The following are some general strategies that can be used to make integration a reality.

Fundamental Knowledge

Knowing what experiential learning is already happening on campus is valuable but you should not stop there. Knowledge that could be useful to your integration efforts includes:

1. **Know basic information about experiential learning theory and practice--learning from experience--including where and how it is appropriate.** Although you cannot possibly know how experiential education initiatives can be designed for all course content areas and subject matter on campus, it is essential to have a basic understanding of the general objectives and knowledge common to experiential learning and most curricular design. For example, cognitive development is a common objective of most courses and curriculum as well as experiential education. A review of the relationship between cognitive development and experiential learning theory and their application will be critical to your ability to engage in discussions with faculty about the design of experiential components.

chapters 5 & 9 of this revision of *Strengthening* also provide you with theory and research that should further equip you as an experiential education professional. Particularly helpful is a review of the four elements in Kolb's (1984) experiential learning model: concrete experience, reflective observation, abstract conceptualization and active experimentation. These four elements provide a framework through which students learn experientially, and insight into what must be considered when experiential activities are designed for courses and programs. Beyond theory, much can be learned by reviewing the "Eight Principles of Good Practice for All Experiential Learning Activities" outlined by NSEE (1998) and through exemplar examples of already proven experiential techniques and programs. Selected sources for further review are found in the References and Resources section at the end of this chapter.

2. **Know and understand the mission and values of your institution.** In addition to the inventory suggested earlier, the chapter in this resource book titled "Mission and Values" outlines the information about the institution's goals and objectives that you should gather and assess. As emphasized in chapter 5, take advantage, whenever possible, of attending and participating in open meetings and committee hearings that are addressing curricular issues. Listen, learn and contribute.

3. **Know and understand the goals and objectives of your general education curriculum, as well as the curriculum of individual departments and programs.** At the course level, relevant records from curriculum committee meetings are often accessible via shared electronic databases on campus. The minutes and agendas from meetings provide initial information about new courses being offered and issues/faculty concerns that might be raised related to curriculum standards and reform at the department, school or institutional level. Determine which programs and courses have earned a reputation as effective in meeting the institutions curricular goals and objectives. These could provide opportunities to introduce experiential learning practices, to collaborate or to identify experiential programs.

4. **Know the quality and quantity of current experiential education practice in your institution (see inventories Appendix in this chapter).**

5. **Know the strategic planning that is taking place or has taken place on your campus recently, including assessment and accreditation endeavors.** Often such initiatives focus on revisiting the goals and objectives of the institution as well as proposing new initiatives tied to curriculum. It is likely that collecting data/evidence of demonstrated learning outcomes and program effectiveness will be part of these initiatives. Once this information is gathered and developed, utilize your knowledge about the institution and experiential education to engage others in informed and academic discussions about experiential education, its relevance to higher education and to your particular institution.

6. **Know the key allies and advocates of experiential education within your institution, including those who staff and make use of your Center for Teaching and Learning.** The obvious place to start is with faculty who already believe in and use experiential methods in their teaching. You will also find potential advocates among faculty who have a reputation for being collegial and open-minded about their teaching practices. Most institutions have centers for teaching and learning, directed by faculty, with the mission to share and improve pedagogy on campus. Lastly, approaching faculty who serve on curriculum and/or assessment committees will be helpful. Their commitment is pivotal to engaging other faculty in discussions and in pushing initiatives forward.

7. **Know and be prepared to address potential arguments or general points of contention.** For example, when speaking with faculty about experiential practices in the classroom (e.g. role-playing, simulations, field trips, semester long projects), understand that the academic calendar can be viewed as a roadblock to creativity and ingenuity in the classroom. Some faculty hold tight to the idea that they must "cover" a certain amount of content in their courses; therefore, dedicating classroom time to experiential projects can seem like a significant commitment in a semester. Using examples from this book and literature on "engaged teaching" and AAC&U's rubrics, be prepared to engage in helpful and thoughtful dialogue about effective teaching and learning.

The institution's course scheduling practices may also dictate the nature and time available for experiential activities. For example, a teacher receives a request from a local science lab to conduct a field project with her students in December through February but the semester ends in December. The challenge becomes whether or not the students would want to continue the project after the semester officially concludes. One possible solution is to run the science course as an independent study to gain more flexibility in structuring the length of the course. This is only a short-term solution unless the institution develops a course numbering system specifically for experiential learning courses. Furthermore without integration the independent study option becomes less desirable because faculty rarely receive compensation for independent studies.

Securing service-learning and internship sites is another point of contention for faculty. The time it takes to establish and maintain partnerships with community organizations becomes a possible hurdle for faculty. There are most likely a number of university policies, related to things such as confidentiality, medical insurance, transportation, that must be reviewed prior to earning approval from administration for study-abroad, service-learning, internships, and other experiential activities. See chapters 6 & 7 for strategies to support faculty in minimizing these obstacles.

Think about and talk through these and other issues with advocates and those familiar with the 'practical' blocks to integrating experiential learning so that you can be prepared to address these and similar issues when they arise.

All of this is to suggest that the challenges are both microscopic and macroscopic, but the learning outcomes and success for your students is more than worth the preparation to meet those challenges. Consideration of the above will help you identify opportunities and support systems for introducing *and expanding* experiential education in your institution *and the curriculum of your institution.*

Leadership

Integration of experiential education into the curriculum will be more likely with support from leadership at your institution--whether it is the provost, vice president for academic affairs, an academic dean or a department chair. In some cases, it is you who will recognize and introduce the need to integrate experiential education, but your vision and plan will be better received when communicated through leadership. The knowledge gained from the examples and information you collect will reveal the best opportunities and possible timing for curriculum change. Additionally, the resources and process used to collect and analyze the information will lend credibility to any of the proposed initiatives. As a result, support and action from leadership becomes more viable.

Opportunities of particular interest to institutional leadership are those introduced through articles and national reports on higher education. President Obama's goal to increase the percentage of college graduates in the United States from 40 to 60% by 2020 has generated much attention and put a spotlight on the issues within higher education that have existed for years. For example, topics such as student retention and dropout rates that point to students' lack of engagement reinforce the benefits and need for integrating experiential education into the curriculum. Also, reports from the AAC&U are extremely helpful and support experiential education. In fact, to address student engagement, the AAC&U recommends that all general education include a number of what they call, high impact practices such as undergraduate research, service-learning, internships, and freshman and capstone experiences (Association of American Colleges and Universities, 2011).

This national movement for institutions of higher education to commit to and build a broad base for experiential learning across the institution is clearly demonstrated by the number that have chosen experiential learning as the focus for their quality enhancement plan (QEP) in meeting regional accrediting agencies' requirement for an institutional improvement strategy. The QEP initiative is requiring that institutions of higher education carefully design an institution-wide, focused plan for enhancing student learning. A quick review of university web sites reveals a growing number of institutions that have selected experiential learning as the focus topic for their QEP. One such example is the University of North Carolina-Wilmington, which has worked directly with the NSEE to provide faculty training in best practices for their experiential learning classroom components. Institutional leadership is taking heed of the critical role of experiential education in enhancing student learning.

Many believe that a paradigm shift in higher education is happening and this shift is deeply rooted in the foundations of experiential education. The leadership of your institution will likely be very interested in integration when you can demonstrate connections between this shift and the principles of experiential learning. Our experience is that presidents, deans, and other leaders are aware of and can be further influenced by linking your institution's mission, the emerging AAC&U initiatives and the value of experiential education pedagogy to the educational success of your students.

Faculty Involvement

Change is not always an easy thing, especially when it relates to teaching, the livelihood of most faculty. Therefore, the credibility of whatever changes or new experiential initiatives you propose is perhaps most critical when garnering faculty involvement. The need and opportunities for change must be clearly stated and supported with documentation from sources that are respected and credible. Even with the support of leadership, without this clarity faculty will likely view your proposed initiatives as a possible waste of their time and energy, or another grandiose idea from administration.

Sharing the process with faculty will help them feel more involved. Faculty then can contribute to the discussions and ultimately provide additional insight and assistance in implementing experiential education into their curriculum. (See chapter 3 of this sourcebook entitled "Increasing Faculty Involvement in Experiential Education.")

Once faculty are on board and your experiential education initiatives have been integrated into the curriculum, *let go and allow the academic departments to take ownership*. The faculty are the closest to the curriculum and they will best control the implementation and assessment of the experiential courses and programs.

But remain involved in the process of supporting faculty as faculty support students within the broad range of experiential education strategies by sharing information, mentoring, and coaching, identifying field/community experiences, or simply asking: "how can I be of assistance?"

You are encouraged to also look to professional associations for support in this work both for yourself and your faculty. Of particular note is the growing demand for and development of NSEE's Experiential Education Academy, offering national, regional, and local workshops in areas such as experiential learning theory, ethical and best practices, legal issues, assessment and reflection, among others. Through these workshops, not only do you and your faculty develop expertise, but you also are building networks and identifying resources for continued development and support beyond your institutions. Nearly every campus has a center for teaching and learning, and each of those is most often connected to the national Professional and Organizational Development in Higher Education (POD) association that offers print and on-line resources, as well as workshops and national meetings. Discipline-specific professional associations can also provide excellent resources and add credibility to this work. With the growing support for experiential, active and applied learning, research and resources are continually being produced. Involvement with these professional associations gives you and your faculty access to experts in the field, the latest research, the most relevant information, strategies for integration and program development, as well as a venue for sharing knowledge through presentations and publications. These are some of the ways that experiential education professionals can enhance and expand the offerings of their institutions as well as their own professional reputations.

Summary

We have reviewed, reiterated, and expanded upon the original chapter in *Strengthening Experiential Education Within Your Institution*. Nothing is more critical than curriculum integration. However, as we have endeavored to communicate, and the following case study illustrates, the curriculum must always be viewed as part of a very complex system. We think that Purdue University Calumet illustrates that complexity, as well as demonstrates how far the field of experiential education has progressed since 1986, and the extent to which NSEE has contributed to these changes.

A Success Scenario: Purdue University Calumet, Hammond, Indiana

In March 2007, the Faculty Senate at Purdue University Calumet (PUC) unanimously passed a resolution to establish a graduation requirement of ExL, what they call experiential learning, for all students beginning fall 2008. Students are required to complete two ExL courses during their academic career. Faculty members mentor students throughout the entire ExL process, helping them to apply the theories and knowledge they learn in the classroom through undergraduate research, service-learning, cooperative education, internships, practicum, and design projects. I asked Janice Golub-Reynolds, Manager of Experiential Learning at PUC, about the integration process. As you will read in her comments below, the integration steps taken by PUC mirror many of those recommended in this chapter.

--Beth

Q: How and why did the integration process at PUC start?

A: In 2005, our Chancellor, Howard Cohen, enlisted a committee to explore a way to distinguish Purdue University Calumet from other local institutions, with the intent to go from "Good to Great". During the committee's assessment of teaching practices at PUC, it was discovered that many of our faculty were teaching experience-based courses. In 2006 the Faculty Senate approved of a faculty task force to study experiential education (to learn more about the theory and practices), define components and create an inventory of experiential education courses offered at PUC. In the fall of 2006 three task force members wrote and received a 1.7 million dollar grant from the U.S. Department of Education for faculty development in the creation of standards for and promotion of experiential education at PUC. In March of 2007, the Faculty Senate established the graduation requirement of ExL for all undergraduate students entering as of fall 2008. The graduation requirement stated: "All undergraduate students entering Purdue University Calumet beginning with fall 2008 must complete two Experiential Learning designated courses before graduation." One month later, the Faculty Senate established a Curriculum Education and Policy Subcommittee for Experiential Education to serve as "quality control" and to establish a designated process for course proposals. The Eight Principles of Good Practice as set by NSEE were required to be integrated into any course that was to receive the ExL designation and therefore count as meeting the graduation requirement. We were on our way!

Q: Who was involved in the process?

A: The Chancellor, Faculty within Nursing, Education, Engineering, Technology, Management and Liberal Arts that were long supporters of experiential education offering field experiences, internships, co-ops, service-learning, etc. for many years. Administrators in Academic Affairs and internship coordinators, and career service staff were also minimally involved.

Q: What do you believe were the keys to successful integration?

A: Faculty involvement from the beginning! Engaging faculty and the governance process from the start were keys to our success. Faculty Senate support and approval was also critical in the process. Going to every academic department meeting and every governance body to discuss the merits, theories and purpose behind experiential learning were an important part of that process. Additionally, we attended the Northeastern University Summer Institute on Experiential Education at Martha's Vineyard in 2007, and we held open forums for faculty, staff and clerical support to raise awareness. The Chancellor and Senior Leadership Team were also supportive and promoted the importance of experiential learning to our students. Overall though, the program begins and ends with faculty involvement and support. Faculty create the courses, and the Faculty Senate Subcommittee designates and monitors quality of the experience. Academic Affairs administrative and professional staff support is very important as they support the faculty in ongoing workshops, development opportunities, community partner relations and an annual faculty development award (Experiential Learning Course Design and Development Award) is given as a summer stipend and release time during the academic year for ExL curriculum and program development.

Q: What does PUC continue to do now that ExL was successfully integrated since 2007?

A: We continue to promote successes and offer development and recognition opportunities to our faculty. We host an annual recognition lunch for faculty that are teaching experiential courses and/or are recipients of the annual Experiential Learning Course Design and Development awards (mentioned above). The Chancellor presents each faculty award recipient with a framed certificate at this luncheon. In addition, we have an annual Experiential Learning Expo. The goal of the Expo is to bring together current and potential community partners with our faculty to network and develop additional experiential learning engagements. We also partner with our career services office to provide faculty with networking opportunities with community partners. The Faculty Senate Subcommittee on Experiential Learning is also in the process of creating experiential learning assessment processes and rubrics for designated ExL courses. We continue to strategically partner with NSEE to offer regional workshops to our faculty. Since the inception of the degree program requirement at PUC, more than 2,100 students have enrolled in at least one of the approximately 100 ExL courses designated by the Faculty Senate. We continue to strive towards increasing the number of courses over every discipline by coordinating opportunities (e.g. luncheons, updates to campus community, blackboard experiential learning module, etc.) for faculty to engage in conversation about ExL at PUC.

Appendix A

NSEE - Revised 4/ 19/ 06

National Society for Experiential Education Description of Experiential Education

"Experiential Education refers to learning activities that involve the learner in the process of active engagement with, and critical reflection about, phenomena being studied."

Types and Forms of Experiential Learning

The items listed below may potentially be classified within the description above, but not necessarily.

Programs/Courses	Components	Techniques or Processes
Cooperative education	Contextual learning	Group learning activities
Field study, fieldwork, field research	Field observations	Laboratory work
Independent study	Field projects	Problem-based learning
Internships	Field trips	Role playing
Practica	Oral interviews	Simulation games and exercises
Service-learning	Participatory observations	Student-led class sessions
Study abroad	Site visits	Other forms of active learning
Work integrated learning	Situated learning	
Others	Use of primary source or raw data	

Appendix B

Examples of Goals of Experiential Education Courses and Programs

Experiential education has the potential to transform the lives of students while at the same time helping them reach the desired learning goals established by the institution. Below is an initial list of categories and associated learning goals. Most of the learning goals on this list are shared between recent teaching and learning initiatives, such as the LEAP Essential Learning Outcomes (AAC&U, 2005), and those historically outlined by Angelo and Cross (1993) and Kendall et al (1986) in the original edition of this book.

1. **Academic Discipline-Related Knowledge and Skills**
   - Acquire, test, apply, integrate and evaluate a body of knowledge or the methodology of an academic discipline
   - Improve understanding of subject, concepts and theories
   - Use subject-related materials and tools, perspectives and values of subject
2. **General, Liberal Education Skills**
   - Develop the foundations and skills to engage in self-directed, lifelong learning
   - Acquire the skills necessary to be a responsible and contributing citizen, including how to understand and analyze social and community issues
   - Foster understanding and openness to different cultures
3. **Generic, Cognitive Skills**
   - Acquire generic living skills: interpersonal interaction, goal setting, time management, coping with ambiguity
   - Acquire intellectual and practical skills including: written and oral communication, inquiry and analysis, problem-solving, teamwork, critical and creative thinking, integration and application of learning across general and specialized studies
4. **Ethical and Moral Values**
   - Develop and apply ethical and moral reasoning or judgment in a complex situation
5. **Personal Development**
   - Foster personal growth and maturation: self-understanding, self-esteem and confidence, personal values, purpose and goals, self-perception and self-reliance
   - Establish a commitment to values, respect for others, emotional well-being
6. **Work & Career Preparation**
   - Explore career options and acquire documented work experience in an occupation
   - Develop and demonstrate competencies, both knowledge and skills, specific to an occupation, profession or organizational setting
   - Acquire leadership and organizational skills, the ability to work productively with others and to follow instruction and direction

Appendix C
(Revised, based on 1986 edition of *Strengthening*)
Inventory of Experiential Education Programs and Courses
Ask each faculty or staff member responsible for a program or course relating to experiential learning to complete a separate inventory form.

Academic or administrative unit _____

Program or course title _____

Name of faculty sponsor(s) _____

Name of staff coordinator _____

Year program or course began _____

Program/Course goals
An experiential learning program or course typically has multiple goals. For all that apply to this program or course, put a "1" beside the most important goal below, a "2" beside the second most important, a "3" beside the third most important, etc...:

____ To acquire, test, apply, integrate and evaluate a body of knowledge or the methodology of an academic discipline

____ To improve understanding of subject, concepts and theories

____ To use subject-related materials and tools, perspectives and values of subject

____ To develop the foundations and skills to engage in self-directed, lifelong learning

____ To acquire the skills necessary to be a responsible and contributing citizen: understanding of social and community issues

____ To foster understanding and openness to different cultures

____ To acquire generic living skills: interpersonal interaction, goal setting, time management, coping with ambiguity

____ To acquire intellectual and practical skills: written and oral communication, inquiry and analysis, problem-solving, teamwork, critical and creative thinking, integration and application of learning across general and specialized studies, think holistically

____ To develop and apply ethical and moral reasoning or judgment in a complex situation

____ To foster personal growth and maturation: self-understanding, self-esteem and confidence, personal values, purpose and goals, self-perception and self-reliance

____ To establish a commitment to values, respect for others, emotional well-being

____ To explore career options and acquire documented work experience in an occupation

____ To develop and demonstrate competencies, both knowledge and skills, specific to an occupation, profession or organizational setting

____ To acquire leadership and organizational skills, the ability to work productively with others and to follow instruction and direction

Academic Status

	Yes	No
1. Does this program or course have the respect of the other faculty or staff in your unit?	____	____
2. Does it have the respect of students (not seen as an easy way to earn credit)?	____	____

3. Is the program/course recognized outside your unit by administrators, faculty, and/or students?   ____   ____

4. Is the program/course required in a plan of study or as a graduation requirement?   ____   ____

	Yes	No
5. Does it provide academic credit?	____	____
6. Are letter grades provided?	____	____

7. If credit is awarded, how is it recognized?
   ____ for general education requirements
   ____ in the academic major
   ____ as an elective outside the major

8. What is the average number of academic credits earned in one academic period for this program/course?
   ____ semester hours   ____ quarter hours

9. If letter grades are provided, who makes the final recommendation for credit and the grade?
   ____ faculty sponsor   ____ faculty committee
   ____ program or course coordinator   ____ site supervisor
   ____ other, specify: _____

10. How is the learning recorded on student transcripts?
    ____ not recorded

    ____ course labels and credits that cannot be distinguished from those obtained from classroom learning

    ____ course labels and credits that are designated as experiential learning

    ____ credits labeled by subject are with no specific course label or title

    ____ credits aggregated and labeled in a block as experiential learning with no course title or subject area

    ____ competency statements

    ____ narrative description of work performed or other achievements

    ____ other, specify: _____

Program Participants

1. How many students participated in the program/course during the past academic year? In the summer? _____

2. What was the total number of academic credits generated by the program/course in the past year, including the summer? _____

3. What is the predominant academic classification of participating students?
   ____ Lower Division/Level

   ____ Upper Division/Level

___ Graduate

4. What are the minimum requirements for participation?

5. Is the program restricted to particular majors? Yes ___ No ___

6. If the program is not restricted to particular majors, what are the predominant majors of participants?

Program Staffing

	Yes	*No*
1. Does the program have a faculty sponsor?	___	___
2. Does the program have a coordinator?	___	___

3. How are these roles recognized? Check the appropriate level for each column below.

	For faculty sponsor	*For program coordinator*
No institutional recognition	_____	_____
Institutional recognition but with no reduction in other responsibilities such as advising or committee work	_____	_____
Institutional recognition through overload compensation	_____	_____
Institutional recognition as part of regular work load	_____	_____

4. What is the percentage of time allocated for program responsibilities for the period the program or course is being offered?
___ % for faculty sponsor   ___ % for program coordinator

Program/Course Operation

1. How do students generally find out about the course or program?
   ___ listing in catalog
   ___ listing in class schedule
   ___ campus newspaper
   ___ campus/department/program website

   ___ publicity materials/strategies (brochures, email announcements, etc.)
   ___ class announcements or presentations
   ___ other, specify:
   _____

	Yes	*No*
2. Are formal learning plans/goals used in the program?	___	___

3. If yes, are they required?   ___   ___

4. Are handbooks/support materials available for:
     students   ___   ___
     faculty   ___   ___
     field supervisors   ___   ___

5. Who arranges the field site for experiential learning?
     ___ student
     ___ administrative personnel
     ___ faculty
     ___ other, specify: _____

6. How many hours a week does a student typically spend in the experiential, non-classroom component during the academic term? _____ hours

7. How many weeks is the usual experience? _____ weeks

8. What procedures are used to prepare students prior to program/course participation?
(check all that apply)
     ___ no specific preparation required
     ___ required course for credit
     ___ optional course for credit
     ___ required non-credit seminar
     ___ optional non-credit seminar
     ___ required workshop
     ___ optional workshop
     ___ one-to-one advising or tutorial
     ___ self-instructional materials or software
     ___ other, specify: _____

9. Which of the following are typically used to monitor student's progress?
(check all that apply)
     ___ telephone conversations with students
     ___ computer mediated conversations with students via web/email/discussion boards, etc.
     ___ telephone, Skype, video conferences, conversations with field supervisors
     ___ on-site visits
     ___ individual conferences with students on campus
     ___ seminars concurrent with the experience
     ___ papers, journals, or reports submitted periodically by the student
     ___ written reports by field supervisor
     ___ other, specify: _____

10. Which methods are commonly used to evaluate students' learning? *(check all that apply)*
     ___ performance tests (such as work samples, observations of students in the work setting)
     ___ simulations or situational tests (such as academic games, role playing, case studies, in-basket exercise)

___ product assessment (such as evaluation of paintings, poetry, proposals, writing samples, interview tapes, special projects)
___ student self-assessment (such as job inventory checklists, self-evaluation instruments)
___ interviews
___ written reports or content papers
___ oral presentations or reports
___ supervisor evaluations
___ portfolio documenting achievement of learning goals
___ other, specify: _____

11. Who evaluates the learning acquired? *(check all that apply)*
___ faculty sponsor   ___ a faculty committee
___ outside expert (s)   ___ program or course coordinator
___ site supervisor   ___ the student
___ other, specify: _____

12. How is the program or course funded? *(check all that apply and indicate percentage of each)*
___ regular institutional funds (____ %)
___ special developmental funds from the institution (____%)
___ grants (____%)
___ other, specify % and nature: _____

13. Which resources are specifically provided for program administration?
___ travel funds for site visits
___ funds for long-distance telephone calls
___ clerical support
___ travel funds for professional/faculty development
___ other, specify: _____

	Yes	No
14. Are there formal, written policies at the departmental level?	___	___
At the institutional level?	___	___
15. Is there a faculty committee with oversight or advisory responsibilities for the program?	___	___

16. If there is a faculty committee, what are its functions? Is it elected or appointed? By who? To whom does it report? What is the academic status of its members? Please respond on a separate page.

17. If there are unique features of the program or course which were not covered in this inventory, please elaborate on a separate page.

Program Plans

1. How was your program or course originally established? By whom? For what purpose? Please respond on a separate page.

2. Has the purpose of the program or course changed over time? How?

3. Of the goals noted under "Program Goals" at the beginning of this inventory which is a goal that should be given more priority in the future?

Name of person completing inventory_____

Title _____

Date completed _____

Appendix D
(Revised, based on 1986 edition of *Strengthening*)

Inventory for Experiential Components, Techniques and Processes

Your engagement with experiential learning may fall more clearly in the category of a component, technique or process within a course or program. The following inventory may be useful in gathering data about this level of use of experiential activity.

Component/Techniques/Process

An experiential component typically has multiple goals. For all that apply to each component or technique put a "1" beside the most important, "2", etc....:

___ To acquire, test, apply, integrate and evaluate a body of knowledge or the methodology of an academic discipline

___ To improve understanding of subject, concepts and theories

___ To use subject-related materials and tools, perspectives and values of subject

___ To develop the foundations and skills to engage in self-directed, lifelong learning

___ To acquire the skills necessary to be a responsible and contributing citizen: understanding of social and community issues

___ To foster understanding and openness to different cultures

___ To acquire generic living skills: interpersonal interaction, goal setting, time management, coping with ambiguity

___ To acquire intellectual and practical skills: written and oral communication, inquiry and analysis, problem-solving, teamwork, critical and creative thinking, integration and application of learning across general and specialized studies

___ To develop and apply ethical and moral reasoning or judgment in a complex situation

___ To foster personal growth and maturation: self-understanding, self-esteem and confidence, (personal values, goals, self-perception, purpose) and self-reliance

___ To establish a commitment to values, respect for others, emotional well-being

___ To explore career options and acquire documented work experience in an occupation

___ To develop and demonstrate competencies, both knowledge and skills, specific to an occupation, profession or organizational setting

___ To acquire leadership and organizational skills, the ability to work productively with others and to follow instruction and direction

Academic Status

	Yes	No
1. Does the assignment/activity have respect of other faculty or staff in your unit?	___	___
2. Does it have respect of the students (not seen as just an easy way to earn credit?)	___	___
3. Is the component, technique, or process recognized outside your unit by administrators, faculty, and or students?	___	___
4. Is the activity required to complete the course?	___	___
5. Is the activity graded?	___	___

6. If a letter grade is provided, who makes the recommendation for the grade?

7. How many participated in the activity? _____

Component/Activity Operation:

	Yes	No
1. Are support materials available to help the student prepare for the activity?	___	___

2. What are these?

3. Who arranges the field site for the activity (if applicable)?

4. How many hours will the student typically spend in this activity per term?

5. What procedures are used to prepare the student?

6. How does the student demonstrate their achievement of the learning goals identified for this activity?

7. Who evaluates the learning required?

8. What funds are provided to support the component/activity (if applicable)?

9. If there are unique features of the activity/component that were not covered in this inventory, please elaborate on a separate page.

Name of person completing inventory _____

Title _____

Date completed _____

References & Resources

Angelo, T. A., & Cross, P. K. (1993). Classroom Assessment Techniques: A Handbook for College Teacher, Second Edition. San Francisco: Jossey-Bass.

Association of American Colleges and Universities (2011). *Liberal Education and America's Promise (LEAP)*. Retrieved from http://www.aacu.org/leap/.

Barr, R. & Tagg, J. (1995). From teaching to learning: A new paradigm for undergraduate education. *Change*, 27(6), 12-25.

Chickering, A.W. & Gamson, Z. F. (1987). Seven Principles of Good Practice in Undergraduate Education. *American Association for Higher Education Bulletin*, 39(7), 3-7.

Cross, P. K. (1998). What do we know about student's learning and how do we know it. Presented at the *AHHE National Conference on Higher Education*, Atlanta, Georgia.

Dewey, J. (1933). *How we think*. Boston: D.C. Heath and Company.

Dewey, J. (1938). *Experience and education*. New York: Collier Books.

Duley, J. S. (1977). Service as Learning, Life-Style, and Faculty Function. In W.B. Martin (Ed.), *Redefining Service, Research, and Teaching: New Directions for Higher Education, No. 18*. San Francisco: Jossey Bass.

Ewell, P. T. (1997). Organizing for learning. American Association for Higher Education Bulletin, 50(4), 3-6.

Keeton, M. T. (1980). Defining and Assuring Quality in Experiential Learning. In *New Directions for Experiential Learning, No. 9*. San Francisco: Jossey-Bass.

Inkster, R. & Ross, R. G. (1995). The Internship as partnership: A Handbook for Campus Based Coordinators and Advisors. Raleigh, NC: National Society for Experiential Education.

Inkster, R. & Ross, R. G. (1998). *The Internship as partnership: A Handbook for businesses, nonprofits and government agencies*. Raleigh, NC: National Society for Experiential Education.

Kendall, J (1986). *Strengthening Experiential Education Within Your Institution*. Raleigh, NC: National Society for Internships and Experiential Education.

Knowles, M. S. (1975). *Self-directed learning: A guide for learners and teachers*. Englewood Cliffs: Prentice Hall/Cambridge.

Kolb, D. A. (1984). *Experiential learning: Experience as the source of learning and development*. Englewood Cliffs, NJ: Prentice Hall.

Little, T. C. (1983). Making Sponsored Experiential Learning Standard Practice. In *New Directions for Experiential Learning, No. 20*. San Francisco: Jossey-Bass.

National Society for Experiential Education (1998). *Eight Principles of Good Practice for All Experiential Learning Activities*. Retrieved from http://www.nsee.org/about_us.htm#sop

Polanyi, M. (1958). *Personal Knowledge: Towards a Post-Critical Philosophy*. Chicago: University of Chicago Press.

Ross, R. G. (2000). Enriching the academic experience of the SCSU British Studies Program: The development of the international 199 and international 299 courses. *Excellence in Teaching, vol.6, 4-31*. A publication of the SCSU Faculty Center for Teaching Excellence.

Ross, R. G. (2000). *Developing the Leadership of America's Next Generation of Nonprofit Leaders: An Introduction to Intern & Mentor Professional Development Institutes;* A Joint Project of: National Society for Experiential Education, Regis

University and the Center for Creative Leadership. Alexandria, VA: National Society for Experiential Education.

Ross, R. G. & Montrose, L. (2001). NSEE's joint project: Developing the leadership of America's next generation of nonprofit leaders service-learning and career exploration through internships. *NSEE Quarterly, fall.*

Sheehan, B., McDonald, M., & Spence, K. (2009). Developing students' emotional competency using the classroom-as-organization (C-A-O) approach. *Journal of Management Education,* 33(1), 77-98.

Sheehan, B., & McDonald, M. (December 2011). An examination into the impact of an experience-based course on students' emotional competency development. *Sport Management Education Journal,* 5(1), 49-75.

Spence, K., Hess, D., McDonald, M., & Sheehan, B. (2009). Designing experiential learning curricula to develop future sport leaders. *Sport Management Education Journal,* 3(1), 1-25.

Tagg, J. (2003). *The Learning Paradigm College.* Bolton, MA: Anker Press.

Authors

ROSEANNA G. ROSS, Ph.D. is a Professor of Communication Studies at St. Cloud State University, Minnesota. She was department Chair for 9 years, department Internship Director for over 18 years, and Director of the Faculty Center for Teaching Excellence for 5 years. Roseanna taught on and/or directed education abroad programs in Denmark, Japan and England. Roseanna is co-author (with Robert Inkster) of two NSEE publications: "The Internship as Partnership: a Handbook for Businesses, Nonprofits and Government Agencies," and "The Internship as Partnership: A Handbook for Campus-Based Coordinators and Advisors." As Senior Associate in the "Developing the Leadership of America's Next Generation of Nonprofit Leaders" joint project of the National Society for Experiential Education (NSEE), Regis University and the Center for Creative Leadership, Ross developed and facilitated a series of institutes for interns and mentors, and published a summary/outline of those institutes (available through NSEE). She has presented and facilitated workshops on NSEE's Best Practices for Experiential Learning for campuses across the U.S. and in Turkey and South Africa. Dr. Ross was the recipient of the 2012 Outstanding Individual in Communication and Theatre Award given by the Communication and Theatre Association of Minnesota and the SCSU 2010 College of Fine Arts and Humanities Leadership Award. She is the recipient of the National Society for Experiential Learning 2006 Pioneer in Experiential Learning Award and the 1999 Young Leader in Experiential Learning Award. Roseanna received the 1998 MnSCU Center for Teaching and Learning Star Leader Award. Ross has received teaching awards including the Central States Speech Association Outstanding Young Teacher Award and the Ohio University Department of Education Distinguished Alumni Award. Roseanna Ross earned a BS in English/speech and theatre education at Ohio University, and a Master of Arts in communication theory from Ohio State University and is a Doctor of Philosophy in communication, interpersonal and small group theory, and higher education from Ohio University.

BETH J. SHEEHAN, Ph.D. is an Associate Professor and acting Director of the College Unbound program at Southern New Hampshire University (SNHU). She was a member of the Sport Management faculty for six years before taking a three-year retreat to serve as Director of College Unbound@SNHU. College Unbound@SNHU is a three-year intensive experiential bachelor's degree program built around internship and project-based learning. Beth's professional certifications include the Experiential Education Academy Certificate from the National Society for Experiential Education. She is a manuscript reviewer for the Journal of Experiential Education, Journal of Management Education, and the Sport Management Education Journal. Dr. Sheehan's publications include Sheehan, E., McDonald, M. A. (December 2011), An examination into the impact of an experience-based course on students' emotional competency development. *Sport Management Education Journal, 5(1), 49-75;* and Sheehan, B., McDonald, M., and Spence, K. (2009), Developing students' emotional competency using the classroom-as-organization (C-A-O) approach. *Journal of Management Education*, 33(1), 77-98. Beth served on the SNHU General Education Committee and as the chairperson for the Tuffy Phelps Scholarship Committee. She is a board member for the Center for Entrepreneurship and Social Innovation at SNHU and completed three years of service on the Board of Directors for Big Brothers Big Sisters of Greater Manchester (2009-2012). Beth received her Bachelor of Arts in Rhetoric and Writing from Mount Saint Mary's College (now University) and her Master of Science in Sport Management and her Doctor of Philosophy in Sport Management from the University of Massachusetts, Amherst.

Chapter 3
INCREASING FACULTY INVOLVEMENT IN EXPERIENTIAL EDUCATION

Garry Hesser
Augsburg College, Minneapolis, MN

Outline
Prologue
Bringing It Home: Seven Legitimating Resources for Faculty Engagement

PROLOGUE [Abstract]

The thesis of this chapter on "increasing faculty involvement" is quite simple: *There has been a "sea change" in higher education since the 1986 edition was published. NSEE contributed to and has benefitted immensely from that change. One corollary or consequence of this profound change is that experiential education professionals, with or without faculty status, will be more effective in increasing the quantity and quality of faculty involvement in experiential education if we exploit the resources and legitimating entities that currently exist and are emerging daily. Few of us in 1986 were bold enough to predict the prominent place that community-based learning and research, civic engagement, high impact practices, and engaged learning in the classroom would assume.*

This revised chapter offers you information and sources that I have found to be effective in my 25 years of conducting faculty workshops. An effective strategy for faculty engagement is to immerse oneself in the current and ongoing conversations in K-16 concerning learning and teaching. This includes "pedagogies of engagement", "the learning paradigm", and "high impact practices". Equipped with an understanding of these new resources, along with NSEE's principles of effective practice in experiential education, your approach might then be to ask your faculty colleagues: *"How can I be of assistance to you in creating the kind of learning centered department that you want to become?"* Or *"How can I help you make fuller use of what the research reveals about quality learning outcomes and how can we make use of NSEE's effective, quality experiential education practices and resources to assist you in moving closer to the vision you have for your department and your own courses?"*

In other words, we should see ourselves as valued colleagues who can assist faculty as they grapple with assessment and effectiveness with regard to the learning outcomes they desire. For example, George Kuh's "high impact practices/pedagogies" are excellent places to start [www.aacu.org/leap/hip.cfm], along with AAC&U's LEAP initiative [www.aacu.org/leap] and the related "bringing theory to practice" [www.aacu.org/bringing_theory]. These new endeavors are discussed in this chapter along with other chapters in this revision, especially 2 and 4. These initiatives identify and underscore the legitimacy of what our National Society for Internships and Experiential Education [NSIEE] colleagues were advocating as part of the 1980's FIPSE project and the initial 1986 publication of *Strengthening*. And both of these efforts were instrumental in bringing about many of the changes that provide us with a very different context for our work.

A review of the contents and strategies found in the original chapter on faculty involvement reveals that it is still very valuable for our work with faculty today. For a quick overview, take a look at Appendix 1 at the end of this chapter and the original itself. The original represents a solid approach and a valid "check list" of strategies for engaging faculty and expanding collaboration with and between faculty colleagues. Building upon that foundation, my strategy for this revision has been to provide you with an overview and access to some of the best resources that have emerged since 1986. It is my hope that this approach will enhance your own growth and offer you resources that will assist you in increasing the quantity and quality of faculty involvement. I have sought to link you to resources that did not exist when the original book was written, as well as to offer a history of this "sea change". My goal has been to provide you with a sense of the changes and a context for what is happening today. I also encourage you to make use of all the other chapters in this new edition as you engage your faculty and administrative colleagues. Note that over half of our authors are or were tenured faculty members. And most have played and are playing significant roles in faculty development and the quality movement in higher education.

As you build upon and exploit this "sea change" to deepen and expand your own dialogue and collaboration with faculty at your institution, consider the *"Rubin Principle"*. Sharon Rubin, one of the original FIPSE consultants was a co-author of the original version of *Strengthening Experiential Education* and is the author of the revised chapter 5. Sharon has been a servant-leader mentor to many of us as we joined with her, Jane Kendall and other colleagues in leadership roles during the 1980's and 1990's. The last three sections of the original chapter "put legs on" the *Rubin Principle*, including a list of "21 Things To Do". Put simply, become a *resource person* for faculty and work closely with whatever office or program that your campus or institution has created for "faculty development", i.e., your "Center for Teaching and Learning". Sharon urges us to g*ive away* the sound and effective NSEE practices, resources and other information we find or are given. And, paradoxically, the corollary to the *Rubin Principle* suggests that the more we "give away", the more we will increase our own esteem and authority.

First step suggestion: Start with, or deepen, your existing work with an inner core of advocates and "champions" with whom you can share this chapter and the articles it identifies for conversation and planning. If you have not already done so, create an "advisory" committee of faculty colleagues who respect and value experiential education. Ideally they should also come from a wide range of disciplines. It is all the better if they have legitimacy as a recognized faculty committee or Dean's advisory group. Utilize chapters 2, 4, 5, 6 & 7 for more ideas, along with the original chapter 3. Strengthened by what you create together, all of you can, in turn, exercise the "Rubin Principle" with other faculty colleagues, passing on the resources that you and they uncover and share with each other as a "learning organization" (Senge et al 2004).

Bringing It Home: Seven Legitimating Resources for Faculty Engagement

It is my sincere hope that this overview of current resources and the historical context will provide you with information and tools that are usable and helpful. I trust that you will find many new ideas, as well as some additional ways to make use of what you are already familiar with, as you work with your faculty colleagues. I have chosen to highlight seven different types of resources that experiential education [EE] professionals and faculty advocates can make use of as we work together to enhance the quantity and quality of EE in every educational institution:

> *1) Context, Context: Precursors to Experiential Education's Legitimation*
> *2) Organizing for Learning: Peter Ewell (1997)*
> *3) High-Impact Educational Practices: A Brief Overview*
> *4) Carnegie, SoTL & POD: Interrelated Resources for Experiential Educators*
> *5) AAC&U: LEAP, BTtoP, and Effective Practice*
> *6) American Commonwealth Partnership [ACP] and "A Crucible Moment"*
> *7) Other Higher Education Initiatives & Collaborations*

Context, Context: Precursors to Experiential Education's Legitimation

Higher Education Engagement

When I entered the faculty realm in the early 1970's, experiential educators were piloting community internships and urban semester programs, often in direct response to the "urban crisis", Harrington's *The Other America*, and Martin Luther King, Jr.'s assassination. Programs and people that shaped NSIEE's creation in 1971 include Tim Stanton, Dwight Giles and their colleagues at Cornell; Jane Permaul and UCLA's Field Study Program; Jim Feeney's work at New College; Steve Brooks and the GLCA Urban Semester; John Duley's Experimental College at Michigan State; Dick Couto's work at Vanderbilt; and Bob Sigmon's North Carolina Internship Program. It is also important to note that none of these colleagues had tenured faculty positions. Joel Torstenson and HECUA's domestic and international urban immersion programs may have been unique in that regard, but even at HECUA, the teaching role evolved into a consortia endeavor with non-tenured faculty. In other words, these remarkable programs still remained largely "marginal", i.e., not "institutionalized". Exceptions were Cooperative Education programs at places like Antioch, Northeastern and LaGuardia.

However, higher education was beginning to take notice of experiential education, beginning in the 1970's. One stellar example was the establishment of the Jossey-Bass series on *New Directions for Experiential Learning,* edited by Pamela Tate and Morris Keeton. Keeton was himself an Academic Dean and faculty member at Antioch. Scholars, including many of our founders, began to document the value of experiential pedagogies. On other fronts, James Coleman, later President of the American Sociological Association and author of the famous "Coleman Report", along with William Gamson and Wilbert McKeachie, who later served as Presidents of the American Sociological Association and American Psychological Association respectively, focused their research on effective teaching and learning outcomes, including experiential education. In addition, David Kolb's initial introduction of his "four-stage learning cycle" first appeared in 1976 in the Jossey-Bass quarterly publication *New Directions for Experiential Learning.*

Then, in 1984, Kolb's classic *Experiential Learning: Experience as the Source of Learning and Development* significantly enhanced research and theory in our field, providing a critical framework for the first edition of *Strengthening,* along with the FIPSE proposal and project itself. The quality of Kolb's theory development and quantitative research, along with his status as a professor of organizational development at Case-Western University, played a seminal role in legitimating experiential education, as well as advancing EE in the academy. William Gamson's development of *SimSoc* represented another major advance in practice and research related to classroom experiential pedagogies. *SimSoc* was an intensive classroom simulation that challenged traditional modes of instruction. Gamson, and his wife Zelda, brought their prominent faculty status and prestige to experiential pedagogy and "learning-centered" teaching. Bill's role as a President of the American Sociological Association and faculty member [Michigan and then Boston College] and Zelda's co-authorship of the *Wingspread Principles* and leadership of the New England Resource Center for Higher Education [NERCHE] were quite significant. Zelda also served on NSEE's Board of Directors. As recently as August of 2012, Bill told this author that his most important current project is updating *SimSoc* for expanded use. One more example illustrates what was emerging in higher education at the same time that *Strengthening* first appeared in 1986. Patricia Cross at the Educational Testing Service [ETS], Bill McKeachie, Michigan Psychology Professor and President of the American Psychological Association, and Russ Edgerton, AAHE President, brought "learning" and "engagement" into prominence in higher education and underscored the questions being asked by NSIEE leaders. All concurred with Derek Bok, President of Harvard University, who challenged higher education to stop focusing primarily on "<u>what</u> students should learn" and give equal or greater attention to "<u>how</u> students learn" (*Higher Learning* 1986). This led to Bok's engaging Richard Light, a prominent evaluation researcher at the Harvard Kennedy School, to do extensive research on "how learning happens." Light further documented what Bill McKeachie and K. Patricia Cross had found, namely that students learn best when they are actively engaged, and especially when they teach each other.

NSIEE was, indeed, taking part in something of which we [were] both witnesses and creators (cf.Ryszard Kapuscinski). This "chicken and egg" process led to the FIPSE proposal in the mid 1980's and an even more extensive interaction with the new thinking that was emerging in higher education and given voice and prominence in the *Wingspread Principles.* <u>Consequently, one "talking point with faculty colleagues today</u> is that NSIEE/NSEE was an active player in the fundamental changes that happened in higher education in the 1970s and 1980s. Our pioneering leaders wisely synthesized their own experiences with the ideas and research that others were producing to document how experiential education pedagogies contribute significantly to student learning and development. *In other words, NSEE is not just now jumping on a "band wagon", but has been a key player and agent of change for the past five decades.*

Wingspread Principles

In 1986-87, several years after the FIPSE consulting had begun and the year <u>after</u> *Strengthening* appeared, AAHE, the Education of Commission of States, and Wingspread brought together the leading researchers in the field of undergraduate education. Arthur Chickering and Zelda Gamson summarized their consensus in an article that first appeared in the American Association

for Higher Education's *AAHE Bulletin* [March, 1987] and has been circulating widely and shaping higher education curriculum ever since.
<*http://www.uis.edu/liberalstudies/students/documents/sevenprinciples.pdf*>

The *Seven Principles* were "monumental" for two reasons: 1) they punctuated and outlined what has become the working agenda in higher education ever since, linking learning outcomes to pedagogy; and 2) they prominently validated the critical importance of "active learning" along the approaches that Dewey and Kolb emphasized. Its introduction is as relevant and useful today as it was a quarter century ago:

> These seven principles are not Ten Commandments shrunk to a 20th century attention span. They are intended as guidelines for faculty members, students, and administrators with support from state agencies and trustees--to improve teaching and learning. These principles seem like good common sense, and they are -- because many teachers and students have experienced them and *because research supports them. They rest on 50 years of research on the way teachers teach and students learn, how students work and play with one another, and how students and faculty talk to each other* (Chickering and Gamson, 1987; italics mine).

Like NSEE's founders, who were also active in this milieu, these leaders in higher education sought to answer the question that we continue to ask today: "how can faculty improve undergraduate education?" Their answer continues to be a focusing framework for our dialogue and collaboration with faculty, based on research regarding effective teaching and learning:

Good practice in undergraduate education:
1. Encourages contact between students and faculty.
2. Develops reciprocity and cooperation among students.
3. Encourages active learning.
4. Gives prompt feedback.
5. Emphasizes time on task.
6. Communicates high expectations.
7. Respects diverse talents and ways of learning (Chickering & Gamson, 1987).

1987-1997: A Watershed Decade
The *Wingspread Principles* surfaced within this larger, changing context that was punctuated by the work of two prominent scholars. Their speeches and publications fundamentally redefined the professional expectations for faculty practice related to the teaching and learning enterprise. In 1987, Ernest Boyer, President of the Carnegie Foundation for the Advancement of Teaching published *College: The Undergraduate Experience in America* and Russ Edgerton invited Parker Palmer to keynote the 1987 AAHE meeting in Chicago. Palmer, like Boyer and Edgerton, literally redrew the epistemological and pedagogical landscape with "Community, Conflict and Ways of Knowing: Ways to Deepen Our Educational Agenda". The speech later appeared in *Change Magazine* and can be found in NSIEE's *Combining Service and Learning, Vol I.*

During this same period of time, Russ Edgerton and AAHE made prominent the work of Donald Schoen regarding the "reflective practitioner". Faculty were encouraged to see themselves as experiential learners, also reflecting and learning from their individual and collective experiences. Similarly, K. Patricia Cross invited and urged faculty to embrace the role of "professor as classroom researcher", practicing the same reflective behavior that Kolb, Schoen and others charted for all learners. The 1980s decade ended with another "sea change" publication by Ernest Boyer and his Carnegie colleague, Gene Rice, *Scholarship Reconsidered* (1990). Carnegie's leadership was then expanded, with Patricia Hutchings, previously an Alverno English professor, experiential educator and co-author of *Knowing and Doing* (1988). She took the lead in Carnegie's Scholarship of Teaching and Learning initiatives.

K. Patricia Cross, one of the leading researchers and participants in Wingspread, keynoted an AAHE conference a decade after *Strengthening* appeared. She underscored the legitimacy of experiential education in her summary and conclusion regarding the two major messages from "contemporary research in cognitive psychology". She urged faculty, faculty development professionals, and all who are engaged in the educational enterprise to focus on: 1) the importance of active, as opposed to passive, learning; and 2) to embrace the idea that learning is transformational rather than additive. Cross underscored what Dewey and Kolb had posited: new learning interacts with what we already know to transform and deepen our understanding

1997: Leadership Matters—Russell Edgerton and Lee Shulman
Pat Cross' summary reveals how leading researchers were centering their attention on *pedagogy and learning* toward the end of the 1990s. Lee Shulman, President of the Carnegie Foundation for Teaching and Learning, wrote the following in 2002 reminding us of how important Russ Edgerton was for much that had transpired. Following his FIPSE years, Russ led AAHE for19 years, and concluded his service to higher education at the Pew Foundation. Shulman emphasized that Edgerton was at the "root of this work" and wrote:

> About five years ago [1997], when Russ Edgerton was serving as education officer for The Pew Charitable Trusts, he produced a terrific white paper, which has propelled many of the most interesting initiatives in higher education today. One of Russ's arguments focused on something he called "pedagogies of engagement" — approaches that have within them the capacity to engage students actively with learning in new ways. He wasn't talking only about service-learning, though service learning was an example; he was talking about an array of approaches, from problem-based and project-based learning to varieties of collaborative work and field-based instruction. Russ used the rubric "pedagogies of engagement" to describe them all (Shulman 2002).

Russ Edgerton's longer *White Paper* also makes excellent reading for faculty when you want to engage them in understanding and practicing EE in the context of higher education. Edgerton and Shulman were instrumental in setting the stage for much of the work of AAC&U today. In 1997 Lee Shulman began to talk about "pedagogical content knowledge" while Russ Edgerton was stressing the "pedagogy of engagement". You will also find Shulman's essay, "Making Differences: A Table of Learning" very helpful, and it is summarized in John Duley's Prologue to this revision [http://www.carnegiefoundation.org/elibrary/making-differences-table-learning>].

To summarize, the decade of the 1990's was marked by the widespread utilization of the *Wingspread Principles*, which were given even greater legitimacy by Ernest Boyer's now classic *Scholarship Reconsidered* (1990). His successor, Lee Shulman, insisted that faculty also develop a "pedagogical competency and scholarship" and Donald Schoen's image of teachers as "reflective practitioners" became additional markers alongside Pat Cross' advocacy of the "teacher as classroom researcher". Parker Palmer and Steven Brookfield, to name a few others, brought the art of teaching to prominence in additional ways, underscoring along with Pat Cross and her Wingspread colleagues, "the importance of active as opposed to passive learning". I trust that this brief historical overview will assist you in engaging your faculty colleagues in ongoing conversations and collaboration regarding learning and teaching.

Organizing for Learning: Peter Ewell (1997)

In this context *Peter Ewell* and his colleagues set to work doing a comprehensive review of the literature of "cognitive science, human learning and development, teaching improvement, curricular and instructional development, organizational restructuring and quality improvement". Ewell, the consummate assessor and evaluator, found "a remarkably consistent" picture based on the evidence from educational research. I have been using Ewell's "Organizing for Learning" publication in nearly every one of the 60 plus faculty workshops that I have conducted since it appeared in 1997 in the *AAHE Bulletin*. It is my recommendation that you do the same with your faculty colleagues. It is an excellent "conversation starter" for dialogue with faculty colleagues. Ewell's work continues to be as valid and focused as any resource I have found for faculty who are being encouraged to embrace the "learning paradigm" or do "backward design" for a particular course or are creating an "engaged curriculum" overall.

Ewell clearly and supportively assists faculty in becoming "reflective practitioners" (Schoen) and "pedagogical scholars" (Shulman). Ewell articulates very clearly "What We [Actually] Know About Learning" and validates what NSEE and experiential educators have asserted since Dewey, Piaget, Lewin, and Kolb. Ewell spells it out this way:

> To get systemic improvement, we must make use of what is already known about learning itself, about promoting learning, and about institutional change…A decade of path breaking research in the field of cognitive science suggests that indeed big differences exist between knowledge based on recall and deeper forms of understanding. That research forces us to recognize that all learning is rich, complex, and occasionally unpredictable. Building effective environments to foster it must rest on collective knowledge and active discussion of this complexity (Ewell, 1997: 4ff).

Drawn from his thorough assessment of the considerable body of research, Ewell cogently identifies seven "consensus" research findings about learning that can and should frame our discussions and engagement with faculty:

1. The learner is not a "receptacle" of knowledge, but rather creates his or her learning actively and uniquely.
2. Learning is about making meaning for each individual learner by establishing and reworking patterns, relationships, and connections.
3. Every student learns all the time, both with us and despite us.
4. Direct experience decisively shapes individual understanding.
5. Learning occurs best in the context of a compelling "presenting problem."

6. Beyond stimulation, learning requires reflection.
7. Learning occurs best in a cultural context that provides both enjoyable interaction and substantial personal support (Ewell, 1997: 3-4).

These conclusions, based on solid research, echo Dewey and Kolb, along with NSEE's Principles of Effective Practice, elaborated in chapter 2 & 4. They also sound almost "identical" to what our founders were contending and documenting anecdotally. Take note that Ewell did not come to these conclusions because he is an experiential educator. He is a hardnosed, "show me the evidence" assessor and evaluator who believes that teaching and learning can best be enhanced with systemic improvement if we "make use of what is already known about learning itself, about promoting learning and about institutional change" (1997: 3). Ewell further contends that:

> Taken individually, each of these insights about the nature of learning isn't much of a surprise. But colleges and universities remain "novice cultures" in developing approaches consistent with these "obvious" insights. Rather than being guided by an overall vision of learning itself, established through systematic research and the wisdom of practice (both hallmarks of an "expert culture"), reform efforts tend to be particularistic and mechanical.

> Yet decades of experimental work in educational psychology and instructional design have taught us a lot about the relative values of specific pedagogical settings and approaches. In parallel with what cognitive science tells us about the nature of learning, this body of work suggests that the following six "big ticket items" are good places to start in remaking instruction (1997: 5).

In light of the research findings, Ewell strongly recommends the following six "big ticket" items related to effective teaching and learning. Note the centrality of <u>experience, application, collaboration, and reflection.</u> He insists that faculty should, wherever possible, make use of:
1. Approaches that emphasize application and experience.
2. Approaches in which faculty constructively model the learning process.
3. Approaches that emphasize linking established concepts to new situations.
4. Approaches that emphasize interpersonal collaboration.
5. Approaches that emphasize rich and frequent feedback on performance.
6. Curricula that consistently develop a limited set of clearly identified, cross-disciplinary skills that are publicly held to be important (Ewell, 1997: 5).

Ewell concludes with an "invitation" that we can extend to our faculty colleagues as we work with them to deepen and expand the quality of learning that we all want for our students. These are also outcomes that accrediting agencies are expecting all of us to deliver in every aspect of teaching and the curriculum. Rob Shumer's chapter on "Assessment and Evaluation" and all the other chapters in this revision underscore this as well. Making Ewell and Shulman's essays available to faculty can help you, as an EE professional, to operationalize your commitment to the "Rubin principle" as you assist faculty and academic departments in becoming more successful.

Ewell contends that our meager gains in overall improvement of student learning is closely related to the failure to heed the research on the nature of learning itself and to work together systemically, with a focus on student learning. This echoes what Jane Kendall, her colleagues in the original FIPSE project, along with the first edition of *Strengthening,* were all about. You will also find this stressed in chapter 7 on "Institutional Change" and chapter 4 on "Quality". Ewell's words, like virtually all of *Strengthening* (1986), have a classical ring when he states that "in the last analysis":

> Every system is perfectly constructed to produce the results that it achieves, long-term observers of organizational dynamics often say. That higher education is currently underperforming — both in its own eyes and in the eyes of others — should come as no surprise then, given its extant organizational structures, values, and patterns of communication.

> Explicit recognition that the current system is a system — intact and self-perpetuating because of a complex network of existing values and supports — is thus fundamental for change. Only by beginning from a new point of departure can we hope to break the constraints on both thinking and action that this system imposes. In the last analysis, this is what "organizing for learning" is all about (1997:6).

The good news is that, while we still have a long way to go, we have made considerable progress since Ewell offered his clear summary that underscores and legitimizes experiential education throughout the academy. Kuh's research, AAC&U's LEAP initiative, and the *Crucible Moment* represent and underscore that more change is underway and that we have a lot more allies, support, and legitimacy for our work with faculty than was the case in 1986.

High-Impact Educational Practices: A Brief Overview

George Kuh, Chancellor Professor and Director Emeritus of Indiana University's Center for Postsecondary Research, was the keynote speaker at the 2010 NSEE conference. He continues to provide us with further "talking points" and ongoing research regarding High-Impact educational practices [HIEP]. This phrase has become a buzz word in educational effectiveness discussions. Kuh and his colleagues refer to these "high impact practices" as "teaching and learning practices [that] have been widely tested and have been shown to be beneficial for college students from many backgrounds". Kuh provides a Chart of High-Impact Practices (pdf) showing the learning and developmental impact that he, like Ewell, distills from surveying the considerable research on learning and pedagogy. Kuh's list includes:

High Impact Educational Practices [HIEP]

First-Year Seminars stressing Common Intellectual Experiences and Learning Communities
Writing-Intensive Courses
Collaborative Assignments and Projects
Undergraduate Research
Diversity/Global Learning/Study Abroad
Service Learning, Community-Based Learning
Internships

Capstone Courses and Projects (Kuh, 2008)

This list of HIEP pedagogies reflects a "developmental" sequencing, beginning with engaging pedagogies that can and should be introduced early and often to achieve the "essential learning outcomes" that AAC&U advocates (see below). This array of high impact "programs" could also be intimidating if you see the list as constituting competing programs and endeavors on your campus. However, I urge you to see those programmatic and engaged pedagogical endeavors as *allies* and *colleagues*. Viewed this way, the "Rubin Principle" invites you to see other colleagues and the faculty as rich resources and "sources of abundance" as you work together.

High impact pedagogical practices embrace a continuum of experiential and engaged forms of learning. AAC&U's embracing and promoting of these high-impact, experiential pedagogies offer validation for what you and I are doing to institutionalize EE in our institutions. In other words, these high impact practices underscore what NSEE has been promoting since its beginning, namely that experiential learning is *necessary* and *essential—not just desirable*. Kuh, AAC&U, Campus Compact, the "Crucible Moment" and American Commonwealth Project are further testimony to NSEE's claims that experiential pedagogy is essential if the lofty "educative" outcomes needed for all students, professionals and citizens are to be achieved.

You will be well served to explore the websites associated with High-Impact Pedagogies and George Kuh <High-Impact educational practices>. Increasingly I find that Faculty Development Centers are also making use of Kuh. This provides you and me with further links and bridges for collaboration with faculty. For example, check out the University of Wisconsin, Madison: <https://tle.wisc.edu/solutions/engagement/summary-high-impact-educational-practices-monograph>). In summary, Kuh's High Impact Educational Practices provide us with another excellent starting point as we seek to increase faculty involvement.

Carnegie, SoTL & POD: Interrelated Resources for Experiential Educators

As a sociologist, I am trained to look for systemic changes, patterns and new organizational ways in which ideas are supported and advanced. And the organizational environment has changed in other fundamental ways since *Strengthening* was published in 1986. While there are many, many organizational influences, there are four that provide major legitimacy and partnership opportunities for experiential education: 1) The Carnegie Foundation for the Advancement of Teaching; 2) the Scholarship of Teaching and Learning movement, including the International Society for the Scholarship of Teaching and Learning [ISSOTL]; 3) the Professional and Organizational Development Network in Higher Education [POD]; and 4) AAC&U and its affiliated initiatives. These are national and international in scope. They all offer many resources and considerable legitimacy to aid you in your faculty engagement and collaboration.

The Carnegie Foundation for the Advancement of Teaching
[http://www.carnegiefoundation.org/]

The Foundation describes itself in this way:

Founded by Andrew Carnegie in 1905 and chartered in 1906 by an act of Congress, the Carnegie Foundation for the Advancement of Teaching is an independent policy and research center. Improving teaching and learning has always been Carnegie's motivation and heritage. Our current improvement research approach builds on the scholarship of teaching and learning, where we: *Learn from each other, Improve on what we know works, Continuously create new knowledge, Take what we learn and make it usable by others.....*

Scholarship of Teaching and Learning. Carnegie has a long history. But it was Ernest Boyer's and Lee Shulman's writings, speeches and "bully pulpit" that gave impetus to rethinking the importance of the scholarship of teaching and learning in *Scholarship Reconsidered* (Boyer, 1990) and "pedagogical scholarship" (Shulman, 2002). In addition to these two presidents and the role they played, Gene Rice, Patricia Hutchings and Mary Huber also have played critical roles in birthing and supporting the "Scholarship for Teaching and Learning" [SoTL] movement. In *The Scholarship of Teaching and Learning Reconsidered: Institutional Integration and Impact* (2011), Pat Hutchings and her colleagues at Carnegie draw on the experiences of individuals, campuses, and professional associations associated with Carnegie and its Institutional Leadership Program. They examine and recommend critical areas where engagement with the scholarship of teaching and learning can have significant effect, especially when there is institution-wide collaboration. Note that this is precisely the underlying thesis of the original *Strengthening,* as well as this 2013 updated version. It is also noteworthy that Pat Hutchings, before going to Carnegie, co-authored the seminal work, *Knowing and Doing: Learning Through Experience* (1988) with her Alverno colleague, Alan Wutzdorff, who also served on NSEE's Board and as NSEE's Executive Director during the 1990s.

Community Engagement Elective Classification. Also of great importance to the field of experiential education is Carnegie's creation and oversight of the *Community Engagement Elective Classification.* In 2006, Carnegie created the classification and continues to promote and oversee it. The *Community Engagement Elective Classification* gives prominence to all forms of community-based educational endeavors and the commitments of colleges and universities. Carnegie's website describes the process and invites further applications: <<u>http://classifications.carnegiefoundation.org/descriptions/community_engagement.php</u>>

The National Advisory Panel [serves] as consultants in the review process to the classification team at the New England Resource Center for Higher Education of *John Saltmarsh* and Consulting Scholar *Amy Driscoll*....Of the one-hundred fifteen (115) successfully classified institutions, sixty-one (61) are public institutions and fifty-four (54) are private; thirty-seven (37) are classified in Carnegie's Basic Classification as research universities, forty (40) are master's colleges and universities, twenty-eight (28) are baccalaureate colleges, six (6) are community colleges, and four (4) institutions have a specialized focus - arts, medicine, technology. The classified institutions represent campuses in thirty-four (34) states....

Community engagement offers often-untapped possibilities for alignment with other campus priorities and initiatives to achieve greater impact—for example, first-year programs that include community engagement; learning communities in which community engagement is integrated into the design; or diversity initiatives that explicitly link active and collaborative community-based teaching and learning with the academic success of underrepresented students. There remain significant opportunities for campuses to develop collaborative internal practices that integrate disparate initiatives into more coherent community engagement efforts (from the Carnegie website).

Many campuses report that the process of securing or renewing this Community Engagement classification was another way to deepen and expand engagement with faculty and academic programs, as well as add legitimacy to the experiential education enterprise. I encourage you to consult Carnegie's website and consider applying if you have not already done so. <http://classifications.carnegiefoundation.org/descriptions/community_engagement.php>

SoTL: Scholarship of Teaching and Learning

Kathleen McKinney identifies SoTL as a "movement" that came into being around 2000, emerging out of Boyer's Scholarship of Teaching, along with K. Patricia Cross' pioneering work related to "teacher as classroom researcher." SoTL is grounded in nearly every academic discipline. McKinney's book, *Enhancing Learning Through the Scholarship of Teaching and Learning: The Challenges and Joys of Juggling* (2007) provides an excellent understanding of the history and practices that have become so widespread and institutionalized in K-16 education. SoTL also has an international expression in the International Society for the Scholarship of Teaching and Learning [ISSOTL; www.issotl.org] which describes itself as:

> The **International Society for the Scholarship of Teaching & Learning (ISSOTL)** serves faculty members, staff, and students who care about teaching and learning as serious intellectual work. The goal of the Society is to foster inquiry and disseminate findings about what improves and articulates post-secondary learning and teaching.

ISSOTL was organized in 2004 by many of those associated with SoTL and Carnegie to:

- Recognize and encourage scholarly work on teaching and learning in each discipline, within other scholarly societies, and across educational levels
- Promote cross-disciplinary conversation to create synergy and prompt new lines of inquiry
- Facilitate the collaboration of scholars in different countries and the flow of new findings and applications across national boundaries
- Encourage the integration of discovery, learning and public engagement
- Advocate for support, review, recognition, and appropriate uses of the scholarship of teaching and learning.

Since 2004, ISSOTL has met annually, with an average of 500 scholars from many countries. Those of us who wish to engage faculty more fully would be well served to network with SoTL.

Professional and Organizational Development Network in Higher Education [POD]

In general, this organization promotes and supports "faculty development" professionals and represents another rich resource and network, both in our own institutions and with other educational institutions. Their website [www.podnetwork.org] is a rich resource for you in your work. There you will find the following:

> POD supports a network of nearly 1,800 members - faculty and teaching assistant developers, faculty, administrators, consultants, and others who perform roles that value teaching and learning in higher education....[through a] POD Network—developing and supporting practitioners and leaders in higher education dedicated to enhancing learning and teaching.

While the specific uses of the term "faculty development" often overlap, the POD Network contends that "the common goal of these programs has been to develop the potential of the existing resources and structures of institutions by viewing and using them in creative ways. These resources include the faculty and staff, the courses and programs, all of which can become self-renewing once we become aware of the possibilities".

I urge you to learn more about Carnegie, SoTL and POD. Nationally, regionally and locally, their campus leaders, expressions and resources could and should be, if they are not already, some of your very best new resources and networks of people who can help you deepen and expand faculty engagement on your campus. As noted in chapter 1 of this revised edition,

> This "new era" in which we work is very much the result of NSEE's role as a significant player and collaborator over the years. Just how successful we will continue to be at building experiential education more deeply into the mission, values, and practices of K-16 education is closely linked to two responses on our part: 1) our ability to see and activate the synergy among the supportive, overlapping, and changing cultural contexts [including Carnegie, SoTL, and POD] ... and 2) our effectiveness in assisting our faculty colleagues in deepening student learning by means of the sound experiential pedagogical practices that are, and have been, espoused by NSEE and throughout the two editions of *Strengthening*. **In other words, this "new" emphasis on community-based pedagogies, engaged learning and high-impact practices provides experiential education both with greater legitimacy in the academy and underscores the need for competent experiential education professionals "now more than ever".**

AAC&U: LEAP, BTtoP, and Effective Practice

The American Association of Colleges and Universities

The American Association of Colleges and Universities [AAC&U], under the leadership of Carol Geary Schneider, has played an impressive leadership role relative to educational reform, with powerful implications and support for all forms of experiential education. AAC&U's LEAP Initiative and the closely related "From Theory to Practice" endeavors illustrate a fundamental shift in K-16 education. They are a "crest in the waves in the sea change" that I am encouraging all of us to embrace, ride and contribute to. Schneider and AAC&U's leadership took up the mantle of AAHE. They have played, I contend, a central role in continuing and expanding the changes in higher education that began in the 1960s and gave birth to NSIEE. AAC&U's core commitment to the liberal arts makes their embracing of experiential education, high impact pedagogies and effective practice all the more remarkable, even "radical". You be the judge. But it seems to me that their *"Liberal Education and America's Promise"* [LEAP] embraces experiential education in virtually every element of its wide ranging scope as it welcomes and promotes "high impact pedagogies," "effective practice", and "from theory to practice".

Liberal Arts and America's Promise: LEAP Initiative

In 2005, after extensive listening and interviewing of stakeholders, AAC&U rolled out their LEAP initiative. LEAP challenged the traditional practice of providing liberal education to some students and narrow training to others. LEAP, like NSEE since its founding, seeks to engage the

> "public with core questions about what really matters in college; connects employers and educational leaders as they make the case for the importance of liberal education in the global economy and in our diverse democracy; and helps all students achieve the essential learning outcomes" [see AAC&U website, www.**aacu**.org].

This author finds the language and literature of LEAP to be one of the best ways I have found to engage faculty in conversations on how experiential education can, and should, play a major role in operationalizing the claims made by Ewell and Wingspread. You and I will be well served to embrace and make use of LEAP's goals, namely "that all students receive the best and most powerful preparation for work, life, and citizenship".

The four elements of LEAP are, I contend, fundamentally linked to EE. They are:

- Essential learning outcomes—as a guiding vision and national benchmarks for college learning and liberal education in the 21st century
- High-Impact educational practices—that help students achieve essential learning outcomes
- Authentic Assessments—probing whether students can apply their learning to complex problems and real-world challenges
- Inclusive Excellence—to ensure that every student gets the benefits of an engaged and practical liberal education.

The "essential learning outcomes" that LEAP promotes require the kind of experiential engagement long promoted by NSEE, namely outcomes:

- *-Focused by engagement with big questions, both contemporary and enduring*
- *-Practiced extensively, across the curriculum, in the context of progressively more challenging problems, projects, and standards for performance*

- *-Anchored* through active involvement with diverse communities and real-world challenges
- *-Demonstrated* through the application of knowledge, skills, and responsibilities to new settings and complex problems [AAC&U, 2007]

LEAP's goal of preparing all students to become "intentional learners" who are prepared "as fully as possible… for the real-world demands of work, citizenship, and life in a complex and fast-changing society" comes very close to the goals of NSEE and experiential education. The "essential learning outcomes" that are identified by the LEAP initiative make it crystal clear that experiential education has come into the "center ring" of K-16 education. Our challenge, it seems to me, is to take advantage of this development and its supportive materials. In addition, experiential education professionals have much to offer as collaborators in the learning enterprise as we work with faculty colleagues to increase the learning potential of high impact practices.

While it is certainly accurate to say that AAC&U's goals and mission are not singularly focused on experiential education, it is my contention and belief that the "Essential Learning Outcomes" and "Principles of Excellence" resonate with virtually everything that advocates of experiential education have been striving for, going back to John Dewey, David Kolb and NSIEE's founders. I do not think that we could advocate for the importance of community-based, experiential education any better than is done in the Introduction to *College Learning for the New Global Century* (pdf) [2007]. Furthermore, it would be difficult to assemble a more impressive collection of advocates than those assembled for the LEAP Leadership Council.

Finally, it is no accident that LEAP is tied closely to George Kuh's high impact practices. Simply put, achieving LEAP's outcomes require pedagogy that is "experiential and educative", as Dewey put it. LEAP's learning outcomes are linked to pedagogical "design principles" along with Authentic Assessments criteria, rubrics and Inclusive Excellence. If you can read *College Learning for the New Global Century* and its Essential Learning Outcomes and not see new entry points for engaging in conversations with your faculty colleagues in a new way, then, as my wife and partner frequently says to me "Garry, go back again and look with both eyes". LEAP and "high impact practices" clearly place experience and engagement at the center of learning. What NSEE brings to the table is its long history and emphasis on "effective principles" that have been stressed and made operational since its beginning, all of which is further underscored by BTtoP.

Bringing Theory to Practice www.aacu.org/bringing_theory/

Led by Donald Harward, the *Bringing Theory to Practice Project (BTtoP)* "encourages colleges and universities to reassert their core purposes as educational institutions, not only to advance learning and discovery, but to advance the potential and well-being of each individual student, and to advance education as a public good that sustains a civic society". The Project is sponsored by the Charles Engelhard Foundation of New York City and the S. Engelhard Center and developed in partnership with the Association of American Colleges and Universities.

I can hear our founders applauding BTtoP's goals of supporting "campus-based initiatives that demonstrate how uses of engaged forms of learning that actively involve students both within and beyond the classroom directly contribute to their cognitive, emotional, and civic development." Their work and piloting endeavors on campuses are linked by collaboration and replication. BTtoP also reminds me of the original FIPSE project designed by Jane Kendall that resulted in the original edition of *Strengthening.* Certainly, BTtoP represents another opportunity for experiential educators to cheer and to expand our effectiveness with faculty colleagues.

As you read their materials and surf their website, note that BTtoP continues to offer publications, project funding and conference opportunities, such as:

> *Civic Provocations* **monograph** is composed of informal essays and provocations that support and deepen inclusive and intentional campus-based consideration of an institution's own civic mission and the civic mission of higher education today. It is the first in a series of monographs that will raise questions and provide perspectives on fundamental issues about the civic mission of higher education. The full monograph is available [by clicking here (pdf)].

> …**Proposals** are requested for projects that will promote engaged learning, civic development and engagement, and psychosocial well-being of college and university students. We are especially interested in efforts that will enable students to have transformational educational experiences, and for institutions to transform and sustain their priorities and practices.

> [Their] 2nd National Bridging Conference. "Bridging Institutional Divides: Practical Applications for Strengthening Campus Cultures for Learning, Civic Engagement and Psychosocial Well-being," addressed patterns of campus divide and dissonance that restrain the full expression of higher education's core purposes and offered practical strategies for maximizing campus resources to more directly connect mission to action and to strengthen campus cultures for engaged learning, civic development and psychosocial well-being of students.

Effective Practice & the Liberal Arts: *AAC&U and Clark University*

Clark University and AAC&U have also collaborated on an "Effective Practice" initiative. It is led by Richard Freeland, former Dean at Northeastern University, one of the early and long standing Cooperative Education institutions. This initiative has convened symposia and conferences to examine the false dichotomy between liberal learning and engaged learning. This endeavor seeks to further link LEAP, BTtoP, and community engagement. Carol Geary Schneider, AAC&U's President, describes the initiative this way:

> In the twentieth century, proponents of liberal learning drew a sharp dividing line between "practical" or career studies and the "true liberal arts." Today, we contend, we need to erase that distinction and insist that liberal education is, among its other virtues, practical. In a turbulent economy where industries are awash in change and where the combination of inventiveness and judgment is key to any organization's future, the most practical possible education is one that prepares students to make sense of complexity, to chart a course of action that takes full account of context, to engage in continuous

80

learning, and to take responsibility for the quality and integrity of what they do.

In the words of the Clark/AAC&U conference [participants] whose papers are synthesized in [an issue of *Liberal Education*], a good liberal education should take pride in preparing students for "effective practice." And how well it actually does that needs to become one of the hallmarks of excellence in this new global century. [To access symposia papers, go to: **http://aacu.org/liberaleducation/le-fa09/le-fa09_index.cfm**]

The entire collection of symposia papers, including one by former NSEE Board member, Janet Eyler, represents another sterling set of brief essays by faculty at leading institutions. Each essay advocates for increased integration of experiential education throughout the curriculum. Any one of them would be an excellent "think piece" and catalyst for discussion with and among your faculty colleagues. They are available free of charge by clicking on the link above. Appendix 2 offers an elaboration and includes excerpts from Richard Freeland's overview and challenge.

American Commonwealth Partnership [ACP] and "A Crucible Moment"

The American Commonwealth Partnership [ACP]

The American Commonwealth Partnership [ACP] is a collection of initiatives close to the heart of NSEE's mission and founding. ACP is led by faculty, administrators and students from throughout higher education. The initiative focuses on the fundamental mission of higher education as it relates to democracy and citizenship. As a collaboration of the White House, the U.S. Department of Education, the Kettering Foundation and a wide array of higher education associations, ACP provides us with many fundamental linkages to our own work and what we do with faculty. The ACP website describes the Partnership this way:

The American Commonwealth Partnership (ACP) is an alliance of community colleges, colleges and universities, P-12 schools and others dedicated to building "democracy colleges" throughout higher education. A Presidents' Advisory Council, composed of distinguished college and university presidents who have long been leaders in engaged higher education movement, offers continuing counsel and wisdom [see the list of Presidents in Appendix 3 along with more details and links related to ACP].

Launched at the White House on January 10th, 2012, the start of the 150th anniversary year of the Morrill Act which created land grant colleges, signed by President Lincoln in 1862, ACP uses the concept of democracy colleges from land grant and community college history. Democracy colleges convey the idea of colleges and universities deeply connected to their communities, which make education for citizenship a signature identity.....

The White House meeting, "For Democracy's Future – Education Reclaims Our Civic Mission", marked a new stage of coordinated effort to bring about a commitment to civic education and education as a public good. It was organized in partnership with the White House Office of Public Engagement, the Department of Education, the Association of American Colleges and Universities, and the Campaign for the Civic Mission of the

Schools.

At the White House, the Department of Education also released its "Road Map" and a "Call to Action" on civic learning and democratic engagement. The scope of ACP was described in remarks by Secretary of Education Arne Duncan. In addition, the National Task Force on Civic Learning and Democratic Engagement released *A Crucible Moment,* a report to the nation on the need for a shift in civic learning from "partial" to "pervasive."

A Crucible Moment: College Learning and Democracy's Future

This report from the National Task Force on Civic Learning and Democratic Engagement called on the nation to reclaim higher education's civic mission. Commissioned by the Department of Education and released at a White House convening in January 2012, the report pushes back against a prevailing national dialogue that limits the mission of higher education to workforce preparation and training while marginalizing disciplines basic to democracy. To view footage from January's White House event, "For Democracy's Future: Education Reclaims Our Civic Mission," you can click here and here. Their website provides this overview:

> *A Crucible Moment* calls on educators and public leaders to advance a 21st century vision of college learning for all students—a vision with civic learning and democratic engagement an expected part of every student's college education. The report documents the nation's anemic civic health and includes recommendations for action that address campus culture, general education, and civic inquiry as part of major and career fields as well as hands-on civic problem solving across differences.... *A Crucible Moment* was developed with input from a series of national roundtables involving leaders from all parts of the higher education and civic renewal communities (ACP website).

Once more, these documents and YouTube videos associated with ACP and *A Crucible Moment* provide you and me with "starting points" to engage our faculty colleagues. In addition, the ACP initiative enables us to reaffirm the role that NSEE has played over the years related to Dewey's assertion concerning the relationship between experiential learning and educating for democracy and community building.

Other Higher Educational Initiatives & Collaborations

Appendix 4 provides you with access to many of the major educational associations, along with AAC&U, NSEE and Campus Compact, that are also supporting the experiential education agenda in a wide variety of ways: American Council on Education [ACE]; The American Association of State Colleges and Universities [AASCU]; the American Association of Community Colleges [AACC]; the Council of Independent Colleges [CIC]; The Council for Advancement and Support of Education [CASE]; The Carnegie Foundation for the Advancement of Teaching and others. Each promotes and sponsors major initiatives and faculty development related to civic engagement and community-based learning.

You can discover the breadth and depth of that involvement and support by surfing their websites. To begin exploring the extent to which experiential education has moved into the mainstream, I suggest that you visit:
1) AASCU's American Democracy Project [< http://www.aascu.org/programs/ADP/>];
2) AACU's "Institutionalizing Service-Learning in Community Colleges"
[<http://www.aacc.nche.edu/Publications/Briefs/Pages/rb02012002.aspx>];
3) AAC&U's initiatives relating experiential education and the liberal arts (see above); and
4) Campus Compact (www.campuscompact.org).

Conclusion

When I review the materials identified in this chapter, I find it somewhat overwhelming to be "flooded" by what seems to be a never ending stream of research and documentation supporting a continuum of experiential learning. This abundance was rare when the original version of *Strengthening* was first written. In addition, many more examples came across my desk and computer screen as I was finalizing this draft. But what a gift this is. This plethora further underscores the claim that current research and practice continue to validate NSEE's founders' vision and further substantiate Ewell's research-based summaries. Examples in the Reference section include Fitzgerald's 2 volume *Handbook of Engaged Scholarship* (2010), Saltmarsh's collaborations (2011), Butin's initiatives (2010), Barkley's *Student Engagement Techniques: A Handbook for College Faculty* (2010), Robert Connor's "Let's Improve Learning, OK, but How?" (2011), Thomas and Brown's *A New Culture of Learning* (2011), Parker Palmer (2010), Randy Stoecker (2012), and Peter Levine's, "What Do We Know About Civic Engagement?" in *Liberal Education* (2011, Spring, vol 87, no. 2). And this list is just a beginning.

In 1986 Jane Kendall, John Duley, Tom Little, Jane Permaul, and Sharon Rubin punctuated our journey when they wrote and gave us *Strengthening Experiential Education Within Your Institution.* These colleagues and their NSIEE cohort advanced the field and broke new ground. Very little of what this chapter and the entire revision lift up was known or widely supported. As noted above, the original *Strengthening* was grounded in the FIPSE sponsored consulting endeavors involving 20 institutions. That watershed process and publication helped to set the stage by clearly identifying what they had learned and what was also emerging relative to experiential pedagogy. We have definitely come a long way from Frank Newman's assessment which accurately reflected the context for the original chapter: "The faculty has been extremely negative....We have a major task on our hands to convince the faculties of this country that they've got to change their ways on this issue [the development of civic leadership]".

This is, indeed, a *new era.* Consequently, I propose a "Hesser Principle" which is implicit, if not explicit, in the "Rubin Principle". It involves "jumping on the band wagon" that NSEE and our educational allies have created. We can, and should, take full advantage of all that has changed in our environment, along with all that NSEE continues to offer. We will be well served to capitalize on these opportunities and resources as we strive to deepen and expand our work with faculty. Being "opportunistic" and collaborative will, I am convinced, further the goal of institutionalizing and strengthening experiential education within our institutions and throughout the educational enterprise.

Hopefully, this chapter provides you with new and valuable awareness and access to a range of key and usable materials, as well as a framework to enhance your collaboration with faculty. While we "suffer" from being inundated by materials on engaged pedagogy and active learning, that is a wonderful "curse" compared to what our founders had available. So, make use of these resources to expand or start your "advisory" group or committee of "champions". Strive to become a "learning organization" that seeks to be the change you hope to help create. Exploiting this growth of information and our more supportive milieu, I encourage you to start new conversations by asking your faculty colleagues: "*What is the best thing you have read recently about teaching and student learning?*" and take off from there on a lively journey together.

Happy travels, and remember what Myles Horton and Paulo Freire reminded us with their last book's title: "we make the road by walking." Best wishes, and be sure to make use of NSEE in your ongoing efforts by attending our conferences, participating in the EE Academy, using our publications, and engaging in dialogues with EE colleagues as we all grow and serve together.

References & Resources

Association of American Colleges and Universities. (2012). *A crucible moment*: *College learning and democracy's future*. Washington DC: AAC&U.

Association of American Colleges and Universities. (2007). *College learning for the new global century* (pdf). Washington, DC: AAC&U.

Bailey, T., Hughes, K., & Moore, D. (2004). *Working knowledge: Work-based learning and education reform.* NY: RoutledgeFalmer.

> A very sophisticated example of triangulating methodologies to assess the asserted impacts of work-related EE, nuancing the claims and giving major attention to the quality of pedagogical practice and oversight/preparation as the critical/obvious contributor to learning. Along with *Where's the learning in service-learning?* by Eyler and Giles, this book illustrates the evolution of EE, along with K-16 education overall, in theory, research and assessment. [David Moore wrote the Theory chapter in this revision.]

Barkley, E. (2010). *Student engagement techniques: A handbook for college faculty.* SF: Jossey-Bass.

> Following a decade of administrative work, a formerly successful teacher was overwhelmed by the challenges and changes that marked the classroom, including the shift from lecturing. This book is good example of the proliferation of active modes of learning and teaching that build upon conceptual frameworks, the research on teaching and learning, and the experiences of the author and others. Linking motivation and active learning pedagogy, she offers 50 learning activities to enhance classroom teaching across the curriculum.

Battistoni, R. et al. (2003). *The engaged department toolkit.* Providence, RI: Campus Compact.

Bok, D. (1986). *Higher learning.* Cambridge, MA: Harvard University Press.

> Bok, from his powerful position as Harvard University, challenged higher education to stop focusing only on "what students should learn" and give equal or great attention to "how students learn. This led to his engaging Richard Light, a prominent evaluation research at the Harvard Kennedy School, to do extensive research on "how learning happens," identifying what Bill McKeachie found, namely that "students learn best when they are actively engaged, and especially when they teach each other."

Boyer, E. (1996). The scholarship of engagement. *Journal of Public Outreach* 1,1,11-20.

Boyer, E. (1990). *Scholarship reconsidered: Priorities of the professoriate.* Carnegie.

Boyer, E. (1987). *College: The undergraduate experience.* NY: Harper.

Brooks, S., & Althof, J. (1979). *Enriching the liberal arts through experiential learning.* SF: Jossey-Bass.

> Number 6 in the quarterly series *New directions for experiential learning*, edited by Morris Keeton and Pamela Tate illustrating the depth and sophistication that CAEL and NSIEE brought to theories and pedagogy overall and EE in particular and quite early.

Butin, D. (2010). *Service-learning in theory and practice: The future of community engagement in higher education.* Palgrave Macmillan.

Colby, A., Ehrlich, T., Beaumont, E., & Stephens, J. (2003). *Educating citizens: Preparing America's undergraduates for lives of moral and civic responsibility.* SF: Jossey Bass.

> A major contribution of scholars associated with the Carnegie Foundation. The authors summarize the research on civic and moral development and offer a wide variety of examples and designs that have moved civic engagement toward the center of the academic enterprise. They "describe in detail what it will take to build a more engaged and public-spirited academy" [Carol Schneider, AAC&U].

Connor, R. (2011). Let's improve learning, OK, but How? *Chronicle of Higher Education,* Dec 21, 2011.

> A candid assessment by a Teagle Foundation advisor about what we know about teaching practices that improve learning outcomes, identifying four clusters that make a difference: interactions, challenge and expectations, diversity experiences, and high order, integrative, reflective learning. Example of the candid and data based assessments.

Cross, K.P. & Steadman, H. (1996). *Classroom research: Implementing the scholarship of teaching.* SF: Jossey-Bass

An updating of the original work by Cross and Angelo and linking it to the SoTL endeavors that grew out of Cross and Carnegie, e.g., Boyer, Shulman and Hutchings. See also: Cross, K. P. & Angelo, T. (1993) *Classroom assessment techniques: A handbook for faculty*. 2nd ed. San Francisco: Jossey-Bass. The website article provides an elaborated description of "classroom research" from the Washington Center/Evergreen work on learning communities:
http://www.evergreen.edu/washcenter/resources/acl/c1.html

Duncan, D. & Kopperud, J. (2008). *Service-learning companion*. Boston: Wadsworth Centage.

A student source to guide and support effective learning and citizenship, with CARC.

Edgerton, R. (1997). *Education white paper*. Washington DC: Pew Forum on Undergraduate Learning.

What has come to be one of the most influential and synthesizing summaries and prescriptions for higher education, introducing the prophetic and now ubiquitous phrase "pedagogies of engagement". Edgerton was an early FIPSE staff member who laid the groundwork for NSEE's successful grants that produced *Strengthening*. After 19 years of reshaping higher education as President of AAHE, he led the Pew Forum on Undergraduate Learning.

Ewell, P. (1997). Organizing for learning: A new imperative. *AAHE Bulletin*. December, 3-6.

Eyler, J. (2009). The power of experiential education. *Liberal Education*, 95 (4), 22-26.

Experiential education, which takes students into the community, helps students both to bridge classroom study and life in the world and to transform inert knowledge into knowledge-in-use. A solid overview that demonstrates how EE has become central to the HE dialogue on effective practice in teaching and learning.

Eyler, J. & Giles. D. (1999). *Where's the learning in service-learning?* SF: Jossey-Bass.

One of the most cited research assessments of the strengths, limitations and effective practices associated with service-learning as an experiential education "pedagogy of engagement". Another example of work that emerged in the 1990s framing and re-framing experiential learning and the "pedagogy of engagement."

Faculty Leadership and Institutional Change, *Liberal Education*, 93 (4), entire issue.

This issue offers recommendations for strengthening faculty governance, examines campus practices and policies that can reverse or slow current trends impeding faculty leadership, and explores the complex interplay among organizational structures within higher education. Also included are articles on public health, the impact of teacher-scholars, a program focused on poverty, and an argument against the syllabus.

Fitzgerald, H., Burack, C., & Seifer, S. (2010). *Handbook of engaged scholarship:*

Contemporary landscapes, future directions, institutional change, Vol 1. (Transformation in higher education). East Lansing: Michigan State University Press.

Fitzgerald, H., Burack, C., & Seifer, S. (2010). *Handbook of engaged scholarship: Community-campus partnership, Vol 2. (Transformation in higher education).* East Lansing: Michigan State University Press.

Freeland, R. M. (2009). The Clark/AAC&U conference on liberal education and effective practice. *Liberal Education,* 95 (4), 3-7.

> How well do the learning experiences we offer align with our professed goals of preparing engaged citizens, effective professionals, and, more broadly, adults equipped to make significant contributions to society?

Freeland, R.M. (2009). Liberal education and effective practice: The Necessary Revolution in Undergraduate Education. *Liberal Education,* 95 (1), 4-8.

> Campus-level efforts to connect liberal education with practice are designed to nurture engaged, effective, constructive professionals and citizens. And they implicitly question whether learning experiences that cultivate analytic skills in classroom settings constitute the most effective way to enact this traditional mission of liberal education.

Harward, D.W. (2007). Engaged learning and the core purposes of liberal education: Bringing theory to practice". *Liberal Education,* 93 (1), 3-8.

> Founded on the premise of a connection between the neglect of the core purposes of undergraduate liberal education, on the one hand, and certain patterns of disengagement exhibited by students, on the other, the Bringing Theory to Practice project provides support for campus programs as well as for research on the connection of certain forms of engaged learning to student health, well-being, and civic development.

Horton, M. & Freire, P. (1990). *We make the road by walking.* Philadelphia: Temple University Press.

Howard, J. (1994-present). *Michigan Journal of Community Service Learning.* University of Michigan.

> One of the premier examples of the advancement of the field of community and civic engagement. A peer reviewed journal that brings together the Scholarship of Teaching and Learning, Service-Learning, and Civic Engagement, including its evolution in practice and emphases over the years of the "sea change" chronicled in this chapter.

Huber, M., Hutchings, P., Gale, R., Miller, R., & Breen, M. (2007). Leading initiatives for integrative learning. *Liberal Education,* 93 (2), 28-33.

Through initiatives such as the national Integrative Learning Project, the higher education community is gaining significant experience in fostering integrative learning through changes in the curricula, pedagogy, assessment, and faculty development.

Hutchings, P., Huber, M.T. & Ciccone, A. (2011). *The Scholarship of Teaching and Learning Reconsidered: Institutional Integration and Impact.* SF: Jossey-Bass [Wiley].

Drawing on the experience with the individuals, campuses, and professional associations associated with the Carnegie Academy for the Scholarship of Teaching and Learning and the Institutional Leadership Program, this important resource examines four critical areas where engagement with the scholarship of teaching and learning can have a significant effect. This book is intended for a broad audience of campus leaders, faculty, and people in foundations and other education associations with an interest in supporting new directions in teaching and learning.

Hutchings, P., & Wutzdorff, A., (1988). *Knowing and doing: Learning through experience.* SF: Jossey-Bass.

Rationale for EE and Alverno faculty articulating their understanding and practice.

Jacoby, B. (2009). (Ed). *Civic engagement in higher education: Concepts and practices.* San Francisco: Jossey-Bass.

Updated version of earlier classic on Service-Learning concepts and practices.

Jacoby, B. (1996) (Ed). *Service-Learning in higher education: Concepts and practices.* SF: Jossey-Bass.

Combines theory and practice as comprehensive guide for curriculum and student affairs. Other salient books by Barbara Jacoby of relevance to faculty engagement include *Civic Engagement in Higher Education* (2009) and *Looking In, Reaching Out* (2010).

Keeton, M. (1980). *Defining and assuring quality in experiential learning.* SF: Jossey-Bass.

Number 9 in the quarterly series *New directions for experiential learning,* edited overall by Morris Keeton and Pamela Tate. The entire series illustrates the depth and sophistication that CAEL and NSIEE brought to assessment, quality and pedagogy overall and EE in particular what later came to be named "pedagogies of engagement". Also illustrates that Jossey-Bass, as a major publisher, saw a significant market in EE.

Kolb, D. (1976). On management and the learning process. *California Management Review. 18(3), 21-31.*

Kolb's earliest published account of his ubiquitous "four-stage learning cycle.

Kolb, D. (1984). *Experiential learning: Experience as the source of learning and development.* NJ: Prentice-Hall.

Kolb's ground breaking theory and empirically based validation of experiential learning and the pedagogical practices associated with experiential learning based on his ongoing research related to "learning styles". Became the "bible" to many in NSIEE and widely utilized by the authors of the first edition of *Strengthening.*

Kuh, G. (2008). *High-Impact Educational Practices: What They Are, Who Has Access to Them, and Why They Matter.* Washington, DC: AAC&U.
    This publication defines a set of educational practices that research has demonstrated have a significant impact on student success. Kuh presents data from the National Survey of Student Engagement about these practices and explains why they benefit all students, but also seem to benefit underserved students even more than their more advantaged peers. The report also presents data that show definitively that underserved students are the least likely students, on average, to have access to these practices.

LEAP articles in *Liberal Education.* (2005-2011). http://www.aacu.org/liberaleducation/leapseries.cfm

See AAC&U website for listing of articles that have appeared related to the LEAP.

Levine, P. (2011). What do we know about civic engagement? *Liberal Education* 87, (2).

Good example of the supportive but questioning and "evidentiary" approach that exemplifies the best research and surveys of research literature in search of valid and reliable findings.

McKeachie, W. J. *Teaching Tips.* (8th Ed.) (1986) Lexington, Mass.: Heath.

The classic book on teaching by the former President of the American Psychological Association and leader in AAHE and developer of NCRIPTAL at the University of Michigan. Marilla Svinicki and Wilbert McKeachie's *Teaching Tips,* first published in 1950 and now in its 13th edition (2011), offers a hearty bread-and-butter treatment of college teaching that will both sate hungry first-time instructors and give veterans plenty to chew on. The book's strengths are its humorous, practical voice; its clear summaries of research and theory about student learning; and its concrete tips and suggestions for central elements of college teaching.

McKinney, K. (2007). *Enhancing learning through the scholarship of teaching and learning: The challenges and joys of juggling.* SF: Jossey-Bass/Anker.

An overview history of the Scholarship of Teaching Movement by one of its leaders in the field of Sociology and higher education overall. Introduction by C. Patricia Cross places book in context as Cross was one of it "founders" with her "teacher as classroom researcher" work with Angelo. Book includes rationales and suggestions for how to engage in SoTL, ethics, et al.

McKinney, K. & Heyl, B. (2009). *Sociology through active learning: Student exercises (2nd Ed)* LA: Pine Forge/Sage.

An example of how experiential learning has infused into the curriculum as active learning and experiential education has developed since the 1987 Wingspread identification of "active learning" as one of the seven principles of Good Practice. Provides examples referred to in chapter 2 of this revision, with descriptions, learning goals, rationales, instructions, worksheets for a wide range of active learning done by individuals, small groups, over weeks and during class. Illustration of sources to use to engage faculty.

Meisel, W. (2007). Connecting cocurricular service with academic inquiry: A movement toward civic engagement. *Liberal Education*, 93 (2), 35-38.

At the colleges and universities working with the Bonner Foundation to build and sustain civic engagement initiatives, students are committed to significant, ongoing involvement in community issues and to engaging other students to join with them in such endeavors.

National Task Force on Civic Learning and Democratic Engagement. (2012). *A crucible moment: College learning and democracy's future.* Washington, DC: AAC&U.

Palmer, P. (1987). Community, conflict and ways of knowing. *Change Magazine,* 19 (5), 20-25.

The published speech from the AAHE meeting that has become a classic in higher education and experiential education, also appearing in *Combining Service and Learning,* vol I (pp. 105-113).

Palmer, P., et al. (2010). *The heart of higher education: A call for renewal.* SF: Jossey Bass.

Peters, S. et al. (2010). *Democracy and higher education: Traditions and stories of civic engagement. (Transformation in higher education).* East Lansing: Michigan State University Press.

Saltmarsh, J. & E. Zlotkowski (2011). *Higher education and democracy: Essays on service-learning and civic engagement.* Philadelphia: Temple University Press.

Saltmarsh, J. & Hartley, M. (2011). (Eds). *"To serve a larger purpose": Engagement for democracy and the transformation of higher education.* Philadelphia: Temple University Press.

Schneider, C.G. (2009). The Clark/AAC&U challenge: Connecting liberal education with real-world practice. *Liberal Education*, 95 (4), 2-3.

If the nation is going to make a huge new investment in postsecondary learning—as it must—then we need, as a society, to establish a clear understanding of the kind of learning that will build meaningful opportunity for Americans and a vibrant future for our society

Schneider, C.G. The proof is in the portfolio. *Liberal Education*, 95 (1), 2-3.

Let's band together as a community and insist that it is high time to break free of the reductive focus on standardized testing of "general skills," quantitative metrics for achievement, and the national obeisance before the false gods of comparable scores and faux rankings.

Schneider, C. (2007). President's message: It's not just the economy. *Liberal Education*, 93 (1), 2-3.
New surveys of employers and recent graduates reveal strong support for the core LEAP assertion that the skills and knowledge developed through a liberal education are essential to economic success. Yet they also provide further evidence that higher education has failed to establish the essential connections between democratic freedom and college learning.

Senge, P. et al. (2004). *Presence: Human purpose and field of the future.* NY: Crown/Random House

Shulman, L. (2002). *Making differences: A table of learning.* Palo Alto, CA: The Carnegie Foundation for the Advancement of Teaching.
A classic distillation of what we know about "pedagogies of engagement" (Edgerton) that integrates the best research on teaching and learning with Bloom, Perry, et al. Along with Ewell's essay, this 12 page essay could be the basis for faculty conversations about "not whether", but how and when pedagogies of engagement will be expanded and deepened at any institution. As John Duley points out in the prologue, this "table/taxonomy" embraces motivation, commitment and seems more dyamic, holistic and "integrative" than Kolb's model.
Also: "Making Differences: A Table of Learning," in *Change*, November/December 2002. Volume 34, Number 6. Pages 36-44.

Sigmon, R. (1996). *Journey to service-learning: Experiences from independent liberal arts colleges and universities.* Washington DC: Council of Independent Colleges.
Combining theory with practice, and drawing on the work of nearly 200 private liberal arts colleges and universities, this new book from CIC offers suggestions and strategies for faculty and administrators seeking to develop, structure, and sustain programs in service learning.

Stanton, T. (1987). *Integrating public service with academic study: The faculty role.* A Report of Campus Compact: The Project for Public and Community Service. Providence, RI
Game changing position paper that changed the direction of founding Presidents from volunteer service to service-learning with a major role for faculty and learning outcomes. Stanton provided leadership to Cornell and Stanford Universities during the early and formative years of S-L and Campus Compact and was a NSIEE/FIPSE consultant.

Stoecker, R. (2012). *Research methods for community change* (2nd Ed). Sage.

Strand, K. (2003). Principles of best practice for community-based research. *Michigan Journal of Community Service Learning.* 9 (3), 5-15.

Distillation of book on community-based research written by leading scholars and practitioners in this promising field of engaged research and high impact practices that rests on assumptions that the community should identify the research question, control and share in the interpretation of the findings, and be strengthened empowered as a result of the research, moving toward greater justice and equity.

Tagg, J. (2003). *The learning paradigm college.* Bolton, MA: Anker

Thomas, D. & Brown, J. (2011). *A new culture of learning: Cultivating the imagination for a world of constant change.* Self-published.

Mixing erudite concepts with simple anecdotes and examples, *A New Culture of Learning* begins with some familiar notions about the value of intuitive learning—the way the Harry Potter phenomenon excited children to continue to explore ideas about geography and history (albeit fictional) through fan blogs and wiki sites; the way multiplayer online games like World of Warcraft connect gamers worldwide in common quests for solutions; even the way students have learned to read and dissect Wikipedia entries. Those "learning-based approaches" to education work better than "teaching-based approaches," write Brown and Thomas, because they engage the imagination.

Zlotkowski, E. (1996). *Successful Service-Learning Programs: New Models of Excellence in Higher Education.* Bolton, MA: Anker.

Zlotkowski, E. (1996-2000) Disciplinary series on Service-Learning, 20+ volumes, AAHE-Campus Compact

Zlotkowski, E. (1996). Linking service-learning and the academy: A new voice at the table. *Change* (Jan-Feb)—see entire Disciplinary series edited by Zlotkowski, AAHE-Campus Compact
Introduces the AAHE-Compact disciplinary based series on Service-Learning in the Disciplines

Appendix 1: Original Chapter Outline & Contents

Increasing Faculty Involvement in Experiential Education [1st Edition, 1986]
I.   <u>*Why Active Faculty Involvement Is Critical*</u>
    A.   The Faculty is the primary group responsible for teaching
    B.   Faculty are needed in order to integrate experiential education into the curriculum
    C.   Faculty are needed for quality control
    D.   Students listen to faculty
    E.   Faculty members are significant role models for students [and other faculty]
II.   <u>*What Faculty Gain from Experiential Education*</u>
    A.   Pleasure of taking on new role of facilitator of learning, of listener, consultant, coach
    B.   Sense of new clarity in their expectations of students, e.g., "Backward Design"
    C.   Development of new set of skills
    D.   Excitement of seeing students become less passive, more motivated, empowered learners and active members of society
III.   <u>*Faculty Concerns and Barriers to Involvement*</u> [10 to start with]
    A.   Concern about faculty control of academic quality
    B.   Lack of awareness of EE as pedagogy & lack of theoretical knowledge in pedagogy
    C.   Lack of familiarity with techniques for assessing experiential education
    D.   Lack of understanding of how experiential learning help students test the concept of disciplines
    E.   A belief that application is only useful when it follows theory
    F.   Concern about faculty compensation for sponsoring students in experiential education
    G.   Concern about whether involvement in EE helps with tenure, promotion, and merit increases
    H.   Fear of the world outside the campus
    I.   Lack of priority [placed] on student development
    J.   Limitations of the 50 minute class
IV.   <u>*Assessing Faculty Involvement in Experiential Education*</u> [17 "Things to Do"]
V.   <u>*Building Faculty Support and Involvement in Experiential Education*</u>
    A.   Feed information about ee/experiential learning to the faculty continuously
    B.   Act as a catalyst to link faculty from different departments

C. Organize informal discussions

D. Find out what people's concerns are

E. Work through supportive opinion leaders on the faculty

F. Establish a faculty committee on experiential education

G. Let students speak for the value of experiential education

H. Conduct workshops or sponsor speakers on campus

I. Give away money and authority

J. Reinforce excellence in faculty support of experiential education

K. Help academic advisors to understand and promote experiential learning as an integral part of the curriculum

VI. *Faculty Enrichment*

A. Arrange faculty internships

B. Have a summer study group of faculty focusing on experiential learning

C. Create a rotating faculty position in the EE "central" office

D. Take faculty on site visits

E. Ask faculty to design & implement research projects related to experiential learning

F. Help key faculty members arrange sabbaticals that involve experiential learning

G. Establish "Field Study Coordinatorships" like Teaching Assistantships for students

H. Offer senior faculty opportunities to take on leadership roles in EE as renewal

I. Establish a library of resources for faculty about teaching more experientially

J. Take faculty to professional meetings for experiential educators [NSEE, AAC&U]

K. [Provide & encourage other opportunities for overall faculty development

L. Look for opportunities to give their work visibility among faculty, college, discipline]

VII. *Special Considerations for Those Who Are Not Faculty Members*

A. Redefine your roles, especially as advocates for EE & learning, i.e., broadly as a resource person to faculty

B. Work as a consultant to departments, enlarging understanding of EE & learning

C. Give away power and authority to faculty across campus

Appendix 2
Effective Practice, Teaching & the Liberal Arts: AAC&U Initiatives

I.*The Clark/AAC&U Challenge: Connecting Liberal Education with Real-World Practice*
Liberal Education, Vol. 95, No. 1 (Winter 2009)

Liberal Education and Effective Practice
This issue examines how the vision for college learning outlined in the 2007 report from AAC&U's Liberal Education and America's Promise (LEAP) initiative is being enacted by particularly effective forms of educational practice and explores some of the ongoing challenges to implementation.

http://aacu.org/liberaleducation/le-fa09/le-fa09_index.cfm
http://aacu.org/liberaleducation/le-wi09/le-wi09_index.cfm

Liberal Education and Effective Practice: The Necessary Revolution in Undergraduate Education
By Richard M. Freeland

Something remarkable is happening in programs of liberal education all over the country. The longstanding notion that learning should occur almost exclusively in classrooms is being amended to give a much more prominent place to various forms of experiential education. The belief that liberal education should focus on a narrow range of intellectual qualities is being revised to include an emphasis on connecting ideas with action. These developments constitute a profoundly important, indeed revolutionary, challenge to the version of liberal education that has dominated American higher education since the early years of the twentieth century.....

There is much at stake in seeking wider appreciation of the value of linking liberal education and effective practice as well as greater understanding of the role experiential education can play in establishing that link. The pedagogical claims advanced by advocates of community service and internships are too important merely to be tolerated at the margins of our thinking about liberal learning. We need to take a hard, fresh look at the qualities needed for effectiveness as professionals and as citizens, to compare those qualities to the outcomes we cultivate through the arts and sciences, and to design educational formats that will empower our graduates to translate the values and skills we nurture into constructive social action. As Carol Geary Schneider has argued in championing a heightened emphasis on practice, the challenges our country faces in the twenty-first century are too great for us to rest comfortably with any lesser educational goal. " http://aacu.org/liberaleducation/le-wi09/le-wi09_freeland.cfm

President's Message
The Clark/AAC&U Challenge: Connecting Liberal Education with Real-World Practice
By Carol Geary Schneider
If the nation is going to make a huge new investment in postsecondary learning—as it must—then we need, as a society, to establish a clear understanding of the kind of learning that will build meaningful opportunity for Americans and a vibrant future for our society.

The Clark/AAC&U Conference on Liberal Education and Effective Practice
By Richard M. Freeland
How well do the learning experiences we offer align with our professed goals of preparing engaged citizens, effective professionals, and, more broadly, adults equipped to make significant contributions to society?

Wisdom, Intelligence, and Creativity Synthesized: A New Model for Liberal Education
By Robert J. Sternberg
WICS is a framework that can help us get beyond self-fulfilling prophecies in admissions, instruction, and assessment.

Engaged Learning: Enabling Self-Authorship and Effective Practice
By David C. Hodge, Marcia B. Baxter Magolda, and Carolyn A. Haynes
A carefully sequenced and developmentally appropriate curriculum can help students develop self-authorship while in college.

The Power of Experiential Education
By Janet Eyler
Experiential education, which takes students into the community, helps students both to bridge classroom study and life in the world and to transform inert knowledge into knowledge-in-use.

Liberal Arts Education and the Capacity for Effective Practice: What's Holding Us Back?
By Diana Chapman Walsh and Lee Cuba
We offer this brief case study to suggest the complexity of leading a faculty through a process of institutional change.

Race-Conscious Student Engagement Practices and the Equitable Distribution of Enriching Educational Experiences
By Shaun R. Harper
What is possible when educators and administrators take seriously the responsibility to engage diverse student populations in educationally purposeful ways?

II. *Bringing Theory to Practice*

The Winter 2007 issue of *Liberal Education* (Vol. 93, No. 1) provides an overview of the Bringing Theory to Practice project [BTtoP], an effort to advance engaged student learning and determine how it might improve the quality of students' education, development, health, and commitment to civic engagement. Also included are articles on diversity, a reflection on teaching in a first-year program, and the executive summary of the new LEAP report.

http://aacu.org/liberaleducation/le-wi07/index.cfm

Appendix 3: American Commonwealth Partnership & *A Crucible Moment*

I. *American Commonwealth Partnership and DemocracyU*

The American Commonwealth Partnership (ACP) is an alliance of community colleges, colleges and universities, P-12 schools and others dedicated to building "democracy colleges" throughout higher education. A Presidents' Advisory Council, composed of distinguished college and university presidents who have long been leaders in engaged higher education movement, offers continuing counsel and wisdom (see below). [The following is adapted from the ACP website]

Launched at the White House on January 10th, 2012, the start of the 150th anniversary year of the Morrill Act which created land grant colleges, signed by President Lincoln in 1862, ACP uses the concept of democracy colleges from land grant and community college history. Democracy colleges convey the idea of colleges and universities deeply connected to their communities, which make education for citizenship a signature identity. The work of building democracy colleges draws on a rich tradition, dating back to Abraham Lincoln's presidency.

The White House meeting, "For Democracy's Future – Education Reclaims Our Civic Mission", marked a new stage of coordinated effort to bring about a commitment to civic education and education as a public good. It was organized in partnership with the White House Office of Public Engagement, the Department of Education, the Association of American Colleges and Universities, and the Campaign for the Civic Mission of the Schools.

At the White House, the Department of Education released its Road Map and Call to Action on civic learning and democratic engagement, described in remarks by Secretary of Education Arne Duncan. The National Task Force on Civic Learning and Democratic Engagement released *A Crucible Moment*, a report to the nation on the need for a shift in civic learning from "partial" to "pervasive."

ACP highlighted institutions that have taken steps toward becoming democracy colleges, including community colleges, liberal arts colleges, state colleges and universities, and research institutions. ACP continues to consult with Undersecretary for Higher Education Martha Kanter and her Office of Postsecondary Education on policies to strengthen higher education's public engagement and is also helping to organize state level policy initiatives on the topic.

The ACP coalition promotes several initiatives including:

The Deliberative Dialogue Initiative, in partnership with the National Issues Forums Institute (NIFI), is organizing a discussion on campuses and in communities on higher education's role in America's future. It is to be complemented by a communications effort to convey the potential of higher education in teaching skills, such as listening, deliberation, teamwork, negotiating different interests and views, to work across differences on public problems. Research by NIFI suggests that the public is largely unaware of higher education's contributions to such skill development – seen as an urgent need by citizens of many views and backgrounds in order to turn around the growing divisiveness and polarization in America.

Citizen Alum Initiative, directed by Julie Ellison of the University of Michigan, aims to change the framework of alumni relations, partnering with alumni as "do-ers" as well as donors. Citizen Alum aims to find the hidden treasure—the creative, civic, intellectual, and social capital of alumni – especially recent "gap alums" and alums who opt out of conventional roles, supporting them as contributors to their home communities and as allies in education.

Student Organizing Initiative is a campaign to deepen the civic identity of college students, develop skills of deliberative public work, and strengthen the DemocracyU social media campaign and website as resources for students to share their stories and address their concerns for America's democracy. This initiative is also exploring strategies for putting cross partisan citizen-centered politics back at the center of the highly polarized election campaign of 2012.

Pedagogies of Empowerment and Engagement Initiative is an organizing effort spearheaded by Blase Scarnati of Northern Arizona University. It will identity and collect the details of effective pedagogies of empowerment and engagement across the country that teach skills to work across differences. The group will also recruit new sites and partners.

Public Scholarship Initiative is organized by Scott Peters of Cornell University, Tim Eatman of Imagining America at Syracuse University, and John Saltmarsh of NERCHE (UMASS Boston). The team has begun a participatory research project with various institutions on the work of building democracy colleges in the 21st century.

Campus-Community Civic Health Initiative, coordinated by the American Democracy Project in partnership with the National Conference on Citizenship, is developing ways to assess the impact of colleges and universities on community and campus civic health.

Civic Science Initiative is organized by John Spencer at the University of Iowa, Scott Peters at Cornell University, Molly Jahn at the University of Wisconsin, Rom Coles at Northern Arizona University, and Harry Boyte at Augsburg College and the Humphrey School of Public Affairs, University of Minnesota. Civic science is a framework for understanding scientists as citizens, working with other citizens in ways that respect different ways of knowing, deepening collective wisdom on public questions, and developing civic agency.

ACP Policy Initiative, building on policy discussions with the Department of Education in 2011, focuses on state level policies strengthening engagement, and is consulting with the DOE on an ongoing basis about policies to strengthen engagement.

Presidents' Advisory Council Co-Chairs: Nancy Cantor, Chancellor, Syracuse & Brian Murphy, President, De Anza College **Members**: M. Christopher Brown, President, Alcorn State University; Thomas Ehrlich, President Emeritus, Indiana University; Freeman Hrabowski, President, University of Maryland Baltimore County; David Mathews, President Emeritus, University of Alabama; Paul Pribbenow, President, Augsburg College; Judith Ramaley, President, Winona State University **Inaugural Host Institution**: Augsburg College, Minneapolis **National Coordinator**: Harry Boyte, Director, Center for Democracy and Citizenship

II.   *A Crucible Moment: College Learning & Democracy's Future*

A Call to Action and Report from The National Task Force on Civic Learning and Democratic Engagement [AAC&U website]

A Crucible Moment: College Learning and Democracy's Future (2012)
By The National Task Force on Civic Learning and Democratic Engagement

- This report from the National Task Force on Civic Learning and Democratic Engagement calls on the nation to reclaim higher education's civic mission. Commissioned by the Department of Education and released at a White House convening in January 2012, the report pushes back against a prevailing national dialogue that limits the mission of higher education to workforce preparation and training while marginalizing disciplines basic to democracy. To view footage from January's White House event, "For Democracy's Future: Education Reclaims Our Civic Mission," please click here and here.

- *A Crucible Moment* calls on educators and public leaders to advance a 21st century vision of college learning for all students—a vision with civic learning and democratic engagement an expected part of every student's college education. The report documents the nation's anemic civic health and includes recommendations for action that address campus culture, general education, and civic inquiry as part of major and career fields as well as hands-on civic problem solving across differences. AAC&U credits the Bringing Theory to Practice project and its supporters, the S. Engelhard Center, and the Christian A. Johnson Endeavor Foundation, for funding the design, printing, and dissemination of this publication.

- *A Crucible Moment* was prepared at the invitation of the U.S. Department of Education under the leadership of the Global Perspective Institute, Inc. (GPI) and AAC&U. The publication was developed with input from a series of national roundtables involving leaders from all parts of the higher education and civic renewal communities.

- This entire report is available as a PDF document (see link below) and additional print copies can be purchased through AAC&U's online publications catalog.

- Report (pdf)
- Highlights (pdf)

Highlights From *A Crucible Moment: College Learning and Democracy's Future*
- **Components of 21st century civic learning should include:**
    - Knowledge of U.S. history, political structures, and core democratic principles and founding documents; and debates—US and global—about their meaning and application;
    - Knowledge of the political systems that frame constitutional democracies and of political levers for affecting change;
    - Knowledge of diverse cultures and religions in the US and around the world;
    - Critical inquiry and reasoning capacities;
    - Deliberation and bridge-building across differences;
    - Collaborative decision-making skills;
    - Open-mindedness and capacity to engage different points of view and cultures;
    - Civic problem-solving skills and experience
    - Civility, ethical integrity, and mutual respect.

A Crucible Moment provides specific campus examples illustrating how to move from "partial transformation to pervasive civic and democratic learning and practices."

Appendix 4: Other Higher Ed Associations & EE Initiatives

I. American Association of State Colleges and Universities [AASCU]

http://www.aascu.org/
http://www.aascu.org/programs/ADP/
American Democracy Project
       2003, with NY Times
       "Stewards of Place

II. American Association of Community Colleges [AACC]
http://www.aacc.nche.edu/Pages/default.aspx
Institutionalizing Service-Learning
http://www.aacc.nche.edu/Publications/Briefs/Pages/rb02012002.aspx

III. American Council on Education
http://www.acenet.edu/AM/Template.cfm?Section=Home

IV. The Council of Independent Colleges

http://www.cic.edu/

V. Council for Advancement and Support of Education [CASE]

http://www.case.org/

VI. Carnegie Foundation for the Advancement of Teaching
http://www.carnegiefoundation.org/
Carnegie Community-Engagement Classification
http://classifications.carnegiefoundation.org/
http://www.carnegiefoundation.org/sites/default/files/elibrary/Driscoll.pdf
http://www.carnegiefoundation.org/sites/default/files/elibrary/zuiches.pdf

V. The Council of Independent Colleges

http://www.cic.edu/

VI. Council for Advancement and Support of Education [CASE]

http://www.case.org/

VII. Campus Compact
http://www.compact.org/
http://www.compact.org/category/resources/
http://www.compact.org/resources-for-faculty/ E.g., Syllabi, et al
 http://www.compact.org/category/resources/faculty-resources/ Bookstore:
https://www.e2e-store.com/compact/

Appendix 5: Quotes That Chronicle and Punctuate the Journey

The Roots of This Work About five years ago, when Russ Edgerton was serving as education officer for The Pew Charitable Trusts, he produced a terrific white paper, which has propelled many of the most interesting initiatives in higher education today. One of Russ's arguments focused on something he called "pedagogies of engagement" — approaches that have within them the capacity to engage students actively with learning in new ways. He wasn't talking only about service-learning, though service learning was an example; he was talking about an array of approaches, from problem-based and project-based learning to varieties of collaborative work and field-based instruction. Russ used the rubric "pedagogies of engagement" to describe them all (Shulman 2002).

"I have been observing, studying and participating in higher education for almost 50 years and I have never seen as much interest in teaching and learning at the college level as I have seen in the past decade" (K. Patricia Cross, in Forward to McKinney, 2006). "Students must accept responsibility for and become actively engaged in their own learning. But faculty too must accept responsibility for encouraging students to become active learners, and evidence is accumulating that college teaching practices are changing. The old practice of lecturing, once the reported practice of a majority of college teachers, has tipped to a minority in just the past decade as it is replaced by methods that engage students more actively in their own learning" (Huber & Hutchings, 2005 cited by Cross, 2007, p. xvi).

"Teachers recognize [that lifelong learning has become a necessity]. The Number One teaching goal in both community colleges and four year institutions is to develop the ability to apply principles and generalizations already learned to new problems and situations" (Cross, 2007).

In the twentieth century, proponents of liberal learning drew a sharp dividing line between "practical" or career studies and the "true liberal arts." Today, we contend, we need to erase that distinction and insist that liberal education is, among its other virtues, practical. In a turbulent economy where industries are awash in change and where the combination of inventiveness and judgment is key to any organization's future, the most practical possible education is one that prepares students to make sense of complexity, to chart a course of action that takes full account of context, to engage in continuous learning, and to take responsibility for the quality and integrity of what they do (Schneider, 2009).

Author

GARRY HESSER is the Sabo Professor of Citizenship and Learning at Augsburg College in Minneapolis, MN where he teaches courses on Sociology, Community, Urban Sociology, Urban Planning, Religion and Society, Creativity, and Community-Based Research. He chaired the Metro-Urban Studies program for thirty years and was a Visiting Professor in Planning and Public Policy at the University of Minnesota [Humphrey School of Public Affairs]. In 2004, he was named the Carnegie-CASE Professor of the Year [Minnesota] and in 2002 was named the Distinguished Sociologist of Minnesota by the Sociologists of Minnesota. Garry received Campus Compact's Thomas Ehrlich Award in 1998 and was named a Pioneer by NSEE in 2001. Garry's Ph.D. is from the University of Notre Dame, following a B.A. from Phillips University and a M.Div. from Union Theological Seminary (NYC). He was president of the National Society for Experiential Education (NSEE) and the Higher Education Consortium for Urban Affairs (HECUA). As a member of the NSEE-Campus Compact-AAHE Consulting Corps, he has led workshops on service-learning and experiential education on over sixty campuses and at professional meetings. He is the author of *Experiential Education as a Liberating Art*; "Principles of Good Practice in Service-Learning"; "Examining Communities and Urban Change"; "Benefits and Educational Outcomes of Internships"; and co-editor of *Cultivating the Sociological Imagination: Concepts and Models for Service-Learning in Sociology*.

Chapter 4
Ensuring Quality in Experiential Education

Mary A. King, Ed. D.
Professor Emerita at Fitchburg State University

The Quagmire of Quality: A Look Back

The Quest for Quality: A Look at the Present
> *The Five Keys to Quality*
>> Key #1: *Integration of General Goals*
>> Key #2: *Evidence of Effective Learning*
>> Key #3: *Effective Program Practices*
>> Key #4: *Embedded Levels of Quality Assurance*
>> Key #5: *The Principles & Standards of the Field*

The Question of Quality: A Look Ahead

As we move into the second decade of the 21ˢᵗ century, the matter of ensuring quality in traditional education is foremost and pressing on all agendas—from towns and cities to states and federal governments, from pre-school through graduate school. What it looks like, how it is attained and maintained, and how it is ensured have challenged our communities of educators. When it comes to experiential education, because of its status of non-traditional education practices, the issue of quality has been integral to the field since it took foothold in areas of professional education in the late 19ᵗʰ century. This chapter considers the quality in experiential education beginning in the final quarter of the 20ᵗʰ century, when educators invested intentionally in ensuring quality in high impact experiential education practices.

The Quagmire of Quality: A Look Back

> *Come, give us a taste of your quality.*
> **Hamlet, Act II, Scene II**

The question of quality in American higher education is front and center during the beginning of this 21ˢᵗ century. In late summer, 2010, just as the academic year was about to begin, *The Chronicle of Higher Education* began a multiple part series called *Measuring Stick* (Glenn, 9/3/10). The focus of the series was exploring debates on the issue of quality: how quality in higher education should be measured and whether higher education's quality assurance mechanisms are functioning effectively. Ensuring quality and continuous improvement in experiential education present some unique challenges, and over time the field has evolved to meet them in creative ways.

The challenge to Hamlet is the challenge that continues to face experiential education and all of K-16 education today, just as it was of concern to the authors of the original *Strengthening* publication in 1986. At that time, "quality" in higher education was equated with the type and extent of resources provided for learning activities. Accordingly, the focus was on the money expended per student, the size of the library collection, the academic degrees of faculty, and how much faculty was paid. The argument was that if these resources were provided, quality of learning could be reasonably anticipated. Hence, the guarantor was each faculty member, who in turn was responsible to establish his or her own standards and make individual judgments on student attainment (NSIEE, 1986). "Learning outcomes," as we understand them today, did not factor into the equation at that time in *traditional* American higher education practices. (For further discussion, see *Key 2* in *The Question of Quality: A Look at the Present* later in this chapter).

There are lessons to be learned from our international colleagues in this regard. One such lesson resulted from a series of interviews conducted by Dr. Norman Evans, a leader in British higher education, who visited a number of American institutions and spoke with students, faculty, and administrators to understand our approach to experiential education and how we addressed quality assurance. What was most telling were the responses of faculty who were asked about the *criteria* being used in designing such learning experiences, *how* it was determined that "real" learning was taking place, whether experiential education should be something colleges should be doing. They responded with blank stares, reflecting differences in perspectives on quality assurance in American and British higher education at the time. Instead, the faculty talked about the *quality of the learning environment*. The year was 1983, and at that time, quality was equated with the type and extent of resources provided for learning activities. The argument was that if resources were provided, quality learning could be reasonably expected. So, when students interned at a corporate technology giant or the governor's office, they were assumed to have learned a great deal by virtue of the placement. It was when they were asked about the nature of the work that the issues became apparent (NSIEE, 1986).

While the traditional approach of providing high quality facilities and resources to assure the quality of the students' learning reflected the collective thinking of the academy at the time, it was not an effective tool to use when it came to experiential education (or any pedagogical approach for that matter). Unlike more traditional forms of education, programs steeped in experiential education had to *demonstrate* their value, just as did the clinical and internship programs in such professional fields as education, medicine, and human services. Professional programs with embedded field-based learning had to *guarantee* that their students could demonstrate in *applied practice* what they had learned in the classroom and in the field. By so doing, professional internships and other forms of field-based learning set the operating standards for experiential educational practices.

Morris Keeton provided an alternative perspective on quality assurance in his edited volume, *Defining and Assuring Quality* in the *New Directions for Experiential Learning* series sponsored by the Council for the Advancement of Experiential Learning (CAEL) (1980). He posited that quality depended on three factors: purpose, educational strategy, and effectiveness with which resources are applied to that strategy (Keeton, 1980, p.1). Keeton's instructive and seminal volume reflected the thinking of the authors of the original *Strengthening*. It also highlighted specific areas of quality assurance in experiential learning programs, viz., that the purpose and strategy are defined; that there is an institutional priority to assure quality (p.vii); and, that key human resources (faculty, program managers, learners, and administrators) are considered in terms of their roles, the ways they interact, and the contributions each makes to assure the high quality of experientially enriched education on their campus (p.vii). See Appendix I (#1) for a description of Keeton's *Six Key Areas of Quality Assurance.*

In the original version of this publication (1986), the founders of NSIEE described in detail the emerging practices of the experiential educational movement. That early leadership and understanding led to the FIPSE grant that funded the first edition of *Strengthening*. The practices described by the original authors are the heart of the paradigm shift today: *a focus on learning outcomes as the assurance of quality.* Approaches to quality, then, must be based on the quality of *student learning.*

The Quest for Quality: A Look at the Present

> *Learning is not attained by chance; it must be sought for with ardor and attended to with diligence.*   Abigail Adams, 1780

During the last two decades, service-learning has been mainstreamed within institutions, internships have been flourishing across academic majors, and co-op education has been thriving as have study abroad programs. Additionally, community service and civic engagement are being required in elementary and secondary schools, as well being integrated into academic and student affairs programs across campuses. Even so, experiential education is still often regarded as an innovation, an alternative to the traditional ways of teaching. Consequently, experiential education must make the case for its integrity if it is to be used in academic disciplines steeped in traditional methodology.

Experiential Learning, Professional Studies, and the Liberal Arts
In the provocative article "Pedagogies of Uncertainty", Lee Shulman (2005), then president of the Carnegie Foundation for the Advancement of Teaching, discusses the Foundation's position on professional education, such as that of medicine and law, in relation to liberal arts education. He noted that they were not at odds with each other, nor was professional education "a corrupting influence that must be kept at bay in order to preserve the purity of the mission of liberal education" (p. 1). Rather, it is the Foundation's position that the two fields can inform each other about learning in instructive ways. Historically, the Foundation has had a long relationship with professional education; its first major study, the Flexner Report in 1910, focused on the professional education of physicians in this country and in turn permanently changed how physicians are educated. Today, the Foundation is focusing research in a long-term effort on how professionals are educated, while simultaneously collaborating with the Wabash Center for Inquiry in the Liberal Arts and the Association of American Colleges and Universities (AAC&U) on studies in liberal education (Shulman, 2005).

The value of experiential learning to undergraduate professional studies programs is undisputed; it is the essence of the academic program. Without the learning-through-doing component (Eyler, 2009), the student as an emerging professional would not be ready for the work ahead. With the experiential component, theory meets practice and practice meets theory, knowledge is grounded in its proven usefulness, and skills are developed through application under close and informed supervision. Having withstood the scrutiny of well-structured and expertly supervised field-based course practica and internships, the student emerges as an aspiring professional, prepared in depth and breadth with the knowledge, skills, values, and demeanor of the profession. The impressive history of quality education in the professional studies disciplines was hard earned. Discipline-specific accrediting bodies have long overseen the development of such academic programs, reaching far into the classroom and into field experiences to ensure the highest level of quality. The academy itself has had the responsibility to ensure that these same students are equally prepared with an education in the liberal arts as well.

Experiential education's challenge, then, is not primarily in its application to professional studies programs. Rather the challenge is in its relevance to learning overall, and to liberal education in particular. In this regard, liberal learning can be informed in important ways by the history of professional education. Eyler (2009) notes that experiential education can be of value to liberal learning provided deliberate attention is paid to both the *structure* and the *supervision* of the experience. These are the same two factors in which professional studies faculty invest heavily, developing long-standing, model field sites and excellence in supervisory responsibilities. Otherwise, the intended learning is compromised, as is the integrity of the academic program. In short, professional studies disciplines are driven to excellence—to quality—in order to survive as academic programs.

Eyler's Guidelines for Quality Experiential Programs Across Campus. Whether it's in liberal arts or professional studies programs, academic quality must be ensured if field-based learning is a worthy component of the course or curriculum. That means quality learning must go on in both dimensions—the intellectual dimension and the dimension of work (Eyler, 2009). The guidelines for quality experiential programs and for creating contexts in which students can empower themselves through experience are consistent with the literature on effective liberal education. Some of those guidelines have been identified by Eyler (2009) as:

- Work or service, clearly related to the academic goals of the course or program;
- Well-developed assessments that provide evidence of the achievement of academic objectives;
- Important responsibility for the student;
- Site supervisors who understand the learning goals for the student and partner with the academic supervisor to provide continuous monitoring and feedback;
- An academic supervisor or instructor who pays close attention to the student's work in the field and partners with the site supervisor to provide continuous monitoring and feedback;

- Attention paid to preparing students for both the practical challenges of their placements and for learning from experience;
- Continuous, well-structured reflection opportunities to help students link experience and learning throughout the course to their placements.

Scholarship, Tenure, and Experiential Education

Now that Experiential Education has become an accepted pedagogy and mode of learning for students, the field is moving forward with the next challenge in the academy: demonstrating that Experiential Education is also a valid epistemology for faculty scholarly work that can be assessed as legitimate scholarship for faculty rewards and recognition.

Dwight E. Giles, Jr., NSEE Pioneer &
Professor and Sr. Associate at NERCHE
University of Massachusetts Boston

Through the creation and development of professional associations and the support of private and public grants, thought leaders and practitioners have been developing principles and standards of practice over the past few decades. Ongoing research has been expanding in its foci, publications have been forthcoming in varied and new venues, and scholars have been investing their academic intentions in experiential education-- because of its potential for creating powerful learning contexts. For that, they risked tenure and promotion in the past. But that is changing as well, as Dwight Giles poignantly notes.

A collective attack on tenure during the late 1980s into the early 1990s by multiple factions, including the press, campus trustees, and government officials, resulted in three areas of changes in the tenure system: tenure track positions became more coveted due to fiscal restraints; workplace reforms were put in place, including post-tenure review, parental leave, and stop-the-clock policies; and, scholarship was reconsidered in promotion and tenure processes in terms of what it is and how it is assessed.

Ernest Boyer, a former president of the Carnegie Foundation for the Advancement of Teaching, proposed to the academy and professoriate in *Scholarship Reconsidered: Priorities of the Professoriate* a broadband concept of scholarship "to break out of the tired old teaching versus research debate and define, in more creative ways, what it means to be a scholar….to recognize the full range of faculty talent and the great diversity of functions higher education must perform" (1990, p. xii). Boyer believed that scholarship should have four separate, yet overlapping functions or categories (p.16). These general categories were the *scholarships of discovery, integration, application* and *teaching* (1990, p. xii). In his later publication, *Scholarship of Engagement*, Boyer proposed to extend further his own way of thinking about scholarship to include the scholarship of engagement (1996). He used the term "scholarship" in this instance to refer to practices that cut across the categories of academic scholarship he previously had identified—research, integration, application and teaching—and "engagement" to suggest reciprocity and collaboration in the relationship with the public (Barker, 2004). The

107

scholarship of engagement then engages faculty in academically relevant work that meets the mission and goals of the institution as well as community needs. A scholarly agenda, it "incorporates community issues which can be within or integrative across teaching, research and service" (Sandmann, 2007). Boyer's model of scholarships is described in Appendix I (#2).

The matter of how to assess the quality of scholarship, though, loomed largely over the academy. It was the Carnegie Foundation for the Advancement of Teaching that responded to this need in 1994 with a study on "how shall excellence be sustained" (Glassick, 2000, p.878). Six themes were "derived" from the study, referred to as standards of excellence in scholarship. They were published in 1997 in *Scholarship Assessed* (Glassick, Huber, & Maeroff, p.36) and can be applied to Boyer's four forms of scholarship. Between these two classic publications, the academy had the tools to re-think scholarship as well as the criteria for promotion and tenure (Glassick, 2000, p.879). Descriptions of the standards that follow are found in Appendix I (#3)

Scholarship Assessed: *Standards of Excellence in Scholarship*

For a work of scholarship to be praised, it must be characterized by:
- Clear Goals
- Adequate Preparation
- Appropriate Methods
- Significant Results
- Effective Presentation
- Reflective Critique

Attempts were made on hundreds of campuses to move toward a broader definition of scholarship, one that would include the scholarship of teaching and the scholarship of community engagement as legitimate scholarly work (Saltmarsh, Giles, O'Meara, Sandmann, Ward and Buglione, 2009). By mid-2012, the Carnegie Foundation for the Advancement of Teaching had selected 311 academic institutions for its Community Engagement classification for completing a campus assessment that includes institutional reward policies for various forms of scholarship (G. Clyburn, personal correspondence, 6/4/12). Of note, these 311 recipients are the ones that are "potentially inclined to reward community-engaged scholarship..." (Saltmarsh, et al, p.4) The value that the Carnegie Foundation assigned to the place of community in the academic enterprise is evident in that classification. Referred to as the "value of the local," it is closely associated "with an epistemological struggle over the value of community based practitioner knowledge: *What is legitimate knowledge in higher education, and is there a place for forms of scholarship that value community-based knowledge?*" (Saltmarsh, et al, p. 5).

The Five Keys to Quality

Key #1: Integration of General Goals
Key #2: Evidence of Effective Learning
Key #3: Effective Program Practices
Key #4: Embedded Levels of Quality Assurance
Key #5: The Principles & Standards of the Field

I don't think we recognize often enough the radical nature of the shift from classroom learning to being in charge of your own learning in the field placement. Students will continue to function in the dependency mode unless you somehow reorient them so that they know they're in charge.

John S. Duley, NSEE Pioneer &
Professor Emeritus
Michigan State University

As true today as when John Duley first made his observations about field placements being a powerful context for students to take charge of their learning, John recently observed that "a field placement not chosen by the student will have very little impact because the student didn't choose it." (J. Duley, personal correspondence, 8/10/12). Moving students in the direction of engaged learning is a challenge the entire academy faces at this time. When it comes to experiential learning, the goal of the engaged intern, service-learning student, and practicum student is a given. Guidelines developed to ensure such quality in learning continue to withstand the test of time and continue to be developed with the goal of high impact learning. In this section of the chapter, efforts to ensure that the student is engaged from the beginning of the placement process are described.

In higher education parlance, "quality assurance" referred to institutional activities, policies, and procedures that provided a measure of confidence that what is done academically is consistent with the institution's goals and is likely to affect learning at levels established by the institution and/or by external accrediting bodies (NSIEE, 1986). In today's academy, the term quality assurance, as used in the literature, refers to the assessment of student learning outcomes and using that assessment data to improve teaching, learning and program evaluation (J. Walters, personal correspondence, 3/15/12).

Experiential education's long standing concern with acceptance by the broader academic community and its ongoing investment in quality learning outcomes have reached that point in history where its issues are central to the national discussion of quality. In the sections of the chapter that follow, several conduits for quality are described, including the principles and standards that have been developed to guide the field. These ways to attain quality, when used collectively, will allow the experiential education community to embrace a quest that includes not only *attaining* but also *maintaining* excellence in practice.

If student learning is to be the primary measure of program quality, and it should, it is necessary for the experiential practices to have worthy educational goals, effective outcomes, proven ways to reach them, and effective assessment tools as well. NSIEE's initial publication of this source-book (NSIEE, 1986) resulted in a comprehensive exploration of experiential education by hundreds of colleagues at campuses across the country, yielding the most informed under-standing of the issues and practices of the day. Among the fruits of that seminal effort was the identification of five keys to quality in experiential learning, all of which are as relevant now as they were then: *Program Goals, Learning Outcomes, Program Practices, Levels of Quality Assurance, and Guiding Principles and Standards.* These 5 keys frame the discussions in this chapter.

Key #1: Integration of General Goals

Eight goals emerged from the original *Strengthening* work. General in nature, they appear most often in the goals statements of various types of experiential education courses and programs at the college level. Taken together, these eight general goals provide a framework within which academic departments and campus programs can develop learning outcomes specific to the intent of the work of the academic discipline or purpose of the campus program. Without *intentional* efforts to integrate these general goals into the learning experience, the learning that takes place may have little quality to its substance.

> **1. Body of Knowledge/Methodology**: To acquire, apply, integrate and evaluate a body of knowledge or the methodology of an academic discipline.
> **2. Competency Development**: To develop competencies, both knowledge and skills, specific to an occupation, profession or organizational setting.
> 3. **Appreciation of Differences**: To understand differences across cultures, abilities, orientations, and environments; and to develop empathy and skill to navigate among differences.
> **4. Critical Thinking Skills**: To acquire generic academic thinking skills, e.g., analysis, synthesis, stating a problem.
> **5. Competent Living Skills**: To acquire generic living skills, e.g., oral communication, interpersonal interaction, coping with ambiguity, working in groups, goal setting, and time management.
> **6. Civic Development**: To acquire skills needed for effective citizenship.
> **7. Career Development**: To explore career options and acquire documented work experience in an occupation that requires college-level knowledge and skills.
> **8. Ethical Development**: To develop and use an ethical perspective in a complex situation.

Key #2: Evidence of Effective Learning

> *If you are serious about quality control in experiential learning, then you have to focus not on the experience, but on the learning. What you're trying to assure is that college level learning worthy of credit is taking place. Experience can be an instrumentality for learning, but by itself it's not learning. It may be valuable for a person to put on a resume, and it may do a lot of good things in terms of career exploration, and so forth, but if there isn't learning taking place, it's not worthy of college credit.*
> **John S. Duley, NSEE Pioneer &**
> **Professor Emerita**
> **Michigan State University**

As laudable as the General Goals cited in Key #1 might be, the questions remain whether they *are* being met and *how* that is determined. Very importantly, as John Duley points out, campus sponsors and students may have little trouble documenting that work was done in the field. What they often have trouble documenting is *evidence* that the work they did was a *learning* experience and that the learning was worthy of academic credit.

Although the interns referred to previously (corporate technology giant and a governor's office) had opportunities to *observe* what others did at their field sites, as well observe and experience aspects of the organizational culture, if the interns (only) operated the postage meter and ran errands in the governor's mail room or (only) packed up storage debris and filed paperwork at the corporate technology site, their placements beg the question: Do those experiences necessarily constitute the substantive academic learning that warrants credit and credit at the college level? To address these issues, educators have identified three areas of inquiry.

1. **Awarding of Credit.** Neither the experience in the field nor the amount of hours worked is reason to grant credit. All three parties involved in the experiential learning activity—the campus sponsors, the student, and the site supervisor--must be able to identify specifically *what* was learned, *how much* was learned, i.e., the depth and breadth of learning, and at what academic *level* the learning occurred. Unless these basic criteria are met, the learning is questionable. If the learning cannot be documented, the credit cannot be awarded.

****

Credit for Service

For experiential programs that focus specifically on service, such as service-learning, there are many resources available today to guide decisions about credit for the service. Among the many, there are two sets of guidelines we find instructive and useful in this regard.

Criteria for Credit Appropriateness. Paul Dressel (1971, cited in NSIEE, 1986) advised colleges to determine the appropriateness of a particular service experience for academic credit by evaluating the extent to which the experience:
1. Strengthens the idea of public service as a value worth passing on to succeeding generations;
2. Contributes to the growth, self-development, maturity, and possible career development of the student; and,
3. Adds the breadth, depth, and integration upon which cognition depends.

Criteria for Service-Learning Course Designation. Jeff Howard, editor of the *Michigan Journal of Community Service Learning*, identified three criteria necessary for courses to be considered service-learning (2001):

111

1. Relevant and meaningful service with the community (viz., service is relevant and meaningful to all stakeholders.)
2. Enhanced academic learning (viz., enhances student academic learning in the course)
3. Purposeful civic learning (viz., directly and intentionally prepares one for active civic participation in a diverse democratic society).

****

2. **Evidence of Learning.** Experiential education needs to be able to *demonstrate* evidence of student learning relative to *specific, intentional* and *measurable* learning outcomes for a particular experience, course or program. By way of one example, in the instance of the intern at the governor's office cited previously, examples of learning outcomes in the category *Body of Knowledge* could be to describe: the constitutional powers of the governor; the state's relationship with the federal government in two particular programs; and, the primary policy issues in state economic development at the time.

Although not within the purview of this chapter to provide criteria for determining learning outcomes for each of the eight goals cited previously, there is a strong likelihood that resources are available on your campus to assist with this task. Your colleagues who are involved in professional studies academic programs (such as Education) have the experience and an appreciation for how such criteria can vary by activities, course, and program.

NSEE continues to offer Peer Consultation and the Experiential Education Academy to assist with curriculum, instruction, and assessment design for developing effective experiential learning courses and programs (www.nsee.org).

3. Levels of Learning. It is not sufficient for students to demonstrate that they learned something; it is also necessary for them to demonstrate that what they learned is appropriate for their level of learning. For example, graduate students do not earn academic credit for learning associated with sophomore year undergraduate studies, nor should undergraduate seniors be earning credit for learning outcomes in a senior level course that are typical of those in 1st year courses. Collegiate institutions should *only* provide academic credit for the appropriate level of college learning. While the conceptualization of "college-level" is ultimately a matter for each institution's judgment, there are three general criteria that may be helpful as you think about what is appropriate for your campus:

a. College-level learning requires a conceptual as well as a practical grasp of the knowledge or skill (Willingham, 1977, p.12).
b. College-level learning requires that the learning be applicable outside the specific context in which it was required, i.e., is transferable (Willingham, 1977, p.12).

112

c. College-level learning requires evidence of demonstration of higher-level cognitive skills, such as those identified in standard taxonomies such as Benjamin Bloom's Taxonomy of Educational Objectives (Bloom, 1956) and Sydney Fine's Taxonomy of Skills (Fine, 1972).

Of these three criteria, it is the third one—demonstration of higher-level cognitive skills—that may prove to be the most challenging. Those who oversee or are otherwise involved in the development/management of off-campus learning must have a functional knowledge of cognitive skills development for college levels of learning. Knowing what higher-level cognition looks like in practice and understanding how to guide students in attaining it are necessary for both faculty/staff to be effective in their roles and for courses/programs to meet the criterion of quality. Learning contracts cannot be adequately negotiated without it; field supervisors cannot be guided in the type and depth of tasks they assign without it; and, those monitoring the student's experiences – on campus and in the field-- cannot do so effectively without it. If the preparation of the faculty or professional staff is such that they are not aware of these areas of knowledge and skills, then the quality of their courses and programs will likely be compromised and be mediocre at best. And, the students lose out in learning.

In the Appendix II of this chapter, there is a compilation of principles and standards created by practitioner thought leaders in the field, nearly all of which have been developed since the original publication of this sourcebook. Within those documents are specifics to guide the development of college-level learning outcomes for experiential learning. Similarly, in Appendix I to this chapter, there are four resources provided in this regard: Alverno College's critical thinking skills model (#4), Fine's (#5) and Bloom's (#6) taxonomies of cognitive/affective skills, Bradley's framework (#7) for assessing levels of thinking in reflective assignments, and examples of models that frame the internship experience (#8). Additional resources are likely found on your campus (e.g., colleagues in nursing, education, human services, social work, communications media, physical therapy, occupational therapy programs). In addition, NSEE offers Peer Consultation services to academic institutions, their departments and campus-wide programs (www.nsee.org).

Key #1: Integration of General Goals
Key #2: Evidence of Effective Learning
Key #3: Effective Program Practices
Key #4: Embedded Levels of Quality Assurance
Key #5: The Principles & Standards of the Field

Key #3: Effective Program Practices

The academic degree is an important foundation for one's goals. The strategic planning that supports a career trajectory must include participating in substantive internships. Internships make all the difference as students envision and build experiences that ensure a successful path toward their future.
Lynne Montrose, NSEE Pioneer & Director, Academic Internship Program, Regis University, Denver

From experience, observation, and reflection, practitioners of experiential education continue to clarify and reach consensus on the issues and principles that must be addressed to ensure quality in experiential practices. Lynne Montrose's observation underscores the importance of ensuring for quality: an internship of substance matters both in the students' visions of their future and the foundations that contribute to a successful future.

Another fruit of the original work of the NSIEE team of consultants is a list of tasks that embody both the important issues and the principles of practice critical to ensure quality in off-campus learning. The tasks are offered to the field as guides that deserve serious consideration by institutions engaged in such learning programs. Each institution must decide its own interpretation and the criteria to be met for the issues raised here. The issues and principles are organized by tasks that reflect an integrated 8-step process, each step being interdependent and mutually supportive of the other seven steps. The tasks of these 8 steps take the reader from the beginning point of developing the goals for the course or program through the process of placing students in field settings to the documentation of the student's work once it ends.

8 Steps to Quality Learning

Step 1: Develop Goals for the Course or Program
- State the goals of the course or program in a document that has the official sanction of the institution or the institution's department, division or program which sponsors the experiential learning.
- Be sure these goals reflect the interests of all three parties in experiential education: the academic institution, the student, and the host organization.
- Experiential education can provide multiple benefits to these three parties. Given that all goals may not be of equal importance, the statement of goals should specifically differentiate between primary and secondary goals for each party if such exist, and each of the parties should be aware of and agree to accept and support the primary goals(s) of the other two parties.
- Establish program goals that are measurable. For example, you should be able to derive clear statements of goals from the general educational goals of the course or program.

Step 2: Identify Placement ⬛ Sites for Experiential Learning
- Give students a shared role in the responsibility for securing the field positions/sites for their experiential learning. Faculty, staff, alumni, community organizations, and parents all have natural circles of contacts that can assist students with this task.
- Establish criteria for determining the suitability of particular placement positions (e.g., internship, work, service positions) for accomplishing the goals of the program
- Be sure the placement site provides a site supervisor who will help the student adapt to the site's environment, direct the tasks, evaluate the student's performance, and intentionally support the learning goals of the placement (see *Step 3*)
- Have an ongoing system for evaluating placement sites and field positions, and for evaluating individual site supervisors.
- Have an institutional policy to favor paid work positions for students whenever pay can be arranged in work environments that have the potential for meeting the students' learning goals. Outdated policies that prevent students from being paid for their work if they are receiving college credit are discriminatory because they often preclude participation by low income students. Credit is for what students learn; pay is for work the students provide to the field sponsor. The two are neither mutually exclusive nor conflicting.

Step 3: *Contract for Learning Outcomes*

- Develop a formal statement of the expected and intentional learning outcomes to be achieved by each individual student, *how* this learning is to be *accomplished,* and *how* it is to be *assessed.* Include a description of the placement activities, the learning outcomes, learning resources (site supervisor and co-workers at the site, campus sponsors and other campus professionals, readings, websites, seminars, etc.), the criteria and the procedure for assessing the learning (who, when, how). The learning contract should include learning outcomes consistent with both the goals of the program and the interests of the individual student.
- Establish a system to ensure that the student, campus sponsor, and site supervisor all agree to this learning contract
- Have a procedure in place for making changes to this learning contract to accommodate changes in expectations by /opportunities for the student, the academic institution, and the host organization.
- Identify and discuss with all parties potential risk factors, and develop necessary and effective safeguards; create a written statement of such, either as part of or separate from the learning contract. Areas to consider include but are not limited to risk of student safety (physical and emotional), risk for professional liability and risk for potential ethical conflicts.

Step 4: *Recruit, Select, and Establish Students in Field Sites*

- Communicate the goals of the program, the benefits of participation in the program, the eligibility criteria, and the application procedures to all potential student participants.
- Limit the eligibility criteria to those factors which relate directly to the student's potential for learning and performing in the field, e.g., background knowledge, skills, and aptitudes. The grade point average, though, may or may not be a relevant field-related criterion for all placements.
- Arrange the application process so that it provides the student with experience in preparing a resume, arranging a placement interview, preparing for the interview, conducting the interview, and negotiating the conditions of the placement, all of which will be very useful skills for securing future employment; for some internship students and for most co-op education students, it is employment they seek, hence theirs are employment interviews.
- Keep in mind that assessment is the key to successful student preparation. Develop a procedure to determine whether the student has the knowledge needed to meet the learning outcomes and the minimum competence required for effective performance in the field position.
- Establish with the host site sponsor (the point person for the host organization) the legal conditions for the student's placement and determine whether or not in the instance of an internship it is an employment situation; explore medical insurance, worker's compensation, accident insurance, social security, liability protection as appropriate.
- Require that the field sponsor name a specific site supervisor for the student.

Step 5: *Prepare Students for Performing and Learning*

- Decide with the field sponsor who has responsibility to prepare students for the placement, as well as how and when this preparation is done.
- Include in the pre-field preparation information about the campus program, an orientation to the placement site and its environment, and the site-related skills and knowledge (both technical and generic) the student will develop; and, include information about the expectation for self-directed learning at the site.

Step 6: *Monitor and Support the Learning*

- Build enough variety into the components of the learning support system to accommodate the different learning styles of individual students.
- Design an intentional support system that includes a reflective component to assist students to learn from the experience. Without reflection, learning from direct experience cannot be assumed. The campus has the primary responsibility for providing this support system. Useful avenues could include seminars or colloquia, email, Blackboard, Dropbox, professional networking sites, written reports, journals, logs, simulation exercises, campus interviews, and placement site visits by peers. Students, of course, will create their own support systems in addition to what the campus

provides. If possible, include some group activities in the learning support system, since a group process enhances reflection on experience.

- Require ongoing evaluation of the learning and performance as a necessary component of the learning support system. Performance appraisal when done effectively can contribute to student motivation; distance from the placement site does not negate this principle. The challenges of good supervision by both the campus and the site supervisors have been documented and dealt with successfully by a number of professional studies programs across campuses. Some college sponsors use contemporary professional networking and social media sites such as the internet, web-cam, Facebook, LinkedIn, and Skype as ways to oversee the students' learning. Many campuses use pre-field preparation and debriefing as primary vehicles for conceptualization and analysis; they also monitor the learning on an on-going basis via weekly learning logs submitted via internet or otherwise; and they use competency focused evaluations, written as well as performance based.

- Clearly establish a policy and procedure whereby each party--- the student, academic institution, and host organization --- can address a complaint with another party

Step 7: Assess and Evaluate the Learning

- Assessment and evaluation of the learning outcomes *is* the essence of quality assurance; it is both desired and necessary to ensure excellence in courses and programs. See Chapter 8 by Rob Shumer for extensive discussions of effective assessment practices.

Step 8: Document the Learning (Transcripts and Student Records)

- Ensure that academic credits awarded for experiential learning have the same standing as those awarded for classroom-based learning.

- Use letter grades or other standard measures to ensure that the report of the learning outcomes allows for different levels of achievement to be recorded. Alternatives to letter grades such as pass/fail, satisfactory-unsatisfactory, should only be used if this alternative is also used as the standard way of reporting classroom-based learning.

- Include in the student's academic transcript at least a brief description of the experiential education activity, including the name of the host organization, the placement responsibilities, and the time commitment. For example: "Internship with Central State Hospital, Petersburg, Virginia, as an Occupational Therapy aid for 120 hours." A copy of the learning contract, evaluations by all three parties (college sponsor, student, and site supervisor); a final product(s) can also become part of the institutional file as appropriate.

- If students typically develop placement file/ portfolios for future employment, they should be encouraged to include pertinent original paperwork from their field experience, including but not limited to the learning contract, detailed description of the student's responsibilities at the site, samples/descriptions of products created by the student (as allowed), and measurable attainment of learning outcomes, including evaluations by the campus sponsors and site supervisors of the student's performance and demonstration of competencies.

Sigmon's Principles for Service

In his instructive article, Robert Sigmon (1990, pp. 56-64)) proposes three fundamental principles of service-learning projects that reflect effective program practices. Elemental to these principles is Sigmon's position that learning grows from the service task(s), and that mutuality is an important dimension of learning. He instructs the reader in the importance of having an understanding of Robert Greenleaf's (*Servant Leader*) concept of *service* as it informs Sigmon's thinking:

116

Serve in a way that care is taken to ensure that other people's highest priority needs are being served. Additionally, Sigmon's thinking is rooted in the belief that all persons are of unique worth, have gifts for sharing with others, have the right to understand and act on their own situations, and are dependent on each for survival, i.e., the more able and the less able being able to serve each other (p.62). In the Preface to this revision of *Strengthening EE,* John S. Duley underscores the centrality of this set of values both to the founders of NSIEE and to those of us who continue to lead and institutionalize experiential education in all its forms.

PRINCIPLE ONE:

Those being served control the services(s) provided.

PRINCIPLE TWO:

Those being served become better able to serve and be served
by their own actions.

PRINCIPLE THREE:

Those who serve also are learners and have significant control over
what is expected to be learned.

Ensuring Excellence in the Off-Campus Placement

Although serendipitous learning is part of the internship experience, to ensure quality, the learning must be purposeful, worthy, and meaningful. This calls for a written agreement -- a learning contract -- that reflects learning beyond the student's current knowledge, competencies, and perspective taking. It is important that such an agreement include a plan for responsible supervision as well as on-going contact with the academic institution throughout the internship. Else, the chances of a quality learning experience are just that: by chance.

Mary A. King
Professor Emerita
Fitchburg State University

When designed effectively, the successful integration of the campus program with the community site —be it public or private, non-profit or for-profit—can be an empowering context for learning (King, 1989). When all "systems" are working and all "parts" are in place, the student has the opportunity to engage in meaningful, worthy work at the field site while under the supervision of competent supervisors who collaborate to ensure a quality learning experience. However, effective learning in field experiences doesn't just happen by chance or by following the 8 steps, although not doing the latter will most likely result in a mediocre placement at best, and mediocre is a failed placement for all intents and purposes.

Effective placements are a result of careful attention to a number of factors, including common qualities, operating principles, well laid foundations, responsible relationships, informed mentoring and an awareness of the path and journey of the internship (King, 1989). These factors, with the exception of the latter, are reframed in terms of themes and characteristics in the discussion that follows, after which that path and journey are acknowledged.

A Model Placement Process: Common Themes of Commitment. The policies and practices evident in an effective placement process can be described in common themes that contribute to quality field placements (King, 1989).

- *Commitment to Collaboration:* all parties agree to work together to attain the goals of placement and the intentional learning outcomes, characterized by discussion of issues and a commitment to mutually agreed upon resolves.
- *Commitment to Involvement*: all parties take active and shared roles, with responsibilities from the onset to the goal of the student actualizing their potential through the learning experience.
- *Commitment to Excellence*: all parties commit to excellence throughout the process, with all fully informed of their roles and have a command of the knowledge and skills needed to ensure a quality learning experience (substantive learning contract). Five common characteristics of a commitment to excellence in a field placement are:
    - *Compatibility:* All parties are in agreement with the campus program in philosophy, principles and learning outcomes.
    - *Transparency:* Students and host sites know exactly what is expected of them at all points in the process; evaluations are conducted in ways that involve the student and provide a context for learning; feedback is solicited from the student and the site supervisor in useful formats. Host sites are informed of relevant and current campus information, such as campus literature and links to related sites, including academic program sourcebooks.
    - *Surety:* Risk factors are discussed in such a way that the student recognizes a risk factor for what it is and when it presents itself. In the instance of *risk of student safety,* both physical and emotional factors are identified, such as the obvious circumstances of clients who are violent or when there is known danger in parking areas; plus, the not so obvious circumstances such as being assigned to work with staff who demonstrate less than professional behavior, including incompetence, exhaustion, or prejudice. In the instance of *risk of professional liability*, awareness of potential problems is developed, such as when the site supervisor has excessive expectations of the student's workload, unreasonable expectations of the student's competencies, or when situations expose the student to legal sanctions. In the instance of *risk of potential ethical conflicts*, awareness of potential problems is developed when the student has an existing history of employment with the site, where the student will be paid while interning, or where there is a history of employment with a competing company.
    - *Reflective Readiness:* As the student prepares for the field placement, the student has been afforded opportunities to reflect on their abilities and past field

experiences (volunteer work, employment, community service, service-learning, study abroad, course related practica, other internships), has clarified personal goals and career interests and has considered the need to develop basic, practical skills (interview, resume writing and portfolio skills).

o *Responsible Modeling:* The campus is proud of its affiliation with all the supervisors involved in the placement. They are professional(s) with the expertise, experience, presentation of self, and supervisory abilities worthy of being mentors; as supervisors, they are modeling excellent access to supervisor, supervisory skills, and approaches to supervision (King, 1989).

It is important that the campus sponsors, the site supervisor, and the student have an informed understanding of what to expect in the internship process and experience. There are a number of models that have been developed to explain the path and journey taken by the intern, and they do so in different ways. Some of the models are linear in nature, describing the experience as a step-by-step process; some models describe aspects of the experience, the composite of which is the essence of the student's journey; and, one model describes the phenomenology of the experience, focusing on a journey in learning driven by the intern's concerns. (For additional information, see Appendix I (#8) *Models Framing the Internship Experience: A Sampling*)

Guiding Principles & Steps for Developing a Quality Internship.

> *I have always held that the success of an internship is grounded in the relationship between the site supervisor, the student and the campus advisor. It truly is a partnership, and like any partnership, functions most successfully with clear communication and well-articulated expectations. When all three parties work together, and stay focused on the learning, there is maximum gain for all involved.*

> **Roseanna Gaye Ross, NSEE Pioneer &**
> **Professor of Communication Studies**
> **St. Cloud State University**

The NSEE publication *The Internship as Partnership: A Handbook for Businesses, Nonprofits and Government Agencies* developed by Robert Inkster and Roseanna Ross (1998) was written specifically for those supervising interns at off-campus workplace sites. One premise of the book is that internships are three-way partnerships between the academic institution, the student and host site. The second premise is that host supervisors are busy people and although they want their students to succeed, they have limited time and resources to support their interns or to invest in becoming premier internship supervisors. This NSEE publication, one in a three-part series, was written as a sourcebook for the host organization; it guides the host supervisors in developing a quality internship by providing a plethora of resources such as assessing the feasibility of supervising an intern, working principles and mentoring guidelines to ensure a solid foundation for the internship, and a strong relationship with the student. Three excerpts from these resources are included below. (For full text and commentaries that accompany each of the sections below from that sourcebook, see Inkster and Ross, NSEE, 1998; contact www.nsee.org)

1. *An Internship That's a Success for Everyone Concerned*

Inkster & Ross developed for the field host site six working principles that will ensure a quality experience for all involved. Each principle has a clarifying commentary.

1. *The primary goal of an internship is experiential learning—and both concepts, the experience and the learning, are fundamental.*
2. *Experiential learning needs to be supported by a clear set of learning goals, with tasks and other learning opportunities identified in relation to those goals.*
3. *The learning plan for an intern needs to provide and schedule systematic reflection and self-assessment for the intern.*
4. *Finding just the right level of responsibility for an intern will require a thoughtful audit, careful planning, and continued monitoring and some fine tuning after the internship is underway.*
5. *The host organization shares the responsibility to monitor, support, assess, and provide feedback to the intern throughout the internship.*
6. *The host organization is not just a passive host, but an active, full partner in the educational enterprise, with the potential to participate in improving the curriculum.*

2. *The Four Steps to Assessing the Feasibility of Supervising an Intern*

Although the idea of an intern, or many interns, in an organization may be very appealing to the director or CEO, it may not be feasible to the supervisory staff in light of the energy and resources needed to provide an intern with a quality experience. The authors of this NSEE publication, Inkster & Ross, offer host sites four sets of tasks in step order to help the site assess the feasibility of bringing an intern into the organization. Unless the site is prepared for and committed to the responsibilities of supervising an intern, the quality of the internship is at risk from the onset.

Step #1: Informal Audit
o *Does our organization have the time to support an intern?*
o *What human resources do we have to support an intern?*
o *What physical resources do we have to support an intern?*
o *What financial resources do we have to support an intern?*
o *What could an intern do for us?*
o *What should be our goals if we bring an intern on board?*

Step #2: Drafting a Job Description
Step #3: Marketing the Position
Step #4: Interviewing and Selecting the Intern.

Effective Practices ... *Perspectives from the Field*
Michael T. Van Grinsven, CLU
Director, Field Recruitment Division
Northwestern Mutual
Milwaukee, Wisconsin

"Some internships produce work through people...
our internships develop people through work"

That's the guiding principle that Northwestern Mutual has reinforced since the launch of its internship program in 1967 and what has made the program one of the best in the nation. Our internship program is a cornerstone of our recruiting efforts and one of the key drivers behind our long track record of being able to attract exceptional talent to the company. In fact, for the past 16 years, Northwestern Mutual's internship program has been nationally recognized by Vault.com – the definitive resource of information for students and professionals pursuing and managing their careers. Vault noted that 98 percent of the Northwestern Mutual interns they surveyed found the program to be instrumental or very helpful to their future careers – whether in the financial services industry, sales or other business endeavor.

This success is a testament to our tremendous pride in our ability to develop people – by placing great value in quality above quantity in our aim to empower students both professionally and personally. This is evident in our effort to strengthen the "courage muscle" by offering students a real-world and unique experience, which we believe is the most valuable way to learn and grow in a career that can last a lifetime. At the same time, we get an opportunity to find and train the best and the brightest early in their careers. Many of the company's most successful financial representatives and nearly half of its senior field management are former interns. While we provide the tools and hands-on training, students should view our internships as a test environment that is not just role-playing. Our interns are essentially full-fledged financial representatives that get an opportunity to build relationships, make recommendations and ultimately reap the same rewards as a full-time financial representative – all coinciding with classroom work.

While we provide the tools and hands-on training, students should view our internships as a test environment that is not just role-playing. Our interns are essentially full-fledged financial representatives that get an opportunity to build relationships, make recommendations and ultimately reap the same rewards as a full-time financial representative – all coinciding with classroom work. This approach gives our interns an in-depth look at the profession that gives them a real sense of whether the career is a right fit. And if so, it serves as a jumpstart to their career after college. The end result is a program from which 37,000 students have graduated and one that lays the foundation for success in any profession.

Michael Van Grinsven currently serves as the national director of field internships. He joined Northwestern Mutual as an intern in 1984 and has held various positions with the Agency department. Over the past 20 years he has guest lectured on more than 200 colleges and universities. He has authored articles or has been interviewed by numerous industry and employment related publications. Northwestern Mutual is the marketing name for the Northwestern Mutual Life Insurance Company Milwaukee, WI and its subsidiaries.

3. *The Four Steps to Creating an Effective Relationship with the Intern*

Critical to a quality internship is an effective relationship with the intern. A four-step process is described by Inkster & Ross whereby the host supervisor plays a critical role starting early on in establishing the basis for that relationship.

- **Negotiate and develop a learning plan.** Guidance is given in the areas of what an effective plan looks like, the elements important to a learning plan, incorporating the intern's learning goals, citing the specifics of the agreement or contract and noting additional responsibilities of the three parties not already specified in the learning plan.
- **Train and orient the intern**. Extensive and detailed guidance offered in the areas of sequential tasks, checklists of goals, resources, and activities, and points of information.
- **Evaluate the intern.** Discussion given of the evaluation process, ongoing monitoring and evaluation strategies, and periodic evaluations, including the final evaluation.
- **Supervise and mentor the intern.** The authors provide the host site supervisors with general guidelines in how to develop a responsible mentoring relationship with their interns. Each guideline is augmented with commentary to help the supervisor develop quality practices.
    1. *Know your intern's learning objectives.*
    2. *Provide frequent, specific, descriptive feedback to your intern.*
    3. *Encourage your intern to be an active problem solver.*
    4. *When problems occur, communicate directly with your intern.*
    5. *Be sensitive to the role of power in your relationship.*
    6. *Use the support available from your academic contact* (Inkster & Ross, 1998).

Effective Practices … *Perspectives from the Field*
Karen Zuckerman, LMSW
Associate Vice President Student Internships and Volunteer Services
F.E.G.S Health and Human Services, NYC

I believe strongly in the value of a supervised student internship experience one that stresses a positive learning opportunity for all students, both undergraduate and graduate. A successful internship experience of collaboration, training, and supervision will help prepare a student to become a professional in their field.

An important aspect of a successful internship program is partnering with and developing relationships with community colleges, 4-year universities, and graduate programs so that students can begin to get "hands on experience" throughout their educational career.

Each student needs to have an individualized plan that takes into consideration their educational acumen, their past work and/or volunteer experience, their educational goals and requirements and their availability. It is important that the students be registered for an internship course at an educational institution and have a professor or advisor who will be responsible for reviewing the learning contract and signing a joint agency affiliation agreement. This collaboration strengthens the relationship between the student, the school that they attend, and the organization where they will be placed for their internship.

Student Interns stimulate the existing workforce with their enthusiasm, eagerness, and motivation to learn. Students get a valuable learning experience and build their resumes and confidence as they enter the workforce. When the management of an organization views the success of an Internship program as a positive collaboration, it is a "win/win" situation for the student and the organization.

I have learned that in order for a student to be successful in their internship, both the organization and the school need to be involved and be an integral part of the planning process. In addition, it is the organization's responsibility to have a well thought out and organized assignment description and weekly supervision schedule.

Karen Zuckerman is Associate Vice President of Student Internships and Volunteer Services who, in 1986, created and then developed the F·E·G·S Student Internship program. It has grown to more than 500 students yearly in a wide variety of professional internship experiences. She was awarded the NSEE Experiential Education Corporate Foundation Leader of the Year Award and has presented at numerous Social Work and Experiential Education conferences. She is Adjunct Assistant Professor of Field Work at Columbia University School of Social Work and Smith College School for Social Work.

Key #4: Embedded Levels of Quality Assurance

Critical to quality assurance in programs and services afforded by Student Affairs is the understanding that the choices of experiential education opportunities need to be both educational and developmental in intent and that in our work with students, subsequent evaluations of those experiences reflect both of these dimensions. The field of Student Affairs many times is categorized by some in the academy as "value added" when in truth we are "value laden." Student Affairs work, done correctly through experiential learning practices, provides opportunities for students to genuinely explore themselves through meaningful choice work, group work, and community work as they engage in assessable learning activities.

James Walters, Professor &
Director of Student Life
Montgomery College
Takoma Park/Silver Spring Campus

When it comes to experiential education, it might be useful to consider quality assurance in terms of *who* monitors for quality, *when* this monitoring is done, and *how* it is accomplished. However, as Jim Walters points out, it is also important to have a clear understanding of what it is that should be monitored for quality. In the instance of Student Affairs, it is *both* the educational and developmental dimensions of the experiential activities and experiences that need attention and assessment.

For quality assurance to be comprehensive, it must be well ensconced in each of three levels within the academic community: the individual (faculty/staff professionals); the department; and, the institution as a whole (NSIEE, 1986). (See Chapters 2 and 3 for discussions on the centrality of Faculty and Staff Development/POD and how that links all three levels.) A description of each of these levels follows.

Level One: Faculty/Staff Development

As in any academic endeavor, the first line of quality assurance is the individual faculty/staff professional. Quality assurance at this level involves ongoing attention to be sure that the principles of effective practice are being maintained. At this level, the difficulty with quality assurance is not a lack of good intentions. Faculty/staff professionals who provide experiential options to students have been typically student-oriented. They want the best learning experiences possible for students. Instead, the difficulty is usually that they are not aware of what constitutes quality practice. With traditional academic orientation leaning toward content rather than process, faculty in particular may not appreciate the need to take into account the general goals of the course

124

or program, the steps to quality learning, and the learning outcomes issues, especially those related to cognitive skills development and demonstration.

At this initial level of quality assurance, the task is that of communicating what constitutes effective practice. This has been done in a variety of ways through Faculty Development/POD institutionalization since 1986. Informal faculty discussion groups about quality provide opportunities to share common experiences regarding experiential education. Most institutions and professional associations maintain libraries of literature and resources in experiential education; some institutions provide subscriptions to publications through memberships in professional associations; and, some support professional staff and faculty participation at conferences. Additionally, faculty in professional studies programs on many campus have consulted with liberal studies programs about ways to incorporate experiential activities and programs into their departments and classes. A growing number of colleges and universities have incorporated experiential education into their mission statements and are looking at it as an important area of faculty development. For example, experienced professionals are being called upon to provide information about their models at other campuses. NSEE's Experiential Education Academy is routinely contacted to give workshops on campuses for faculty, staff and administrators on such topics as fundamentals of experiential education, teaching and learning experientially, reflection, assessment and legal issues (www.nsee.org).

Level Two: The Academic Department & The Campus Programs
The second level of quality assurance includes the basic academic and student development units of the institution, typically the academic departments and student affairs' campus programs where experiential learning activities take place, e.g., a centralized internship office, career services, the office of volunteer and community service, student services, and the office of civic engagement. The concern at this level is the control exercised by the community of faculty and staff professionals over the integrity of the experiential offerings:

- *What are the educational goals of the experiential course or program?*
- *Where do they fit in terms of sequence of learning?*
- *What are the prerequisites, if any?*
- *What are the expected learning outcomes?*
- *What academic/developmental/career offerings can be built on these outcomes?*
- *What existing offerings support the experiential courses/programs?*

To address these concerns, quality assurance needs to be integrated into both the academic and student affairs structures:

Academic Affairs: *Course Approval & Academic Review*
To provide a new academic offering with an experiential component or for one that is experientially based, the faculty must demonstrate that the activity can provide quality learning and is integrated with other curricular offerings. The

complexity and length of the course approval process can vary greatly by institution. If the academic unit approves the new offering through its governance structure, it will likely be approved at other points in the institution's course review process. Accordingly, it is important that academic departments formally consider and establish guidelines for experiential course design, pedagogy, learning expectations, and outcomes assessment design, using credible sources to guide the processes and policies.

The academic review process is typically a much less formal activity of faculty reporting to their peers on their teaching efforts and accomplishments. For these reports, faculty instructing experiential courses should be expected to document student learning for the educational goals established for the course and give evidence of the learning outcomes for individual students. As the assessment agenda evolves on each campus, this review process will take on unique expressions, so the experiential educator will want to understand the nuances of how this works on their respective campus, including how such reviews relate to tenure and promotion processes (See Chapter 8 on effective assessment practices).

A solid foundation for developing experiential coursework can be created by using the practices described previously that lead to quality off-campus learning and using the guiding documents listed in Appendix (II) at the end of this chapter, *Documents to Ensure Quality in Experiential Education.*

Student Affairs*: Program Development & Assessment Processes*
In most instances experiential programs supported by Student Affairs are developed using effective practices developed and evaluated by thought leaders in the programmatic area. Internships, service-learning, community-based research, leadership development and other experiential learning opportunities would look to experiential and program specific pedagogy in designing their offerings. In the best of these cases, student learning outcomes would be aligned with institutional mission as programs seek to contribute to those institutional and discipline specific goals Maki (2010). Currently more attention is being paid to the learning that happens outside of the classroom and how that learning can be verified. For Student Affairs offerings more work needs to be done in this area.

Other than the practices mentioned earlier in this document for creating quality experiences and implementing assessment strategies, AAC&U has developed some rubrics which support assessment of more holistic learning outcomes that might be associated with experiential learning programs and the institutional mission statement alignment mentioned above. Additionally, the three references below provide excellent foundational thinking and program examples.

Student services include a variety of programs and activities that support student development and provide avenues for positive interaction with the institution. In some, programs have learning outcomes where activities provide opportunities for developing friendships and building community within the student body. Distinguishing between programs with associated learning outcomes and activities, which foster community, should be the first step in identifying outcomes for assessment.

Just as academic departments define the anticipated skills and abilities a student should develop through participation in learning activities, student services departments and office program managers should address the same concern over experiential activities referenced earlier in this section. The national movement over the past few years is toward relating student learning in these "out-of-class" experiences to the mission objectives of the institution and assessing student progress toward these goals.

Active civic engagement, students acting as agents of positive change within the community both on and off campus, the development of habits associated with lifelong learning and personal change, all have associated skills and understandings that are developed experientially. Those programs should also be regularly assessed to inform understandings of student learning.

Like their academic counterparts, some institutions are organizing around communities of practice that reflect programmatic activity – like access, engagement and student success - rather than maintaining traditional organizational structures. This affords the practitioners an opportunity not only to assess student learning but to relate those student outcomes to program goals that address major institutional objectives. Issues of quality assurance will be addressed by these communities of practice as assessments reveal student development and learning and the associated program strengths and weaknesses that are or not addressing student learning.

The obvious issue then becomes what are the student learning outcomes one should be developing and how might one assess that accomplishment for experiential programs. Astin & Antonio (2012), Bresciani (2006), Maki (2010) and others offer a compelling argument for the focus to be on the assessment of student learning rather than on a more traditional use of assessment data to support alternative institutional goals. While each institution somewhat differently describes these expectations of student abilities and learning as a result of their higher education experience, these programs, classroom and "meta" expectations of the institution as supported by experiential learning methods are the outcomes that need to be assessed. (J. Walters, personal correspondence, 7/31/12).

Level Three: The Institution

When it comes to experiential education programs, career services' professionals often find ourselves at that central connection point between the students, employers, and faculty. We understand each of these stakeholders' points of view, and clearly see the win-win-win of a high quality internship / field placement. As counselors, we see how students grow during their placements, acquiring skills, developing confidence, and making professional connections. As relationship managers, we know how important it is for our employers to benefit from the perspectives, talents, and energy our interns bring to bear in solving their problems / serving their clientele. As educators, we know the faculty very much enjoy having committed, motivated, and engaged students in their classrooms, often resulting from a positive internship experience. And as university administrators, we see how the university benefits in the long term from these high quality experiential opportunities that keep our employers coming back, keep our faculty informed about industry needs, and keep our students in college and motivated to succeed.

Marianna Savoca, Director
Career Center
Stony Brook University -- SUNY

The third level for quality assurance in experiential education is the institution itself. An institution with integrity demonstrates an ongoing concern for any and all educational endeavors pursued in its name. They typically heed this responsibility in two ways: internally, through procedures for the approval of new courses and program offerings; and, externally, through relationships with accrediting bodies for the review of all educational activities.

> *Internal Monitors: Institutional Committees and Reviews.* Academic institutions are beginning to pay attention to quality assurance in experiential education at the institutional level. This emerging shift reflects the inclusion of experiential learning in mission statements due to the civic engagement movement of recent years. One way of attending to the quality issue is through committees focused specifically on experiential learning. Such committees often have different levels of authority. In most institutions, they are advisory committees for campus-wide programs such as service-learning or ad hoc committees appointed by administrators to develop and review policies for experiential education programs or practices. These committees can be of great value in institutional quality assurance if they are given enough authority and status. If the committee is a standing subcommittee of the curriculum and instruction committee, it can (1) establish minimum guidelines for approval of new courses with experiential components, and (2) require as a condition of institutional approval that petitioners demonstrate how these standards will be met. Experiential education practices, whether curricular or co-curricular, should be guided in their development and application by the *NSEE Principles of Best Practices in Experiential Education* and the standards established by NSEE's associate and partner (membership) organization the Council for the Advancement of Standards in Higher Education. An example of using such documents is Purdue University Calumet. See *Case Study of Effective Practices: Purdue University Calumet -- A Matter of Principles* at end of Key 5 for a description of how NSEE Principles are being used to ensure quality at the institutional level.

> *External Monitors.* External accrediting bodies usually review formally only the experiential learning offered through the academic programs which emphasize applied learning, such as nursing, social work, and teaching. However, accrediting agencies do ask for information about innovative, alternative, and special programs related to instructional improvements. This presents an opportunity to provide information on

128

experiential education at your institution. External accrediting agencies also are increasingly demanding evidence of student learning and of using assessment data for program improvement. For instance, with AQIP and newer accreditation bodies, the focus is, indeed, on showing evidence of learning and meeting the mission of educating students, i.e., learning outcomes from classroom and off-campus. In addition, AAC&U's LEAP Initiative goes to the heart of learning outcomes and evidence for "high impact" practices in experiential education. Although not an accrediting body, NSEE works with campuses to assess their readiness for integrating experiential learning and guiding the implementation of experiential practices.

Bowen's Principles for Reviewing Outcomes

Some years back, Howard Bowen (1979) suggested at a conference of the Council on Postsecondary Accreditation seven principles for reviewing outcomes   Three of those principles harkened a bright future for institutional recognition of experiential education, both then and now.

1. The study of outcomes should avoid the common confusion of inputs and outcomes. The only valid tests of outcomes are: *What happens in the development of persons? How do persons change and grow as a result of their college experience?*

2. Assessment should be linked to all the major goals of education and not be confined just to aspects of human development that can be easily measured or that are related to economic success.

3. Educational outcomes should relate to the development of whole persons. Colleges should accept individual differences among their students and encourage their students to develop individually along lines consistent with their unique interests and talents. For any individual, such development inevitably means substantial progress along some lines, no change along others, and regression along still others.

Governance as Monitor. Typically in the past, academic governance has been left in the hands of the faculty and administration, with little or no involvement of governing boards/trustees. However, times are changing the role of governance bodies in higher education. In a report released in late summer, 2010, by the Association of Governing Boards of Universities and Colleges (AGBUC), Katherine Masterson notes that the involvement of leadership and governance are noticeably absent from the process of assuring academic quality. 1300 chief academic officers and chairs of board committees on academic affairs were surveyed in late 2009 as to how they oversee quality of student learning outcomes. A total of 38.5% responded to the survey, with 28% being trustees and 58% chief academic officers. The report makes the point that academic institutions have "two bottom lines—a financial one and an academic one" and that boards have the responsibility to hold the campus administration accountable for the educational quality of the institution (Masterson, *CHE*, Sept. 10, 2010).

At the annual meeting of the AGBUC in April, 2011, in Los Angeles, the Board issued the statement that the boards "should be demanding more information about student-learning outcomes at their colleges, while showing deference to faculty expertise in shaping curricula and creating the tools to assess educational quality. A "2010 association survey of board engagement…found that 62 percent of trustees thought their boards spent insufficient time discussing student-learning outcome." The statement follows years of "growing scrutiny about the value of higher education" (Stripling, CHE: Leadership & Governance, April 4, 2011).

Former college President and trustee board member, and current president of the Teagle Foundation, Richard Morrill, is in agreement with the findings in the report. He considers overseeing academic quality as part of a board's responsibility, as is holding the campus administration accountable for how the mission of the institution is being carried out (Masterson, Sept. 10, 2010). Hence, the Teagle Foundation is actively involved in supporting two of five nationally based quality-of-learning projects that began within the last six years: the *New Leadership Alliance for Student Learning and Accountability* and the *National Institute for Learning Outcomes Assessment.*

Key #1: Integration of General Goals
Key #2: Evidence of Effective Learning
Key #3: Effective Program Practices
Key #4: Embedded Levels of Quality Assurance
Key #5: The Principles & Standards of the Field

Key #5: The Principles & Standards of Experiential Education

Comprehensive descriptions of the guiding principles and instructive standards that steer the field of experiential education can be found in Appendix II of this chapter. Of note, accreditation standards for the academic disciplines have historically informed the faculty of the intellectual functioning levels expected of the students at designated points in the academic program. Many of the principles and standards cited in Appendix II require that students *develop* intellectually per Bloom (1956) and Fine (1972) as well as *learn* while engaged in experiential learning programs such as internships, co-op education, study abroad, and service-learning.

Judith S. Eaton (2010), president of the Council for Higher Education Accreditation (CHEA), points out that accreditation has a notable record of meeting the quality challenge in higher education and has been instrumental in developing very sound academic programs and maintaining, as well as enhancing, quality (Eaton, 2010, p. A12). However, it is not enough to maintain and enhance quality. It must also be guaranteed (NSIEE, 1986). The principles and standards documents identified in this chapter, nearly all of which of which have been developed since the first publication of this sourcebook, have been crafted toward that intent. The reader will find these listed below and in some detail in Appendix II.

Documents to Ensure Quality in Experiential Learning and Education

- **National Society of Experiential Education** (www.nsee.org)
  - *NSEE Principles of Good Practice in Combining Service and Learning (1990)*
  - *NSEE Principles of Best Practices in Experiential Education (1998, 2009)*
  - *NSEE Guiding Principles of Ethical Practice (2010)*
  - *NSEE Position Statement on Paid Internships (1986)*

- **American Association of Higher Education (AAHE)**
  - *Principles of Good Practice for Assessing Student Learning*
    (AAHE Assessment Forum, www.eric.ed.gov*)*
  - *Seven Principles for Good Practice in Undergraduate Education (1987)*

- **Association of Experiential Education (AEE)** (2009, 5th edition, www.aee.org
  - *AEE Accreditation Standards at a Glance: Manual of Accreditation Standards for Adventure, Experiential, & Therapeutic Adventure Programs*

- **Council for Adult and Experiential Learning** (CAEL) (2006, www.cael.org)
  - *Assessing Learning: Standards, Principles & Procedures (2nd edition)*

- **Council for the Advancement of Standards in Higher Education** (2009, www.cas.edu
  - *Student Learning and Development Outcome Domains & Related Dimensions*
  - *CAS Professional Standards for Internship Programs*
  - *CAS Professional Standards for Service-Learning Programs*

- **Forum on Education Abroad** (2011, 4th edition; www.forumea.org)
  - *The Standards of Good Practice for Education Abroad*

- **Michigan Journal of Community Service Learning** (2001, www.umich.edu/`mjcsl)
  - *Principles of Good Practice for Service-Learning Pedagogy*

A CASE STUDY OF EFFECTIVE PRACTICES

Purdue University Calumet: A Matter of Principles

The cornerstone for the ExL program at Purdue University Calumet has been the integration of the NSEE Principles of Best Practices in Experiential Education into the curriculum approval process. Part of the rationale used to adapt David Kolb's Theory of Experiential Learning as an organizational change model was to be transformative; that is, to consider the institution as a "learner" and design the requisite learning activities for the university as a learning organization. Therefore, it was decided early on that faculty development efforts would bring about this anticipated transformation by developing its most valuable resource as the catalyst necessary for the strategic organizational change. A cycle of meta-implementation was implemented that included intensive faculty development workshops on experiential learning as well as a weeklong faculty retreat at Northeastern University's Summer Institute for Experiential Education. It was there that a curriculum review process was designed specifically for approving courses to receive the coveted experiential learning designation. The Faculty Senate soon thereafter approved the formation of a subcommittee on experiential learning under its Curriculum and Educational Policies committee. This ExL Committee crafted a review process similar to what was already being used for general course approval, but modified the document/application to incorporate NSEE's Principles of Good Practice. Still utilized today at PUC, all courses designated to fulfill a two-course graduation requirement in every program of study at the 10,000 student university, has had to demonstrate a strict adherence to the NSEE Principles via this curriculum review process. In addition, faculty development workshops and curriculum redesign grants continue this integration of NSEE principles into the curriculum. (See Appendix III for an expanded discussion of this initiative at PUC)

Ronald J. Kovach, Ed. D.

Assistant Vice Chancellor for Academic Affairs

Purdue University Calumet   **June 13, 2011**

The Question of Quality: A Look Ahead

"We still have a long way to go as an industry in getting to the point of saying, 'This is what quality is, and here's how we'll know it.' "
David Paris, 2011, A10

Experiential education provides a meaningful way for students to learn while pursuing educational goals important to their learning and to the greater society. As experiential educators, we have placed the student at the center of our attention. More than most of those in higher education, we have recognized students' differences and promoted experiential learning as a way to accommodate these differences (NSIEE, 1986). Howard Bowen's three-point charge to the accrediting bodies of American higher education that is described earlier in this chapter constituted a challenge to the experiential education community as well, both at that time and today. Our present challenge is to attend to Bowen's first charge and to do so effectively: **Student learning is the heart of the matter.**

- *What is the quality of this learning?*
- *How can this learning be enhanced by the ways we administer our programs and courses?*
- *What procedures and criteria will we use so we can be confident of this learning?*

When we deliberately direct our attention to these questions, we are answering the question of quality. Bowen is right: neither the questions nor the answers are easy. Unless we speak intentionally to the question of quality, our concern for students will make only a limited contribution to their learning and development (NSIEE, 1986).

Considering Change

"Fundamental to change at both the instructional and organizational levels is recognition that the current system is a system—intact and self-perpetuating because of a complex network of existing values and supports. Only by beginning from a fundamentally different point of departure and thinking systematically about alternatives can we hope to break out of the constraints on both thinking and action that it imposes. In the last analysis, this is what 'organizing for learning' is all about." (Ewell, 1997, p.18)

Experiential education professionals can and should see themselves as *change agents* who develop or demonstrate leadership within their institutions designed to bring about the "institutionalization of experiential education and continuous quality improvement in learning." Peter Ewell (1997) provides insight into such strategic thinking overall and to experiential education professionals specifically. His now classic paper *Organizing for Learning* offers a useful framework for experiential educators to understand what we know about learning as a process and as an experience, as well as what we know about the qualities of curricula and the approaches that promote learning. The fields of organizational re-structuring and continual quality improvement inform the properties that Ewell identified for successful change initiatives

133

when organizing for learning at the organization and culture levels (p.14). Those properties are described below. A comprehensive discussion of these properties can be found in Ewell's paper *Organizing for Learning: A Point of Entry.* (1997, AAHE Summer Academy, Snowbird, Utah). For more information about Ewell's work and organizational change, see Chapters 2, 3, 5 and especially Chapter 7.

Ewell's Properties of Successful Change Initiatives When Organizing for Learning

- *Requires a fundamental shift of perspective for both the organization and its members.* Many academic programs are conceived of as ways to deliver knowledge to the students; Ewell notes that when knowledge itself is at the center of the institution's design, it constructs what its members think they are supposed to do. The shift in perspective that is required puts students and what students need to be successful learners at the beginning of the design process, rather than the academic programs, their resources and structures creating the design. This shift in thinking in turn requires that the organization examine every function, structure and activity that defines it from this new way of looking at how to design for learning (p.14).

- *Needs to be thought about systematically.* Academic institutions need to think *systematically* about activities typically identified for improving learning at the organizational level (e.g., assessment, faculty development, curricular design and instructional technology). Each activity, then, would be considered in terms of how it fundamentally "affects *all* components of the institution and the relationships among them." (p.15). Such "systems thinking" informs the change process of how the components interrelate and "condition" one another's operation. A systematic, formal examination of structures and practices, as well the underlying values and incentives that keep them in place, would be possible and of instructive value. Additionally, Ewell notes the importance of examining elements important to the institution's culture from the system's perspective, such as scholarship and the regard and expectations of faculty and staff (p.15).

- *Requires people to re-learn their own roles.* Those involved in the change process will need to become on-going, open learners themselves by applying the core values of scholarship recursively. This requires an organizational commitment to staff development and recognizing its importance as a "primary key" to transformation. Ewell (1997) notes that from the perspective of organizing for learning, staff development requires a "special character" when it comes to faculty; they need to be provided a "view of learning" grounded in effective practice and conducted in accordance with the principles of good learning used in educating the students. At the same time, the approach to staff development must embed in faculty "a sense of collective accountability" for learning and the learning process no less in quality than what they expect of valued research products. The result of an effective re-learning of roles is a new and collective identity as a learning community that is "recursive and reflexive on all levels, including the learner, instructor, staff, and organizational setting." (p. 16)

- *Requires conscious and consistent administrative and leadership support.* A "revisioned approach" to leadership is required if leaders are to recognize that organizational transformation is basically about individual people, their relationships, and the importance of the quality of their lives. Toward those ends, it is necessary that the institution convene a "critical coalition" of top leadership along with a small group of personnel from throughout the institution who are invested in organizing for learning. This group of "leading learners" will not only model the process of 'learning as a way of being" but also test the waters of visions for change at the institutional level. Relevant stakeholders become involved in the vision as it evolves, with a focus on how they would be expected to go about their work differently as alternatives emerge. Leadership must commit in visible and concrete ways to sustain such initiatives with adequate resources and support (p. 17).

- ***Requires systematic mechanisms for the institution to continuously monitor how it is doing at every level.*** The institution's commitment to "building a learning organization" necessitates the creation of "institutional capacities' for data gathering and collection at all levels. As is the need for people to re-learn their roles, institutions must recursively apply "academic values of systematic investigation and reasoned deliberation." Developing such capacity requires deliberate activities for learning purposes, such as assessment or research, at every organizational level. But, creating a "culture of evidence" demands that information and data be used constructively in decision-making and "to understand and improve collective activities." (p. 18)
- ***Requires a visible triggering opportunity or event.*** Ewell observes that change initiatives tend to emerge from powerful "presenting problems" and that the most successful transformations in organizations grow from a "felt need." Transformational leadership would recognize and capitalize on the triggering events in both of these instances. The power of technology when used to organize learning cannot be overstated: it has the capacity to shatter such instructional traditions as 'classes,' 'semesters,' 'teachers,' and 'disciplinary content,'" and to create opportunities such as learner-centered learning and faculty as facilitators of that learning (p.18).

In examining the traditions of inquiry that supported his paper, Ewell (1997) found themes that were striking in how they embodied parallels at different organizational levels. These themes are the potential tools in bringing continuity to the needed institutional conversations if change is to occur in how a campus organizes for learning. Three potential cross-cutting themes are:

- *a vision of "improvement" as transformational instead of additive;*
- *the need for continuous feedback and reflection on performance*; and,
- *the need for explicit structures for collaboration and support.*

Experiential education professionals continually face the challenge of bringing about institutional change. However, without a "felt need" at the organizational level, Ewell cautions that change in how the institution organizes for learning is unlikely. Given that most members of organizations don't recognize a problem for what it is, the challenge becomes to identify the needs and problems so the process of transformations can begin. An immediate task of experiential leadership today, then, is to identify opportunities to begin that process (p.19).

A second challenge facing experiential educators is making evident the problems with established ways of doing things. Ewell cautions once again that change is unlikely unless those problems are "recognizable and explicit." A master and supervisory teacher echoes Ewell's cautionary warning by pointing out one of the factors contributing to such established ways: colleagues' long-standing attitudes and practices. This is a challenge not to be taken lightly: their power resides in the entrenched perceptions of the staff and faculty, which in some instances they have come by through experience; in other instances, they have been "trained" to think and perceive in such ways (K. Pollak, personal correspondence, 8/4/11). Another immediate task of experiential leadership, then, is to identify sources of entrenched perceptions and long-standing attitudes and practices that contribute to the identified problems with the established ways of doing things on campus.

Expecting the Unexpected

The national conversation about the quality question was captured in the *Chronicle of Higher Education's* series *Measuring Stick* beginning in Sept. 2010 (Glenn, 2010). In addition, the public is demanding to know just what it is they are paying for. Such demands for accountability may well change the role of accreditation according to the president of the Council for Higher Education Accreditation (Eaton, 2010, p.A12). Although it has sustained and reflected the most revered values in higher education (academic freedom and institutional autonomy), accreditation is facing competing and conflicting expectations of quality along with demands for accountability. From Eaton and Glenn's perspective, the questions for accreditors have changed. *"How do we respond appropriately to the call for accountability while assuring the continued health and vitality of quality improvement, peer/professional review, and self-regulation?"* (Glenn, 2010, p. A12)

The range of what is now being considered as legitimate assessment practices illustrates the challenge educators face, but we cannot ignore the realities that are being explored. Standards of competence are being developed, as are various ways of measuring it. The intent is to quantify success, and some systems are using unorthodox approaches to do so. The broadcasting media was reporting in early September 2010, that, after several years of collecting data on the performance of Los Angeles students on standardized testing in Math and English, teachers were graded on the performance of those students using a value added assessment tool; and, their ratings were posted on newspaper website(s). This approach, which seeks to determine how much value the teacher added to the learning and development of the students, is being proposed in higher education as well. For example, in the Texas A & M University System, plans are being discussed to determine the "worth" of the professors based on their salaries and the money they generate from research and teaching. The bottom-line value of the faculty will be calculated based on the salary less the money generated (Mangan, CHE, 9/2/10).

In the quest for quality, examples such as these reflect the challenges facing the academy. When approaches to quality assurance are evolving and are often filled with the unexpected, whether the changing accreditation field or approaches that evoke strong reactions, ensuring quality in assessment practices becomes even more paramount.

Investing In Quality: Experiential Education's Legitimacy and Opportunities

There are three critical elements for experiential learning: the experience, rigorous reflection, and evaluation. All are important for learning, for growth, and for knowledge of impact.

Robert Shumer, NSEE Pioneer &
Research Associate/Adjunct Faculty
University of Minnesota

In response to the questions about quality, our governments and several major foundations are seeking to increase the number of college graduates and to ensure the quality of their degrees. Never has that campaign been more obvious than during the early years of the administration of President Barack Obama. The government's investment in student grants and federal loans and the need for college access and completion reflect the public's outcry for accountability and affordable education (Eaton, 2010, p. A12). Major foundation players are stepping forward and investing in the quality question: Lumina, Teagle, the William and Flora Packett Foundations, and the Carnegie Corporation of New York. Five quality-of-learning initiatives have been created in the last five years in this quest for quality in the years ahead (CHE, Glenn, 2010, p. A15).

Five Quality-of-Learning Projects New this Millennium

o *The Lumina Foundation for Education's Tuning USA* **(2009)**: through faculty led efforts, including discussions, meetings and surveys with a broad array of investors such as alumni, employers, students, and government officials, efforts are underway to define discipline-specific knowledge and skills that can be expected of graduates (www.luminafoundation.org) .

o *New Leadership Alliance for Student Learning and Accountability* **(2009)**: focuses on improved learning and assessment practices by using model campuses that have demonstrated skill in setting clear goals for student learning and effective standards to assess learning outcomes. (www.newleadershipalliance.org)

o *National Institute for Learning Outcomes Assessment* **(2009)**: focuses on assessment practices by conducting surveys and interviews, commission's papers on select topics, and assists campuses in developing learning assessment practices (www.learningoutcomesassessment.org).

o *Voluntary System of Accountability* **(2007)**: generates accountability reports based on learning outcomes data at public 4 year institutions, as a way for families and students to compare institutions with each other (www.voluntarysystem.org).

o *Association of American Colleges and Universities' (AACU) Liberal Education and American's Promise (LEAP)* **(2007)**: supports Kuh's high impact pedagogies which include 1st year seminars and service-learning, 2 of 10 of their identified Effective Educational Practices; established liberal education goals and developed methods to assess learning outcomes based on those goals (www.aacu.org)

Experiential education finds itself at an interesting place in the national discussion about quality. It is no longer in its history as the new kid on the block, marginalized at best. In 2005 the American Association of Colleges and Universities [AAC&U] underscored the "quality gap" in its LEAP initiative, viz., that higher education must "give new priority to a set of educational outcomes that all students need from higher learning, outcomes that are closely calibrated with the challenges of a complex and volatile world." *The Essential Learning Outcomes* identified by the National Leadership Council for Liberal Education & America's Promise (LEAP) are *Knowledge of Human Cultures and the Physical and Natural World; Intellectual and Practical Skills; Personal and Social Responsibility;* and, *Integrative (and Applied) Learning.* These learning outcomes "provide a new framework to guide students' cumulative progress from school through college." (AACU, 2007. 3)

Additionally, principles of excellence have been identified by the LEAP initiative, which offers standards and guidance "for an era of educational reform and renewal." See Appendix I (#9) for a listing of *The Principles of Excellence* (AACU, 2007, p. 4). Ten teaching and learning practices have been identified by the LEAP initiative as effective educational practices; five of those are experientially based (AACU, 2007, pp. 53-54): First-year seminars and experiences; learning communities; collaborative assignments and projects; service-learning, community-based learning; and, internships. Very important to ensuring that experiential education practices are in fact high impact learning experiences are the critical three elements Rob Shumer noted in the beginning of this last section of the chapter. Faculty, staff, and administrators must have a working understanding of <u>why</u> the *experience* itself must be designed and managed for learning, <u>why</u> *reflection i*s crucial to learning experientially and must be designed and managed for learning to occur, and <u>why</u> *evaluation and assessment* are and have been central to effective experiential practices.

This chapter has endeavored to provide the reader with a detailed description of the breadth and depth of changes in quality assurance that have been developed since the original edition of this publication, as well as a look into the future through the work of foundations and initiatives that are contributing to the national landscape today. NSEE has contributed significantly to the dramatic evolution that has occurred and has positioned itself through its Academy to respond to the future needs of experiential educators. As professionals in the field, we and our academic institutions are in positions to benefit immensely from the developments and resources identified in this chapter. There is no question that the field of experiential education can respond convincingly to the calls for better quality assurance; and, there is no question that the field also can respond to the calls for more innovative and active forms of involvement in learning as integral to a quality education. In the history of education in this country, perhaps there is no better time than now for academia to respond to the call for quality and for experiential educators to collaborate in this enterprise of excellence.

References

Alverno College Productions. (1985). Critical thinking: The Alverno model. Milwaukee, WI: Author

American Association of Colleges & Universities (2007). Appendix A: A guide to effective educational practices. Washington, DC: Author.

American Association of Colleges & Universities (2008). Essential learning outcomes. *College learning for a new global century*. Washington, DC: Author.

American Association of Higher Education (1992). Principles of good Practice for assessing student learning. AAHE Assessment Forum. www.eric.ed.gov

Anderson, L. W., & Krathwohl, D. R. (Eds.). (2001). A taxonomy for learning, teaching and assessing: A revision of Bloom's Taxonomy of educational objectives: Complete Ed. New York: Longman.

Association for Experiential Education. (2009). Manual of accreditation standards for adventure, experiential, & therapeutic adventure programs (5th Ed.). Chicago: Author.

Astin, A & Antonio A. (2012) Assessment for excellence (2nd. Ed). Rowman and Littlefield Publishers, Inc.

Barker, D. (2004). The scholarship of engagement: A taxonomy of five emerging practices. *Journal of Higher Education Outreach and Engagement, 9* (2), pp. 123-137.

Bloom, B. (1956). *Taxonomy of Educational Objectives*. New York: D. McKay Company.

Boyer, E. L. (1990). Scholarship reconsidered: Priorities of the professoriate. San Francisco, Jossey Bass.

Boyer, E. L. (1996). "The scholarship of engagement." *Journal of Public Service 1*(1): 11-20.

Bowen, H. (1970). *Evaluating educational quality: A conference summary*. Annual Conference of the Council on Postsecondary Accreditation, Washington, D.C.

Bradley, J. (1995). A model for evaluating student learning in academically based service. In M. Troppe (Ed.), *Connecting cognition and action: Evaluation of student performance in service learning courses*. Denver: Education Commission of the States/ Campus Compact.

Bresciani M. (2006) Outcomes based academic and co-curricular program review. Stylus Publishing, LLC.

Chickering, A.W. & Gamson, Z.F. (1987). Seven principles for good practice in undergraduate education. *AAHE Bulletin*, March.

Council for the Advancement of Standards in Higher Education. (2009). CAS professional standards and guidelines for internship programs. Washington, DC: Author.

Council for the Advancement of Standards in Higher Education. (2009). CAS professional standards for service-learning programs. Washington, DC: Author.

Dressel, P. (1971). *College and university curriculum*. Berkeley, CA: McCutchan Publishing Corporation.

Eaton, J.S. (2010, September 3) Calls for accountability shine harsh light on accreditation [Measuring Stick]. *The Chronicle of Higher Education*, p. A12.

Ewell, P. (1997). *Organizing for learning: A point of entry*. Paper prepared for AAHE Summer Academy, Snowbird, Utah.

Eyler, J. (2009, Fall). The power of experiential education. *Liberal Education, 95* (4): 24

Fine, S. (1972). *Taxonomy of skills*. Dictionary of occupational titles, U.S. Department of Labor, and in the Handbook for analyzing jobs. Washington, D.C.: U.S. Government Printing Office.

Forum on Education Abroad (2011). Standards of good practice for education abroad, (4th Ed.). Carlisle, PA: Author.

Glassick, C.E. (2000). Boyer's expanded definitions of scholarship, the standards for assessing scholarship, and the elusiveness of the scholarship of teaching. *Academic Medicine, 75* (9), pp.877-880.

Glassick, CE, Huber, MT, Maeroff, G. (1997). *Scholarship assessed*. San Francisco, CA: Jossey-Bass.

Glenn, D. (2011, May 20). Presidents are divided on best ways to measure quality. [2 Surveys: Presidents and the Public] *Chronicle of Higher Education*, pp. A8, A9, A10

Glenn, D. (2010, September 3). The new muscle: 5 quality–of-learning projects that didn't exist 5 years ago [Measuring Stick]. *The Chronicle of Higher Education,* p. A15

Howard, J. (2001). Principles of good practice for service-learning pedagogy. Service-learning course design workbook. Companion Volume, *Michigan Journal of Community Service Learning*, pp. 16-19.

Inkster, R. P, & Ross, R. G. (1995). *The internship as partnership: A handbook for campus-based coordinators and advisors*. National Society for Experiential Education.www.nsee.org

Inkster, R.P., & Ross, R.G. (1998). *The Internship as partnership: A handbook for businesses, nonprofits, and government agencies*. Raleigh, NC: National Society for Internships and Experiential Education. (NSEE)

Internship-Net Listserv (1995). M. True (Webmaster) (mtrue@messiah.edu) listserv@listserv.messiah.edu

Keeton, M. (Ed.). (1980). *Defining and assuring quality in experiential learning*, New Directions for Experiential Learning, No.9. San Francisco: Jossey-Bass Inc., and the Council for the Advancement of Experiential Learning (CAEL).

Kendall, J.C. & Associates (1990). *Combining service and learning: A resource book for community and public service.* Raleigh, NC: National Society for Internships and Experiential Education. (NSEE)

Kendall, J.C., Duley, J.S., Little, T.C., Permaul, J.S, Rubin, S. (1986). *Strengthening experiential education within your institution*. Raleigh, N.C.: National Society for Internships and Experiential Education. (NSEE)

King, M.A. (1989). The process of placement: In C. Tower (Ed.), *Field work in human service education.* Council for Standards in Human Service Education Monograph Series, # 6 (64-72).

Maki, P. (2010) Assessing for learning: Building a sustainable commitment across the institution. Stylus Publishing, LLC.

Mangan, K. (2010, September 2). Texas A&M system will rate professors based on their bottom-line value. *Chronicle of Higher Education.*

Masterson, K. (2010, September 9). Many college boards are at sea in assessing student learning, survey finds [Leadership & Governance]. *The Chronicle of Higher Education.*

McCormick, A. (2010, September 3). As literacy declines, faculty members and the media share the blame [Measuring Stick]. *The Chronicle of Higher Education*, p. A12.

National Society for Experiential Education. (1998). Standards of practice: Eight principles of good practice for all experiential learning activities. Presented at the Annual Meeting, Norfolk, VA. Retitled, 2009: NSEE Principles of Best Practices in Experiential Education.

National Society for Experiential Education. (1989). NSEE principles of good practice in combining service and learning. Finalized at the Wingspread Conference, May 10-12, 1989, hosted by the Johnson Foundation. Published in 1990 in *Combining Service and Learning, (I)* 37-55; *(II)*, xxv-xxvii. Raleigh, NC: Author.

National Society for Experiential Education. (2010). NSEE guiding principles of ethical practice. Mt. Royal, NJ: Author.

NSEE Executive Update. (Dec. 2012). *Northwestern Mutual Life Insurance: Internships -- Doing It Right! Q & A with Michael Van Grinsven.* G. McNulty (Editor). Mt. Royal, NJ:

Saltmarsh, J. Giles, D. E. Jr., O'Meara, K. Sandmann, L. R., Ward, E. & Buglione, S. (2009). Community engagement and institutional culture in higher education: An investigation of faculty reward policies at engaged campuses. In B. Moely (Ed.) *Advances in Service Learning Research*, 9.

Sandmann, L. (2007, Oct.22). Engaged scholarship as an expression of community engagement. UMASS-Amherst Symposium: *Beyond Outreach to Scholarly Engagement.*

Shulman, L.S. (1986) Those who understand: Knowledge growth in teaching. *Educational Researcher, 15,* (2), 4-14.

Shulman, L.S. (2005, Spring). Pedagogies of uncertainty. *Liberal Education, 91*(2), 18-25.

Sigmon, R. (1979, Spring). Service learning: Three principles, *Synergist, 8*(I), 9-11, National Center for Service-Learning.

Stripling, J. (2011, April 4). Trustees are pressed to demand data about educational quality at the colleges they serve [Leadership & Governance]. *The Chronicle of Higher Education.*

Sweitzer, H. F., & King, M. A. (1994). Stages of an internship: An organizing framework. *Human Service Education, 14* (I), 25-38.

Sweitzer, H. F., & King, M.A. (1995). The internship seminar: A developmental approach. *National Society for Experiential Education Quarterly, 21* (I), 1, 22-25.

Sweitzer , H.F., & King, M.A. (2014). The successful internship: Personal, professional and civic development in experiential learning. (4th Ed). Monterey: Brooks/Cole, CENGAGE.

Wehlage, G., Stone, C., Lesko, N., Newman, C., & Page, R. (1982). Effective programs for the marginal high school student. Madison, Wisconsin: Wisconsin Center for Educational Research.

Whitaker, Fiddler, & Marieanu (2006). Assessing Learning: Standards, Principles & Procedures. 2nd ed. Chicago: CAEL.

Willingham, W. (1977). Principles of Good Practice in Assessing Experiential Learning, Columbia, Maryland: Council for Adult and Experiential Learning (CAEL) (original publication lead to formation of CAEL and has been reworked into 1989/2006 *Assessing Learning: Standards, Principles and Procedures*).

Appendix I:
Foundational Knowledge

1. Keeton's Key Areas of Quality Assurance (1980)

- *The self-directedness of the learner* to take initiative in the selection of learning goals and methods; best done when encouraged to acquire skills for clarifying goals, finding resources, selecting learning tasks, and appraising progress in the process of learning;
- *Clarification of learning outcomes*, realized when intended outcomes are clear to both parties, appropriate to the purpose of instruction, and if the path to them has been clearly marked;
- *Campus educators who approve credit for experiential learning experiences* assure that standards are fulfilled and experiential learning is recognized or not in their respective disciplines;
- *Tasks of administrators in assuring sound assessment practices* validate the integrity of their institution's practices; ensure that learning is credited at the appropriate academic level and in keeping with instructional goals of the institution; and assess learning in accordance with best practices by trained professionals;
- *Alternative models to self-study* can meet the needs for fail-safe systems to assure program quality, provided the model is on-going, appropriately financed, and earnestly supported throughout the institution;
- *Accrediting process when it emphasizes learning outcomes in the evaluation of quality.*

2. Boyer's Model of Scholarship (Boyer, 1990, p. 17)

- **Scholarship of Discovery**—of knowledge; original research that advances knowledge; disciplined, investigative efforts within the academy that should be strengthened (p.17); investigative tradition of academic life.
- **Scholarship of Integration**— of knowledge; making connections across the disciplines, placing the specialties in larger context, illuminating data in a revealing way (p.18); serious, disciplined work that seeks to interpret, draw together, and bring new insight to bear on original research (p.19); fitting ones' own or others' research into larger intellectual patterns; attention to the scholarly trends of interdisciplinary, interpretive, integrative ways of thinking; synthesizing tradition of academic life.
- **Scholarship of Application**—of knowledge; a dynamic process; moves toward engagement with the community; reflects Zeitgeist of the 19th/20th centuries and early commitment to service by the academy—one that both applies and contributes to human knowledge; for a scholar's inquiry (pp.21-23)

  How can knowledge be responsibly applied to consequential problems?

  How can it be helpful to individuals as well as institutions?

  Can social problems *themselves* define an agenda for scholarly investigation?

- **Scholarship of Teaching** – a dynamic endeavor of transmitting, transforming, and extending knowledge (p. 24); the work of the professor; faculty as scholars and learners; requires a format for public involvement and occasion for application and evaluation by others.

##

3. **Carnegie's** *Scholarship Assessed*:

Standards of Excellence (Glassick, et al, 1997)

- **Clear Goals**

    Does the scholar state the basic purpose of his or her work?
    Does the scholar define objectives that are realistic and achievable?
    Does the scholar identify important questions in the field?

- **Adequate Preparation**

    Does the scholar show an understanding of existing scholarship in the field?
    Does the scholar bring the necessary skills to his or her work?
    Does the scholar bring together the resources necessary to move the project forward?

- **Appropriate Methods**

    Does the scholar use methods appropriate to the goals?
    Does the scholar apply effectively the methods selected?
    Does the scholar modify procedures in response to changing circumstances?

- **Significant Results**

    Does the scholar achieve the goals?
    Does the scholar's work add consequentially to the field?
    Does the scholar's work open additional areas for further exploration?

- **Effective Presentation**

    Does the scholar use a suitable style and effective organization to present his or her work?
    Does the scholar use appropriate forums for communicating the work to its intended audiences?
    Does the scholar present his or her message with clarity and integrity?

- **Reflective Critique**

    Does the scholar critically evaluate his or her own work?
    Does the scholar bring an appropriate breadth of evidence to his or her critique?
    Does the scholar use evaluation to improve the quality of future work?

4. **Critical Thinking: The Alverno Model**

    (Copyright 1985, Alverno College Productions, Milwaukee, Wisconsin)
    Critical Thinking: The ability to apply frameworks in personal, academic, and professional settings <u>and</u> monitor and evaluate that activity.

    Critical Thinking Skills
    1. Analytical thinking and communicating
    2. Synthesis
    3. Judgment

4. Collaborative thinking and communicating
5. Articulating ideas
6. Awareness of values in making choices
7. Asking significant questions
8. Problem solving
9. Organizing
10. Openness to contradictory ideas
11. Evaluation of self and others
12. Creative thinking

Operating Principles
1. That teachers at every level share the responsibility for defining the aspects of critical thinking best developed at their level.
2. That critical thinking is an extensive and expansive concept, process and ability that we develop throughout our lives.
3. That critical thinking needs to be systematically taught and learned in every subject area.

Developing analytical ability within disciplinary frameworks
1. Learning that there are analytic frameworks that determine the direction, focus and scope of analysis.
2. Learning how frameworks determine direction of analysis.
3. Learning to analyze within the full range of an analytic framework.
4. Learning to recognize assumptions of alternate frameworks and is able to articulate how these assumptions might lead to different conclusions.

Developmental Levels of Analysis and Communication

Analysis	*Communication*
1. Observes accurately	1. Assesses own communicating
2. Makes justifiable inferences	2. Communicates with analytic consciousness of the process
3. Relates parts or elements in patterns	3. Communicates with effective control of the process
4. Integrates patterns into coherent systems	4. Integrates effective communication within the framework of academic disciplines
5. Compares and tests frameworks in discipline(s)	5. Develops and applies theoretical perspectives
6. Integrates frameworks into a professional synthesis	6. Integrates communication modes effectively in professional contexts.

Two Cognition Taxonomies

5. Sydney Fine's Taxonomy of Skills
For learning which combines the cognitive and affective domains, which is the case for experiential learning, Fine's Taxonomy of Skills noted below is useful (1972). The dotted line in the chart suggests a dividing line for college-level cognitive skills:

Data	**People**
Synthesizing	Mentoring
Coordinating	Negotiating

Analyzing	Instructing
Comparing	Supervision
	Persuading

Compiling	Speaking-Signaling
Computing	Serving
Copying	Taking Instructions

6. Bloom's Taxonomy of Cognitive Hierarchies (1956)

Bloom, a psychologist, devoted his life's work to the improvement of student learning. The intent of the taxonomy was to develop a way of classifying thinking behaviors considered important in the processes of learning. The taxonomy has become a basic reference for educators at all levels of education and the standard in the field. It is a multi-tiered model of classifying thinking according to levels of complexity, with levels subsuming those before it. Depicted as a stairway, this graphic visual made for an easy separation of lower and higher level thinking skills and was inherently motivating to students who could "see" the "next step."

The Original Bloom's Taxonomy
- Evaluation (judgments)
- Synthesis (creative piecing together)
- Analysis (relationship between parts of knowledge)
- Application (simple usage of knowledge)
- Comprehension (understanding)
- Knowledge (memory)

The Revised Bloom's Taxonomy
The original taxonomy has undergone revisions; one published in 2001 that is being recognized by the field. (Anderson & Krathwohl, 2001, pp. 67-68).
- **Major categories changed from noun to verb forms.**
- **Major Categories Renamed:**
  - *Knowledge* renamed *Remembering.*
  - *Comprehension* renamed *Understanding*
  - *Synthesis* renamed *Creating*
- **Major Categories of the Revised Bloom's Taxonomy**
  - **Creating:** Piercing elements together to form a coherent or functional whole; reorganizing elements into a new pattern or structure through generating, planning, or producing.
  - **Evaluating:** Judging based on criteria and standards through checking and critiquing.
  - **Analyzing:** Dividing content into parts, determining how the parts relate to one another and to an overall structure or purpose through differentiating, organizing, and attributing
  - **Applying:** Carrying out by executing, or implementing.
  - **Understanding:** Creating meaning from messages through interpreting, summarizing, inferring, comparing, and explaining.
  - **Remembering:** Retrieving, recognizing, and recalling knowledge

7. Critical Thinking Skills: Evaluating Student Learning

Bradley's Criteria for Assessing Levels of Reflection (1995)
Level One
1. Gives examples of observed behaviors or characteristics of the client or setting, but provides no insight into reasons behind the observation; observations tend to become dimensional and conventional or unassimilated repetitions of what has been heard in class or from peers.
2. Tends to focus on just one aspect of the situation.
3. Uses unsupported personal beliefs as frequently as "hard" evidence.
4. May acknowledge differences of perspective but does not discriminate effectively among them.

Level Two
1. Observations are fairly thorough and nuanced although they tend not to be placed in a broader context.
2. Provides a cogent critique from one perspective, but fails to see the broader system in which the aspect is embedded and other factors that may make change difficult.
3. Uses both unsupported personal beliefs and evidence but is beginning to be able to differentiate between them.
4. Perceives legitimate differences of viewpoint.
5. Demonstrates a beginning ability to interpret evidence.

Level Three
1. Views things from multiple perspectives; able to observe multiple aspects of the situation and place them in context.
2. Perceives conflicting goals within and among the individual involved in a situation and recognizes that the differences can be evaluated.
3. Recognizes that actions must be situationally dependent and understands many of the factors that affect their choice.
4. Makes appropriate judgments based on reasoning and evidence.
5. Has a reasonable assessment of the importance of the decisions facing clients and of his or her responsibility as a part of the clients' lives.

8. Models Framing the Internship Experience: A Sampling
(Sweitzer & King, 2009)

- Chiaferi, R, & Griffin, M. (1997). *Developing field work skills.* Pacific Grove, CA: Brooks/Cole.
- Chisholm, L. A. (2000). *Charting a hero's journey.* New York: The International Partnership for Service-Learning.
- Cochrane, S. F., & Hanley, M. M. (1999). *Learning through field: A developmental approach.* Boston: Allyn & Bacon.
- Gordon, G. R, McBride, R B., & Hage, H. H. (2011). *Criminal justice internships: Theory into practice* (5th Ed.) Cincinnati, OH: Anderson Publishing.
- Grant, R, & MacCarthy, B. (1990). Emotional stages in the music therapy internship. *Journal of Music Therapy, 27*(3), 102-118.
- Grossman, B., Levine-Jordan, N., & Shearer, P. (1991). Working with students' emotional reaction in the field: An educational framework. *The Clinical Supervisor,* (8), 23-39.

- Inkster, R, & Ross, R (1998/Summer). Monitoring and supervising the internship. *National Society for Experiential Education Quarterly*, (23), 4, 10-11, 23-26.
- Kiser, P. M. (1998). The integrative processing model: A framework for learning in the field experience. *Human Service Education,* 18(1), 3-13.
- Lamb, D., Barker, J., Jennings, M., & Yarris, E. (1982). Passages of an internship in professional psychology. *Professional Psychology*, (13), 661-669.
- Kerson, T. (1994). *Field instruction in social work settings: A framework for teaching. In T. Kerson* (Ed.), Field instruction in social work settings (pp. 1-32). New York: Haworth Press.
- Michelsen, R (1994). Social work practice with the elderly: A multifaceted placement experience. In T. Kerson (Ed.), *Field instruction in social work settings* (pp. 191-198). New York: Haworth Press.
- Rushton, S.P. (200 I). Cultural assimilation: A narrative case study of student-teaching in an inner-city school. *Teaching and Teacher Education*, (7), 147-160.
- Siporin, M. (1982). The process of field instruction. In B. Sheafor & L. Jenkins (Eds.), *Quality field instruction in social work* (pp. 175-198). New York: Longman.
- Skovholt, T. M., & Ronnestad, M. H. (1995). *The evolving professional self: Stages and themes in therapist and counselor development.* New York: John Wiley & Sons.
- Sweitzer, H.F. & King, M.A. (1994). Stages of an internship: An organizing framework. *Human Service Education*, 14 (1), 25-38.
- Sweitzer, H.F. & King, M.A. (1995). The internship seminar: A developmental approach. NSEE *Quarterly 21* (1), 22-25.
- Sweitzer, H. F. and M. A. King (2012). *Stages of an internship revisited.* National Organization for Human Services. Milwaukee, WI.
- Wentz, E. A, & Trapido-Lurie, B. (2001). Structured college internships in geo-graphic
- Wentz, E. A, & Trapido-Lurie, B. (2001). Structured college internships in geo-graphic education. *Journal of Geography*, 100, 140-144.

9. **Liberal Education & America's Promise (LEAP)**
   ## *The Principles of Excellence*   (AAC&U, 2007, p26)
   - **Principle One:**
     Aim High—and Make Excellence Inclusive.
   - **Principle Two:**
     Give Students a Compass
   - **Principle Three:**
     Teach the Arts of Inquiry and Innovation
   - **Principle Four:**
     Engage the Big Questions
   - **Principle Five:**
     Connect Knowledge with Choices and Action
   - **Principle Six:**
     Foster Civic, Intercultural, and Ethical Learning
   - **Principle Seven:**
     Assess Students' Ability to Apply Learning to Complex Problems

Appendix II:
Documents to Ensure Quality in Experiential Education

- **National Society of Experiential Education**

A few years after the NSIEE team of consultants published the original version of this sourcebook (1986), NSEE released the seminal publication *Combining Service and Learning* in 3 volumes (Kendall & Associates, 1990) and in it the NSEE Principles of Good Practice in Combining Service and Learning. This document served to guide experiential education programs toward the goal of being effective and sustained.

Nearly a decade later, in 1998, NSEE released the *Eight Principles of Good Practice for All Experiential Learning Activities* (1998). This document embodied the principles that guide the practice of experiential practices. Given the changes in the field of the previous decade, the Principles document was revisited in part and the title revised to reflect contemporary thinking: *NSEE Principles of Best Practices in Experiential Education* (2009). The document's content is currently under review. In early 2010, a third document was released: *Guiding Principles of Ethical Practice*. This document reflects the fundamental principles of responsible practice in the field of experiential learning and education.

- **NSEE Principles of Good Practice in Combining Service and Learning**
  (See *Combining Service and Learning,* 1990, Vol. I, pp. 37-55; Vol. II, pp. xxv-xxvii)

  - Engages people in responsible and challenging actions for the common good.
  - Provides structured opportunities for people to reflect critically on their service experience.
  - Articulates clear service and learning goals for everyone involved
  - Allows for those with needs to define those needs.
  - Clarifies the responsibilities of each person and organization involved.
  - Matches service providers and service needs through a process that recognizes changing circumstances.
  - Expects genuine, active, and sustained organizational commitment.
  - Includes training, supervision, monitoring, support recognition, and evaluation to meet service and learning goals.
  - Ensures that the time commitment for service and learning is flexible, appropriate, and in the best interest of all involved.
  - Is committed to program participation by and with diverse populations.

- **NSEE Principles of Best Practices in Experiential Education** (1998, 2009)
  Regardless of the experiential learning activity, both the experience and the learning are fundamental. In the learning process and in the relationship between the learner and any facilitator(s) of learning, there is a mutual responsibility. All parties are empowered to achieve the principles which follow. Yet, at the same time, the facilitator(s) of learning are expected to take the lead in ensuring both the quality of the learning experience and of the work produced, and in supporting the learner to use the principles which underlie the pedagogy of experiential education.

1. Intention: All parties must be clear from the outset why experience is the chosen approach to the learning that is to take place and to the knowledge that will be demonstrated, applied or result from it. Intention represents the purposefulness that enables experience to become knowledge and, as such, is deeper than the goals, objectives, and activities that define the experience.

2. Preparedness and Planning: Participants must ensure that they enter the experience with sufficient foundation to support a successful experience. They must also focus from the earliest stages of the experience/program on the identified intentions, adhering to them as goals, objectives and activities are defined. The resulting plan should include those intentions and be referred to on a regular basis by all parties. At the same time, it should be flexible enough to allow for adaptations as the experience unfolds.

3. Authenticity: The experience must have a real world context and/or be useful and meaningful in reference to an applied setting or situation. This means that it should be designed in concert with those who will be affected by or use it, or in response to a real situation.

4. Reflection: Reflection is the element that transforms simple experience to a learning experience. For knowledge to be discovered and internalized the learner must test assumptions and hypotheses about the outcomes of decisions and actions taken, then weigh the outcomes against past learning and future implications. This reflective process is integral to all phases of experiential learning, from identifying intention and choosing the experience, to considering preconceptions and observing how they change as the experience unfolds. Reflection is also an essential tool for adjusting the experience and measuring outcomes.

5. Orientation and Training: For the full value of the experience to be accessible to both the learner and the learning facilitator(s), and to any involved organizational partners, it is essential that they be prepared with important background information about each other and about the context and environment in which the experience will operate. Once that baseline of knowledge is addressed, ongoing structured development opportunities should also be included to expand the learner's appreciation of the context and skill requirements of her/his work.

6. Monitoring and Continuous Improvement: Any learning activity will be dynamic and changing, and the parties involved all bear responsibility for ensuring that the experience, as it is in process, continues to provide the richest learning possible, while affirming the learner. It is important that there be a feedback loop related to learning intentions and quality objectives and that the structure of the experience be sufficiently flexible to permit change in response to what that feedback suggests. While reflection provides input for new hypotheses and knowledge based in documented experience, other strategies for observing progress against intentions and objectives should also be in place. Monitoring and continuous improvement represent the formative evaluation tools.

7. Assessment and Evaluation: Outcomes and processes should be systematically documented with regard to initial intentions and quality outcomes. Assessment is a means to develop and refine the specific learning goals and quality objectives identified during the planning stages of the experience, while evaluation provides comprehensive data about the experiential process as a whole and whether it has met the intentions which suggested it.

8. Acknowledgment: Recognition of learning and impact occur throughout the experience by way of the reflective and monitoring processes and through reporting, documentation and sharing of accomplishments. All parties to the experience should be included in the recognition of progress and accomplishment. Culminating documentation and celebration of learning and impact help provide closure and sustainability to the experience.

Position Statement (2012): *Principles of Best Practices in Experiential Education*
NSEE Principles of Best Practices are grounded in experiential education and reflect the primary tenants of the major theorists in the field of experiential learning and teaching. The Principles are qualitatively derived and form a body of guidance reflecting effective practices in the field at the time of inception; they have continued to do so through the document's last review 2 years ago. The Principles were developed and subsequently reviewed on a number of occasions by nationally recognized experiential education pioneers, scholars, practitioners, and leaders. These are Principles not standards of practice. Principles, by definition, tend not to be empirically tested, although such quantitative analysis would be welcomed by NSEE.

- **NSEE Guiding Principles of Ethical Practice** (2010)
  Introduction:
  The National Society for Experiential Education (NSEE) is an open and pluralistic society of individuals and institutions dedicated to mutual learning and support across the varied roles and responsibilities represented in the field of experiential education. Founded in 1971, the mission of NSEE is to foster the effective use of experience as an integral part of education in order to empower learners and promote the common good. In fulfilling this mission, the Society works to advocate for the use of experiential learning throughout the educational system; to disseminate principles of best practices and innovations in the field; to encourage the development of research and theory related to experiential learning; to support the growth and leadership of experiential educators; and to create partnerships with the community.

  Since the founding of the Society, the Board of Directors, staff, and membership have been governed by policies and practices that guide ethical actions, relationships, and decisions. The distinctive purposes and conditions of experiential learning demand that all those involved in the process of learning through experience are held to the highest standards of mutual respect and responsibility, and that ethical behavior is understood and practiced at every level of the learning process. Experiential educators recognize their responsibility to the student, the community, and the learning process, and are informed and guided by the *NSEE Principles of Best Practice in Experiential Education (1998, 2009)*, as well as ethical principles such as beneficence and justice as promulgated by the *Statement of Shared Ethical Principles* (Council for the Advancement of Standards in Higher Education).

  Furthermore, experiential educators are guided in their research, teaching, and practice by the ethical documents of their professional disciplines and the mission and values of their respective institutions. In addition, NSEE recognizes and embraces the following ethical statements that have special resonance for experiential educators: *Commitments to the Student and to the Profession* (National Education Association); *Statement on Professional Ethics* (American Association of University Professors); and *Code of Ethics for Education Abroad* (Forum on Education Abroad).

  The above documents along with members and friends of NSEE have contributed to the following *NSEE Guiding Principles of Ethical Practice*:

  Principle One: Experiential educators uphold the principles of engaged education and democratic societies, the pursuit of truth, and the freedom of students to express their viewpoints, engage in critical thinking, and develop habits of reflection and civil discourse, listening and learning from those whose experiences and values differ from their own.

151

Principle Two: Experiential educators use recognized, quality standards and practices in the placement and supervision of students engaged in field-based learning experiences and in the creation and maintenance of ethical partnerships with the communities and organizations that host and support these students, maintaining privacy, confidentiality and reciprocity throughout.

Principle Three: Experiential educators recognize the depth of responsibility in teaching and modeling the values, skills, and relationships that foster a spirit of inquiry and fairness without discrimination or disempowerment.

Principle Four: Experiential educators are informed and guided by a body of knowledge, research and pedagogical practices recognized by and specific to the field of experiential education, including reflection, self-authorship, assessment and evaluation, civic engagement, and the development of personal and social responsibility.

Principle Five: Experiential educators are committed to excellence through active scholarship, assessment and instruction, and the creation of shared knowledge and understanding through affiliation with networks and organizations that advance experiential learning.

Principle Six: Experiential educators create informed learning contexts that foster student growth and actualization of potential, achieve academic and civic goals, and reflect excellence in curriculum design and quality.

Principle Seven: Experiential educators are aware of and sensitive to recognized legal, ethical and professional issues germane to the field of experiential education and act in accordance with established guidelines to ensure appropriate practice, for example, *NSEE Principles of Best Practice in Experiential Education* (1998, 2009).

- **NSEE's Position Statement on Paid Internships** (1986)

    Have an institutional policy to favor paid work positions for students whenever pay can be arranged in work environments that have the potential for meeting the students' learning goals. Outdated policies that prevent students from being paid for their work if they are receiving college credit are discriminatory because they often preclude participation by low income students. Credit is for what students learn; pay is for work the students provide to the field sponsor. The two are neither mutually exclusive nor conflicting. (NSIEE, Strengthening, 1986)

- **American Association of Higher Education (AAHE)**

    - **Principles of Good Practice for Assessing Student Learning**
                        (AAHE Assessment Forum. [www.eric.ed.gov])

    Among AAHE's many worthy contributions to American higher education was this 1992 document which embodies a commitment to "high expectations for all students, active forms of learning, coherent curricula, and effective out-of-class opportunities." The principles reflect the vision AAHE held of the need for

152

assessment, i.e., systematic, useable information, to ensure quality in student learning. The following is a list of the principles, without the related commentaries. The full document is available at numerous campus websites and at www.eric.ed.gov and is included in Shumer's chapter 8 on Assessment.

1. The assessment of student learning begins with educational values.

2. Assessment is most effective when it reflects an understanding of learning as multidimensional, integrated, and revealed in performance over time.

3. Assessment works best when the programs it seeks to improve have clear, explicitly stated purposes.

4. Assessment requires attention to outcomes but also and equally to the experiences that lead to those outcomes.

5. Assessment works best when it is ongoing, not episodic.

6. Assessment fosters wider improvement when representatives from across the educational community are involved.

7. Assessment makes a difference when it begins with issues of use and illuminates questions that people really care about.

8. Assessment is most likely to lead to improvement when it is part of a larger set of conditions that promote change.

9. Through assessment, educators meet responsibilities to students and to the public.

- **AAHE Seven Principles for Good Practice in Undergraduate Education**

Developed by Arthur W. Chickering, Zelda F. Gamson and colleagues, with support from the American Association of Higher Education (AAHE), the Education Commission of the States (ECS), and The Johnson Foundation. *AAHE Bulletin*, March 1987.

The Seven Principles: A Focus for Improvement (*AAHE Bulletin*, March, 1987)
These seven principles are not Ten Commandments shrunk to a twentieth century attention span. They are intended as guidelines for faculty members, students, and administrators - with support from state agencies and trustees - to improve teaching and learning. These principles seem like good common sense, and they are - because many teachers and students have experienced them and because research supports them. They rest on 50 years of research on the way teachers teach and students learn, how students work and play with one another, and how students and faculty talk to each other. While each practice can stand on its own, when all are present, their effects multiply. Together, they employ six powerful forces in education: activity, diversity, interaction, cooperation, expectations and responsibility.

1. Good Practice Encourages Student-Faculty Contact

Frequent student-faculty contact in and out of classes is the most important factor in student motivation and involvement. Faculty concern helps students get through rough times and keep on working. Knowing a few faculty members well enhances students' intellectual commitment and encourages them to think about their own values and future plans.

2. Good Practice Encourages Cooperation among Students

Learning is enhanced when it is more like a team effort than a solo race. Good learning, like good work, is collaborative and social, not competitive and isolated. Working with others often increases involvement in learning. Sharing one's own ideas and responding to others' reactions improves thinking and deepens understanding.

3. Good Practice Encourages Active Learning

Learning is not a spectator sport. Students do not learn much just sitting in classes listening to teachers, memorizing pre-packaged assignments, and spitting out answers. They must talk about what they are learning, write about it, relate it to past experiences, and apply it to their daily lives. They must make what they learn part of themselves.

4. Good Practice Gives Prompt Feedback

Knowing what you know and don't know focuses learning. Students need appropriate feedback on performance to benefit from courses. In getting started, students need help in assessing existing knowledge and competence. In classes, students need frequent opportunities to perform and receive suggestions for improvement. At various points during college, and at the end, students need chances to reflect on what they have learned, what they still need to know, and how to assess themselves.

5. Good Practice Emphasizes Time on Task

Time plus energy equals learning. There is no substitute for time on task. Learning to use one's time well is critical for students and professionals alike. Students need help in learning effective time management. Allocating realistic amounts of time means effective learning for students and effective teaching for faculty. How an institution defines time expectations for students, faculty, administrators, and other professional staff can establish the basis for high performance for all.

6. Good Practice Communicates High Expectations

Expect more and you will get it. High Expectations are important for everyone - for the poorly prepared, for those unwilling to exert themselves, and for the bright and well-motivated. Expecting students to perform well becomes a self-fulfilling prophecy when teachers and institutions hold high expectations of themselves and make extra efforts.

7. Good Practice Respects Diverse Talents and Ways of Learning

There are many roads to learning. People bring different talents and styles of learning to college. Brilliant students in the seminar room may be all thumbs in the lab or art studio. Students rich in hands-on experience may not do so well with theory. Students need the opportunity to show their talents and learn in ways that work for them. Then they can be pushed to learning in new ways that do not come so easily.

- **Association of Experiential Education (AEE)**

    - *AEE Accreditation Standards at a Glance: Manual of Accreditation Standards for Adventure, Experiential, & Therapeutic Adventure Programs (October, 2009; aee.org)*

The AEE has developed a manual to guide the accreditation process for its members. The Manual includes instructive chapters on program governance, management, operations and oversight; technical activities on land and water, including solos, service projects, unaccompanied and incidental activities. A glossary of terms is included as well. Standards are described and intentional explanation sections follow each standard; standards are divided into Sections. The AEE standards reflect its commitment to substance and clarity. Sample standards include: philosophy and practice; philosophical, educational and ethical practices; human resources development and management; transportation, environmental impact, and activities such as climbing, hiking, backpacking, with specific attention to winter activities as well as to flat and white water activities. The standards also address games and exercises used by groups when involved in some forms of experiential learning activities. An example is Section 19. *Initiative Games and Problem Solving exercises. (Contact www.aee.org for information about the standards and how to purchase the Manual),*

- **Council for Adult and Experiential Learning (CAEL)**
    - **Assessing Learning: Standards, Principles & Procedures**
      (2006, www.cael.org)

    The Council for Adult and Experiential Learning (CAEL) takes the position that acceptance of experiential education in higher education hinges on the condition of quality assessment. In 1977, the *Principles of Good Practice in Assessing Experiential Learning* was published. This statement of principles, authored by Willingham, was an outgrowth of a three year research & development project at ETS that lead to the formation of CAEL. The book set forth principles, which were reworked in 1989 into *Assessing Learning Standards, Principles & Procedures* by Urban Whitaker. In 2006, CAEL published a second edition of this book (Morry Fiddler, Catherine Marienau, and Urban Whitaker). This most recent edition includes venues such as work-based learning and non-credit-based learning, along with an updated set of standards for assessment of learning and awarding of credit for learning through experience. The publication may be purchased through www.cael.org .

- **Council for the Advancement of Standards in Higher Education (CAS)**
  (www.cas.edu) From *CAS Professional Standards for Higher Education* (7th Ed.). Copyright © 2009 Council for the Advancement of Standards in Higher Education. Reprinted with permission. No part of the CAS Standards and Guidelines may be reproduced or copied in any form, by any means, without written permission of the Council for the Advancement of Standards.

155

The Council was created "to promote the improvement of programs and services to enhance the quality of student learning and development. CAS is a consortium of professional associations who work collaboratively to develop and promulgate standards and guidelines and to encourage self-assessment. CAS has established standards and guidelines across the spectrum of functional areas in higher education. In 2006, CAS first published two documents of specific relevance to experiential education: *standards for both internship programs and service-learning programs. NSEE contributed to the creation and development of both documents.* At the time of this writing, the Standards are being prepared for the 8th revision. Samples of the standards from each of the documents follow and are specific to the Program component of the documents. The documents in their entirety are available at www.cas.edu

- *Student learning and development outcome domains & related dimensions.* The following are desirable and relevant outcome domains in student learning and development for both internship and service-learning programs. Discussions of the domain dimensions can be found at www.cas.edu .
  - *Knowledge acquisition, integration, construction, and application*
  - *Cognitive complexity*
  - *Intrapersonal development*
  - *Interpersonal competence*
  - *Humanitarianism and civic engagement*
  - *Practical competence*

- **CAS Professional Standards for Internship Programs**
  Excerpts: Part 2: PROGRAM

  Learning goals of the internship program must:
    o be clear about the educational purpose and expected student learning outcomes of the internship experience
    o encourage the learner to test assumptions and hypotheses about the outcomes of decisions and actions taken, then weigh the outcomes against past learning and future implications
    o develop and document intentional goals and objectives for the internship experience and measure learning outcomes against these goals and objectives.
    o maintain intellectual rigor in the field experience.

  Internship Programs must:
    • ensure that the participants enter the experience with sufficient foundation to support a successful experience
    • engage students in appropriate and relevant internships that facilitate practical application of theory and knowledge
    • provide the learner, the facilitator, and any organizational partners with important background information about each other and about the context and environment in which the experience will operate
    • articulate the relationship of the internship experience to the expected learning outcomes

- determine criteria for internship sites and train appropriate internship personnel to ensure productive and appropriate learning opportunities for students
- ensure that all parties engaged in the experience are included in the recognition of progress and accomplishment

When course credit is offered for an internship, the credit must primarily be for learning, not just for the practical work completed in the internship. Whether the internship is for credit of not, the focus must be on learning and educational objectives, not just on hours accrued at the site (2008, p.5)

- **CAS Professional Standards for Service-Learning Programs**
  Excerpts: Part 2: Program

  The formal education of students, consisting of the curriculum and co-curriculum, must promote student learning and development outcomes that are purposeful and holistic and that prepare students for satisfying and productive lifestyles, work and civic participation.

  Service–Learning Programs must:
  - allow all participants to define their needs and interests
  - engage students in responsible and purposeful ways to meet community-defined needs
  - enable students to understand needs in the context of community assets
  - articulate clear service and learning goals for everyone involved, including students , faculty and staff members, community agency personnel, and those being served
  - ensure intellectual rigor
  - establish criteria for selecting community service sites to ensure productive learning opportunities for everyone involved
  - educate students regarding the philosophy of service and learning, the particular community service site, the work they will do , and the people they will be serving in the community
  - establish and implement risk management procedures to protect students, the institution, and the community agencies
  - offer alternatives to ensure that students are not required to participate in service that violates a religious or moral belief
  - engage students in reflection designed to enable them to deepen their understanding of themselves, the community, and the complexity of social problems and potential solutions
  - educate students to differentiate between perpetuating dependence and building capacity within the community
  - establish mechanisms to assess service and learning outcomes for students and communities
  - provide on-going professional development and support to faculty and staff members

When course credit is offered for service-learning, the credit must be for learning, not only for service. Whether service-learning is for academic credit or not, the focus must be on learning and educational objectives, not on hours served. Service-learning programs must provide evidence of their impact on the achievement of student learning and development outcomes. (2008, p.4)

- **The Forum on Education Abroad** (2011, 4th edition; www.forumea.org)

  - **The Standards of Good Practice for Education Abroad** The Forum on Education Abroad is an organization that exclusively serves the field of education abroad. It's Standards of Good Practice "are recognized as the definitive means by which the quality of education abroad programs may be judged...." The standards are grounded in queries to ensure "a structure for voluntary, periodic self-evaluation" by institutions and field professionals. The Standards focus on nine areas of inquiry, including but not limited to *Student Learning and Development, Academic Framework, Student Preparation for the Learning Environment Abroad, Student Selection and Code of Conduct,* and *Health, Safety, Security and Risk Management.* (p. 10-12)

    As of September, 2010, The Forum began offering an elective program of Guided Standards Assessments to provide institutions and organizations "a way to assess their education abroad programs, document their success, identify areas for improvement, and share challenges and best practices with others" according to Dr. Brian Whelan, President and CEO. The assessments can be used "as a means to determine how well the programs meet specified areas of the Standards; or, they could be used as part of the self-study requirement of a Quality Improvement Program (QUIP) if the QUIP review is begun within two years of completing a Guided Standards Assessment."

- *Michigan Journal of Community Service Learning* (MJCSL)
  - **Principles of Good Practice in Community Service-Learning Pedagogy**
    (For full discussion of the Principles, see Howard, 2001; www.umich.edu/mjcsl)

    - *Principle 1: Academic credit is for Learning, Not for Service.*
    - *Principle 2: Do Not Compromise Academic Rigor.*
    - *Principle 3: Establish Learning Objectives*
    - *Principle 4: Establish Criteria for the Selection of Service Placements.*
    - *Principle 5: Provide Educationally-Sound Learning Strategies to Harvest Community Learning and Realize Course Learning Objectives.*
    - *Principle 6: Prepare Students for Learning from the Community.*

    - *Principle 7: Minimize the Distinction Between the Student's Community Learning Role and the Classroom Learning Role.*
    - *Principle 8: Re-think the Faculty Instructional Role.*
    - *Principle 9: Be prepared for Variation in, and Some Loss of Control with, Student Learning Outcomes.*
    - *Principle 10: Maximize the Community Responsibility Orientation of the Course.*

APPENDIX III

PURDUE UNIVERSITY CALUMET:
A MATTER OF PRINCIPLES

Objective:
To demonstrate the necessity for establishing first an organizational change model for faculty development in order to transform an institution and improve student success.

Intended Audience:
Any institution that needs to make major organizational culture changes in order to further strategic student success initiatives.

Program Design:
Purdue University Calumet (PUC) is the largest regional campus in the Purdue University system (10,000 students) and is located in the mid-western United States city of Hammond, IN. Since nearly eighty percent of the full-time Purdue University Calumet freshmen do not graduate within six years, student success (student persistence to graduation) became the primary focus of the strategic plan. In addition, seventy-four percent of entering Purdue University Calumet students are first generation college students who historically were graduating with a low percentage having any type of internship, community service, undergraduate research, or study abroad opportunity.

As a result of these demographics, it was apparent that a strategic retention initiative – one that would engage *students* and connect them to the institution and to their discipline – was needed to strengthen learning at PUC. *Faculty* needed additional teaching strategies so as to mentor students and use different teaching pedagogies to better connect the curriculum to practical, hands-on experiences outside of the classroom. An *action plan* was necessary so that college would "make sense" in terms of jobs and careers. It was determined that only then, would the university experience increased graduation rates.

Therefore, PUC developed as one its key strategic goals to improve retention and graduation rates through a comprehensive experiential education program. Both the faculty and administration worked to develop, adapt and implement this program using an organizational change model based on David Kolb's (1981) theory of the Adult Learning Cycle that included: campus-wide research; departmental presentations; informational feedback loops; group and individual consensus; and assessment of the implementers' learning. The process to reach this end goal was bi-dimensional in that the institution utilized individual and organizational learning processes based on Kolb. This bi-dimensional approach was important to utilize because the ultimate goal was to instill a culture of experiential learning and not merely a graduation requirement.

In addition, Purdue University Calumet secured a $1.75 million Title III grant in 2006 that provided the University the opportunity to develop the goal by:
- Creating faculty development programs that enabled faculty to gain expertise in experiential education

- Promoting faculty curriculum development grants that assisted faculty in creating new courses or revising old courses
- Educating advisors to become familiar with the variety of experiences available across disciplines and how these experiences could aid students' career development
- Setting standards of excellence for experiential education that follow the *NSEE Principles of Best Practices in Experiential Education*
- Establishing a two-course experiential learning graduation requirement
- Providing opportunities for faculty members to learn about course construction, write student learning objectives for external learning, and assess the impact of this experience on the student learning
- Starting a new curriculum approval process specifically for experiential learning courses
- Developing in all academic departments a matrix of courses offering experiential education for use by advisors and students
- Establishing the university as a strategic partner as the Midwest Center for the Experiential Education Academy of the National Society for Experiential Education

All of these initiatives for faculty development were designed so as to embed experiential education in the both the culture and the curriculum of the entire university community.

Ronald J. Kovach, Ed. D., Assistant Vice Chancellor for Academic Affairs, Purdue University Calumet, June 13, 2011

APPENDIX IV

NORTHWESTERN MUTUAL:

INTERNSHIPS -- *DOING IT RIGHT!*

Q & A WITH MICHAEL T. VAN GRINSVEN, CLU
Director, Field Recruitment Division
Northwestern Mutual Wealth Management Co.

Northwestern Mutual has been a corporate partner of NSEE for many years, generously supporting the Society in many ways, including donations, gifts, sponsorship of the annual conference, workshops on its internship program research and recently with tours of its corporate headquarters in Milwaukee. Vault has recognized Northwestern Mutual with the ranking of "Top Ten Internship" for the past 16 years.

The following interview was conducted and written by NSEE Board Member Gerald McNulty. It was published in the December 2012 edition of the NSEE Executive Update, of which he is the Editor.

Why are internships so important to Northwestern Mutual?
One of the things our employees value about (the internship program) is a sense that they want to give a student an opportunity; they want to give them a chance to better themselves. Many activities that they do are the same as regular employees... You're sitting down and learning about peoples' personal dreams, and about their financial situations. We use the words 'you need to develop your courage muscle' because it takes you out of your comfort zone... Students are very appreciative of that opportunity.

How big is the Northwestern Mutual Internship Program?
We have reached over 37,000 students. We're doing work that started in 1967. It took us 27 years to get to 10,000 (interns). We're projecting we'll do 10,000 in the next three years. We'll finish with 3,200 this year and we're looking at 3,500 next year.

What makes the Northwestern Mutual internship program unique?
What I think people find unique (I was an intern myself for two years) is that we don't look at what they are capable of doing now, but what they're capable of doing in the future. We've found students are much more capable, if you are willing to work with them. Many companies are not willing to look beyond what students are capable of at the moment.

What measures show the effectiveness of your internship program?
We are very happy with the benefit we get as a company. A bigger value is when we get the feedback from people who didn't join us, and they tell us they went on to do other things but they learned so much (as interns with Northwestern Mutual)...

161

When we hit 40 years we did a survey of our internship alumni. We were impressed to see the amount of positive feedback. Ninety-seven percent of respondents said they would highly recommend it (the program) to a student.

In earlier days we had people who were supportive (of the internship program), but they were not part of it. Now, the major leaders of the company, they themselves were interns – that's how they got their start.

Why does Northwestern Mutual support NSEE?

When we look at who are the key stakeholders and who wants students to succeed, it's NSEE and it certainly is us. If we can align those interests, we're all going to be successful. We're been really pleased with NSEE. We know the motivation and passion matches well with what we're trying to accomplish. When you have a true motive in helping students to grow and develop, you want to support those types of organizations.

What will you focus on in the near future?

We'll be celebrating our 50th anniversary of the internship program in 2017. We're collecting ideas from key stakeholders. We'll probably go back to alumni, survey them, survey internal folks, compile a lot of this stuff and share that in a way that the company would benefit. We're working on figuring out how to use technology effectively in training and development… There are different technologies used in recording and training. Can we use technology for people to see themselves in a live situation and have people be able to critique themselves? How would you do this in a training situation so people could see themselves, have a better conversation and learn what went well. It's so much faster with this new technology.

APPENDIX V

THE "INTERNSHIP-NET" LISTSERV

The "Internship-Net" listserv was created in 1995 following the joint conference of NSEE /CAEL/ICEL in Washington, DC. The NSEE Internship Special Interest Group (Internship SIG) determined that a new mode of communication was needed to keep SIG members in touch with each other more frequently. Michael True, Director of the Internship Center at Messiah College, set it up and invited participants. An initial group of 30 members joined. Today, there are over 950 subscribers - primarily from the U.S., but also from Canada, Europe, Asia and Australia.

The purpose of the Internship-Net listserv is to serve as a forum for all matters related to internships – to discuss relevant issues, offer helpful resources, provide requested advice, and to post job openings.

To join, either send an email to mtrue@messiah.edu requesting to do so or:

1) Send a message to *listserv@listserv.messiah.edu*
2) Keep the Subject line empty
3) In the Body of the email, type "subscribe internship-net" and enter first and last name. Example: subscribe internship-net   Karen Peterson

Author

Mary A. King, Ed.D. is Professor Emerita at Fitchburg State University where she was faculty and coordinator of field placements in Behavioral Sciences, supervised graduate and undergraduate interns in professional studies and liberal arts programs, and instructed service-learning. She has over 30 years of experience working with interns both in the field and on campus. She brings to her academic work backgrounds in teaching, criminal justice, consultation, and counseling psychology, holding several professional licenses. Mary has published in the fields of experiential and human service education; her recent publications include co-authoring *The Successful Internship: Personal, Professional, and Civic Development in Experiential Learning* (2014, 4th edition, Brooks/Coles CENGAGE Learning). Mary has served on several national and regional boards, most recently on that of NSEE as Vice President and as Co-Chair of the Professional Development Committee. She currently oversees NSEE's Experiential Education Academy.

Chapter 5

ESTABLISHING ADMINISTRATIVE STRUCTURES THAT FIT THE GOALS OF EXPERIENTIAL EDUCATION

Sharon Rubin
Ramapo College of New Jersey, Emerita

Abstract:

Although much has changed about the role of experiential learning within institutions of higher education in the United States, there have been, and there continue to be, four basic models used in the administration of experiential programs: a decentralized model, two types of centralized models, and a model with centralized coordination and decentralized control. Each model has some built-in advantages and disadvantages, and there often is an overlap of two or more models within one institution. Although this can result in some models that are less "organized" than others, a certain amount of chaos can result in a chaordic model, which is a harmonious coexistence displaying characteristics of each. Many current organizations use this principle as guidance for creating systems that are hybrids that are neither centralized nor anarchic. However, the overall effectiveness of any of the models depends on the program's goals and its placement within a supportive administrative structure. It is essential that the entire experiential learning programs staff understand how to nurture relationships with administrators and faculty, and become competent in taking leadership to assure the success of their programs.

Outline:
Introduction to Administrative Issues
The Pros and Cons of Four Administrative Models: An Evolutionary Perspective
The Value of Chaos as an Organizational Model
What Has Changed with the New Emphasis on Assessment
Determining How a Coordinating Office and a Department Can Work Together: Toward Efficiency and Effectiveness
Relationships, Relationships: How are Relationships Nurtured?
Leadership and Strategies for Changing Your Administrative Structure to Support Experiential Learning
Illustration and Conclusion

"Part of the complexity of where experiential education fits administratively on college and university campuses comes from the unique nature of experiential education. It does not follow any existing structure. Its functions cut across any department lines or organizational charts that are found on campuses. So it's really a function that requires alliances regardless of the structure. Of the pilot schools in the NSIEE-FIPSE Project, those that have made the most progress have been those that have been the most willing to step outside the traditional ways of looking at organizational charts. The people for whom that is not a problem seem to be the most effective."
-Jane Kendall, Former Executive Director National Society for Internships and Experiential Education

Introduction to Administrative Issues

When I became Vice President for Academic Affairs at Ramapo College of New Jersey in 1993, Experiential Learning and Career Services reported to the Vice President for Student Affairs. It was organized by function: there were staff members in charge of internships, cooperative education, international cooperative education, and community service. The President, knowing of my background, suggested that if I wanted the office to report to me, he would gladly change the organizational structure. I suggested waiting for a while, so I could tell if anything was broken before I stepped in to fix it. Over the years, there were certainly things I would have done differently, but generally, there was a collegial relationship between Student Affairs and Academic Affairs, so I never felt unheard. In fact, I was often asked for advice, usually confidentially, which suited me and the staff members who came for help.

Now, in 2010, the former director of the office has retired. Academic and Student Affairs both report to the Provost, and a new director has reorganized the staff to serve the Schools: American and International Studies, Contemporary Arts, Social Science and Human Services, Theoretical and Applied Science, the Anisfield School of Business, and alumni. The new organization hopes to give students a more seamless experience, from the first day of college through graduation and beyond. The new organization also intends to tie faculty and their needs more closely to staff members and their responsibilities.

Is one of these organizations better than the other? Are students better served by one? Are faculty more satisfied? In the consulting NSIEE representatives did under a grant from the Fund for the Improvement of Postsecondary Education of the US Department of Education, we were amazed at the variety of administrative structures we discovered. During a 1985 conference for the NSIEE-FIPSE pilot schools, representatives of eight different institutions came to a workshop on "Establishing Administrative Structures that Fit the Goals of Experiential Education." At the eight schools, the administrative responsibilities for experiential education were housed in six different types of campus units, and the directors reported to six different types of administrators. Yet all of the representatives felt that their structures were fairly effective. Even for institutions very similar in size and focus, there was certainly no single magic formula that worked for administering experiential education.

What we original five consultants discovered over the course of consulting with dozens of institutions is that experiential education definitely provided multiple benefits to different units of the institution. For *academic affairs*, experiential education served as a powerful instructional tool, a learning source complementing the faculty and the library, and a way to keep the curriculum and faculty in touch with the world beyond the campus. For *student affairs*, experiential education served as a tool for career development and community service. *Institutionally*, it was a means of fostering the town-and-gown relationship, showcasing the institution, serving the larger society, and making contacts for research, fund-raising, and jobs for graduates.

These reasons should have made experiential learning the most popular program at the universities and colleges at which we consulted, but we were often taken aback by administrative unconcern or downright hostility, lack of adequate budget and staffing, faculty disdain, especially in the humanities, and a general feeling of paddling against the current by directors. In fact, we found a number of different problems which led executives of the college or university to want to participate in our grant. Some administrators wished to get rid of an unpopular director; others revealed ambivalence in their proclaimed support for experiential learning while showing unwillingness to provide adequate resources. Others seemed to want a partner who would have the courage to give the bad news that overlapping offices which had developed through the long history of the institution and had ferociously loyal supporters needed to merge.

The landscape has changed dramatically in the last twenty-five years, although many of the tasks and dilemmas facing experiential education administrators have not changed. The value of experiential learning has been accepted by most administrators and faculty, especially in an era of economic downturn and helicopter parents. In addition, accreditation organizations have turned up the heat on institutions to assess all the curriculum, so experiential learning does not seem to be an outlier any more. The assessment of internships and cooperative education is now folded into the assessment of credited coursework within departments; service-learning, sometimes uncredited, is assessed as part of student development, along with learning outcomes.

Although colleges are hotbeds of innovation in many areas, and interdisciplinarity is on the rise, much has not changed in the administration of experiential learning in the last twenty-five years. Although a provost may be in charge of Student Affairs and Academic Affairs, the split between these units seems to be as large as it ever was. There have been, and there continue to be, four basic administrative models used in the administration of experiential programs: a decentralized model, two types of centralized models, and a model with centralized coordination and decentralized control. Each model has some built-in advantages and disadvantages, and there often is an overlap of two or more models within one institution. However, the overall effectiveness of any of the models depends on the program's goals and its placement in the overall administrative structure.

The Pros and Cons of Four Administrative Models:
An Evolutionary Perspective

While the permutations are almost unlimited, there are four administrative models that are dominant, each with its pros and cons. Perhaps the oldest and "most used" administrative model is decentralized management by academic departments for experiential programs and courses granting academic credit. The second is an institutional central office for credited programs in which a program director and staff assume many of the tasks usually performed by faculty. The third model is an institutional office for non-credit programs through career development, community service, financial aid, or some other student affairs office. Finally, the fourth model involves centralized coordination and support combined with departmental control of credited programs and courses.

Decentralized Management through Academic Departments for Experiential Programs and Courses with Academic Credits

There are definitely some *advantages* to this model. First, faculty members are familiar with standards of good practice and can exert quality control. Academic credibility and the better integration of experiential learning into the curriculum can be assured. Resources for instruction and for recognition of faculty work load are provided in a way consistent with the institutional pattern for allocating budgetary resources. Finally, as the number of faculty members who are involved increases, experiential opportunities can be developed and expanded over time. Tom Little, one of the authors of the original book, noted:

> I'm convinced that the quality of learning is best in a highly decentralized model....The experiential education model has to fit the other models of activity and authority in the institution--and the academic model is decentralized....I also think schools have a hard time thinking about 'oddball' models. If a centralized experiential education office is designed as a support unit for the whole campus, the question is whether there are precedents for academic support units--like a reading center--that would have a similar function to an experiential education center. Otherwise it is hard to explain to faculty what an academic support unit does and what it can do for them.

Disadvantages of this model need to be considered by faculty wanting to undertake doing their own placements, curriculum development, and assessment. This model can be inefficient for performing certain tasks, such as institution-wide policy development and the identification and maintenance of worksite opportunities. When a faculty member leaves or retires, an entire small universe of opportunities may be lost. Field work sponsors are often confused by who is responsible, and the failure of some faculty to "hop onto" an opportunity may be frustrating to sponsors as well. Finally, a multiplicity of policies for experiential learning over a number of departments can seem exasperating to students, at the very least, and at worst, unjust. If you have to intern 15 hours a week, delineate specific learning objectives and provide ongoing evidence of learning to receive academic credit in Department A, and your roommate has to intern 5 hours a week and keep a descriptive journal to receive academic credit in Department B, the overall credibility of assessment of experiential education will be problematic. In addition, student frustration, even anger, will continue to grow over time. Finally, if non-credited opportunities are available but departments reject them, student interests and institutional goals that don't fit the major will be ignored.

Institutional Centralization for Credited Programs with a Program Director/Staff

Larger colleges, and those in large metropolitan areas, usually determine that some centralization is useful. A second model is one with an institutional central office for credited programs in which a program director and staff assume many of the tasks usually performed by faculty. These offices are usually found in Student Affairs, sometimes as a part of Career Development, sometimes as independent units, with dual reporting to Academic Affairs. *Advantages* and *disadvantages* are evenly matched. While a centralized office is usually more efficient than the first model, such offices may be inadequately funded in an environment where budgets are departmentally driven. While they are more likely to be more responsive to non-disciplinary

167

academic learning, such as critical thinking, cross-cultural understanding, and other generic liberal arts skills, and are likely to be more knowledgeable about the process of self-directed learning, quality control for discipline-based learning is harder to maintain. Furthermore, faculty usually do not see their interests served, whether research, pedagogical, or enrollment-based, so their recruitment of students is lax. In addition, faculty do not see these offices as having academic credibility since faculty are not in charge.

As John Duley, one of the original authors, noted twenty-five years ago:

> Part of the problem with that model is that a faculty member who has managed internships wonders, 'What does that administrator do? Why does he run an internship program if he does not really offer the internships himself? How does he help me as a faculty member? I'm the one doing it. So why do I need him?' These are real questions that people have on small campuses. If they don't already have a program and somebody wants to start one, they appreciate having someone to turn to. But the problem with justifying some investment of resources in a central office from the faculty's point of view is difficult. At any place where they're cutting back--like at many of the small schools--they wait for faculty to retire and they don't replace them, and departments are losing positions. If you ask for money to coordinate experiential learning, they want to know, "What are we getting that we wouldn't have if we didn't have that person?" You and I know what they're getting--better quality control, professional awareness--but the faculty may not understand that until they see it work.

Thanks to the growing credibility and importance of experiential learning in the academy, there are a growing number of centralized offices that do report to Academic Deans/Assistant Academic Deans as Service-Learning and non-departmental internships are further integrated into the curriculum.

While such offices can provide an impetus for outside funding and can serve as a vehicle for revitalizing the curriculum, Jane Kendall warns that when "people build their centralized empires...they lose the faculty involvement. How does a small school keep that initiative coming from faculty and still have some economy of scale? At too many schools, the faculty say 'It's good that that central person over there does this, so I don't have to do it anymore.'"

Institutional Office for Non-Credit Programs [usually through Student Affairs]

Another centralized model is an institutional office for non-credit programs through career development, community service, financial aid, or some other Student Affairs office. An *advantage* of this type of office is efficiency. The limited goal simplifies interpretation and marketing of the program. Such offices also support the important non-academic learning that occurs through field experiences--career development, knowledge of the work world, appreciation of community needs, interpersonal skills, money management, etc. However, a serious *disadvantage* is that non-credit programs are contrary to the general desire of faculty for an academic and curricular emphasis, and the full educational potential of experiential learning is not being realized or recognized.

Shared Model with Centralized Coordination and Support with Academic Departmental Control of Credited Programs and Courses

Perhaps the most sophisticated model is a shared model, in which there is an office which is in charge of centralized coordination but which supports departmental control of credited programs and courses. This model has some obvious *advantages.* It takes advantage of the discipline-related knowledge of the faculty and places the curricular responsibility where it should be. Furthermore, it relieves the faculty and departments of many of the logistical and administrative concerns associated with experiential education. In addition, it lends itself to positive collaboration and cooperation across different departments and offices, and promotes credibility by assigning responsibilities in a pattern consistent with general institutional and academic practices. In addition, this model enhances the likelihood of the institution developing and overseeing a consistent set of policies and requirements for academic credit for experiential education.

While the *disadvantages* of this model are not serious, it does deviate from tradition, because it provides a focal point for advocacy and expertise about experiential education instead of allowing each faculty member to be the ruler of his/her domain. In addition, it is inter-departmental, so it can create ambiguity and confusion in the assignment of responsibilities and tasks among the central coordinating office, participating departments, and individual faculty members.

Most difficult of all to achieve with this model is selecting the right person to do the coordinating. The coordinator should be able to relate to students, faculty, and administration, and to be open to change, on the one hand. On the other hand, the coordinator needs to provide stability, be credible but not threatening, be assertive and yet flexible, be enthusiastic but not overpowering, be creative but not possessive. This is a tall order for anyone, but at the very least requires competence and considerable self-confidence.

Even twenty-five years later, it is useful to listen to the comments from a representative who benefitted from having such a very special person coordinating her program:

> From the inception of the formal internship program, the dean of our college has been very supportive of having a coordinator of internships. At first, some faculty were protective of their turf. I think it is to the credit of the coordinator that these feelings are almost nonexistent now because we all realize how we benefit from having a coordinator who does placements for us and who works with us to establish policies. She reports to the Academic Dean, and she wants to keep it that way.

> Each department has its own internship program, its own prerequisites and policies regarding papers or readings and its own programs it affiliates with [organizations] like the Washington Center. The campus-wide faculty committee works on issues like quality control. For example, we have worked on the Learning Agreement on the mid-term and

final evaluation forms. We have also planned a workshop on assessment and evaluation [and] developed the option for faculty members supervising internships to be able to have a written abstract attached to the student's transcript.

--Margaret Schram, Chair, Faculty Advisory Committee, and Associate Professor of English, Hartwick College

As the consultants were discussing the role of the coordinator in our original conversations about the project, John Duley noted an especially important role for coordinator: to serve as an administrative aide to the faculty advisory committee.

That's one role that somebody needs to do. It means [he/she] is the communication channel, the [person] who makes sure that the committee meets, that they have the materials ready to review, etc. I don't think those functions are ever clearly understood, but these are responsibilities that won't get done without someone who is keeping up with the whole effort. Another role is to offer an institutional view of quality assurance. It would be good for us to spell out some of those tasks that must be done if experiential education is going to be an acceptable part of an academic program, even though the experiential education person may not be an academician.

Overview of models: An Evolutionary Perspective

There are obviously other possible variations on these four administrative models. The trend of most advanced institutions is to move toward the shared model. However, there is another way of looking at the administrative models, and that is to consider the evolutionary stages in the administration of experiential education.

From our work with colleges and universities across the country, we have observed *three common stages* as experiential education emerges in an institution. In the first stage, individual faculty respond to students' requests, but there are few, if any, institutional policies or programs. In addition, non-credit programs are housed in units such as career development. In the next stage, as student, faculty, and staff interest in experiential learning increases, more departments and faculty get involved on an ad hoc basis. Credit programs begin to be located within some departments. Coordination becomes an issue, and a central office may be designated or established. Finally, in a third stage, there is institutional support and recognition for the multiple outcomes of experiential learning. There is a movement toward emphasis on academic credit, and institutional and departmental policies begin to address quality issues. Finally, there is movement toward a model of shared responsibility between a central administrative unit and academic departments.

While we thought we saw the shared model as being the natural result of an evolution in campus attitudes and policies, there are a few questions to ask when considering the current administrative structure or determining whether a new administrative home seems wise.

-Are the dominant goals of the experiential learning program compatible with and included in the goals of the administrative unit where the program is placed? For instance, if academic learning is the goal of the program, it should probably be housed in Academic Affairs rather than Student Affairs.

-Is experiential education among the top priorities and valued by the administrative unit in which it is placed?

-Does the administrative unit enable the program to meet its multiple goals and perform its varied tasks through collaborative arrangements with other administrative and instructional units on campus and in the community?

-Does the administrative unit have a status within the institution that facilitates, rather than jeopardizes, the advocacy and development of experiential education through the campus?

A positive "yes" to each of these questions seems essential if this or any administrative model is to be effective and efficient.

The Value of Chaos as an Organizational Model

Many years ago, I wrote an article entitled the "The Partial Myth of Efficiency." I believe it is even more valid now than it was when I wrote it. Or perhaps as I've aged, I've become reconciled to the desk that will never be cleared, the organization chart that will never replicate reality, and the creativity that comes out of serendipity when planning has left everyone parched and barren:

> In order to be successful as an experiential educator, you have to be able to tolerate models that do not fit organizational charts. They may be messy and inefficient, and often they do not make a lot of sense at first glance. I've watched people trying to draw charts to explain their complex maze of collaborative relationships across the campus, and they can get very complicated. You have to be able to live in that type of environment, or else you have to get out of the field pretty quickly. And people do get out of the field because they cannot tolerate the ambiguity.

> When I first started as a director of experiential learning, I thought very highly of efficiency. I said, "Why does every department do this differently?" We did have course numbers for the entire campus, but we also had other departmental numbers that some departments used for their majors. And internships in one department were quite different from internships in another department. One department said you had to be a senior, and other said you had to have a 3.0 and take "Introduction to Whatever." My office was a clearinghouse, but we had faculty who kept their own lists of people they talked to. I kept saying, "What a mess! Can't we get organized?" That's where I was. But now I say, "Look, if the goal is to give as many students as possible the opportunity to be involved in experiential learning, then we could all be doing it, and there still wouldn't be enough of us."

> The mess shows that responsibility is shared. People have different policies because they have different goals. In a small institution, it makes sense to have one pattern for experiential learning, because students are generally homogeneous and a small faculty can usually agree on a single model. In a large institution, however, a single model

usually does not work effectively to fit students' varied needs or the curricular models of many different departments. For example, some sort of field work may be mandatory in some of the applied fields, and the number of hours a student is expected to work might be very high. In another department, an internship might be project-centered and might demand fewer hours. A freshman might benefit from a service-learning experience to investigate a potential field of interest for further study, but credit may not be needed or appropriate for that student. On the other hand, a senior might develop a full-time, academically intensive practicum, and what she learns deserves a larger number of credits.

An overlap model can be very strange and delicate to maintain creatively because you don't know who you report to, or you are trying to balance several different reporting structures. However, a model in which a number of programs and courses co-exist in a messy way also has a lot of potential.
(Sharon Rubin, *Strengthening,* p. 100)

A term which expresses this mixture of chaos and order is _chaordic,_ coined by Dee Hock, founder and former CEO of VISA credit cards. It's often described as a harmonious coexistence displaying characteristics of both. Many current organizations use this principle as guidance for creating systems that are hybrids that are neither centralized nor anarchic. As the field of experiential education continues to evolve, the notion of chaordic principles should be kept in mind.

What has Changed with the New Emphasis on Assessment

In the years since 1987, assessment has made the role of faculty and academic departments much more significant and required when it comes to all aspects of the curriculum, including experiential education. (See Chapter 8 on Assessment) Not only are faculty welcomed on advisory boards of offices which may deal with internships, but they are encouraged and even expected to take on administrative tasks which can no longer be done outside of departments.

There are, of course, developmental tasks such as advocacy, research, development of possible new programs, and general leadership in experiential education on and off campus. These tasks may belong in deans' or vice presidents' offices for both Academic and Student Affairs, depending on the specific goals of experiential education. One common characteristic of these tasks is that they are typically performed by administrators rather than faculty. There are exceptions, however, especially in smaller schools.

Then there are coordinating tasks, such as reporting and communicating across courses and programs. These include coordinating the school's relationships with field work sponsors, networking of all people involved, and ensuring quality control. Where do these tasks belong? Again, they may be in Student or Academic Affairs, but perhaps better in both.

However, on issues of standards, policies, and practices, administrators ought not to be in charge. Assessment requires faculty involvement in tasks related to the actual offering of experiential education to students. These functions include recruiting, selecting, and monitoring students;

developing placements; developing relevant coursework; evaluating the learning; and so on. Although experiential learning has a recognized status in the academic community of most campuses, some faculty members still have great ambivalence about recruiting students and developing placements. "This is way outside of what I understand to be my faculty role. Besides, I don't have the skills or time to do this" is sometimes heard from faculty. Yet if the learning is going to be planned, carried out, and evaluated, who else is going to convince students to participate and organizations to put in the effort to make the learning complex and relevant?

If we take the shared model not only as a goal but as a necessity, the question is how experiential learning offices can aid faculty in the tasks they must do to assure that learning of the kind and at the level they need students to accomplish takes place. Chapter 3 further develops ideas related to faculty involvement. I believed in 1985, and I continue to believe, that "where the staff perceives its useful and active alliances is more important than whether it is in Student Affairs or Academic Affairs. No program should use its place in the organizational chart as an excuse for limited alliances." *Building alliances is at the core of the administration of experiential learning.*

Determining How a Coordinating Office and a Department Can Work Together: Toward Efficiency and Effectiveness

It is important to decide who is in charge of what, and who pays for what. It is frustrating to directors of experiential learning to have to negotiate with so many different stakeholders. Consequently, the director of the experiential learning program needs to have ongoing conversations and negotiations with the provost, deans, and department chairs to determine who will be taking care of such administrative tasks as:

Critical Administrative/Leadership Tasks

-Advocating experiential learning among faculty, students, and administrators (making the case for experiential education within the institution).
-Establishing communication mechanisms for faculty to exchange ideas and techniques with colleagues in other departments and other institutions
-Providing administrative support to the faculty and, if applicable, to the faculty committee on experiential education.
-Soliciting input for and making decisions about campus-wide policies.
-Establishing quality controls.
-Monitoring quality.
-Arranging professional development opportunities regarding experiential education for faculty and staff.
-Coordinating the institution's outreach to field supervisors for experiential education.
-Representing the institution's experiential learning programs outside the institution.
-Securing funds for regular program operations.
-Reporting on campus-wide trends and needs regarding experiential education.
-Conducting research regarding experiential education.
-Securing funds for special projects, research, and development regarding experiential education.

-Keeping abreast of the professional literature and other developments in experiential education regionally and nationally.

Dimensions/Steps in the Learning Process

In addition, it is necessary to determine who will handle each part of the learning process in actual courses and programs, namely addressing the quality issues elaborated in Chapter 4:

1. Establishing goals for each program or course.
2. Identifying sites for experiential learning.
3. Helping students establish appropriate learning objectives.
4. Recruiting, selecting, and establishing students at field sites.
5. Preparing students for learning and working.
6. Monitoring and supporting the learning.
7. Evaluating and assessing the learning.
8. Reporting the learning on transcripts and student records.
9. Other issues of importance and/or unique to your institution

Critical Questions to Ask about Each Task

One way of thinking about this set of issues is to try to consider each issue by asking the following questions:

-Is it very clear who is responsible for this task?
-Is it somewhat clear who is responsible for this task?
-Is it unclear who is responsible for this task? (Or is it clear that nobody is responsible for this task?)
-Is it clear that there are adequate resources for this task?
-Is it somewhat clear that there are adequate resources for this task?
-Is it unclear that there are adequate resources for this task?
-Is it clear that there are not adequate resources for this task?
-Who is responsible for evaluation and long-range planning regarding this task?
-Who are the collaborators or competitors with responsibilities related to this task?

It may be particularly useful to have every stakeholder fill out the answers to these questions individually as a precursor to such a meeting. Survey Monkey or Qualtrics surveys may be used to give an opportunity to have everyone fill out the answers anonymously and then share information about the "sense of the group." Finding genuine responses to these issues will be time-consuming and sometimes contentious. However, such candor seems essential if effective and efficient administrative practices are to emerge. Indeed, one of the important outcomes may be to find that there are some tasks that no one is doing or wants to do, and others that are being done by overlapping individuals or groups. As Jane Kendall noted, "If you have one program on campus using its resources to compete with another program on the same campus, then you've got some work to do at the upper level of decision-making. Not many institutions can afford this duplication, but I see it happen all the time." However, with the answers will come both clarity and a shared commitment that should improve the quality of experiential learning substantially.

Relationships, Relationships:
How Are Relationships Nurtured?

We would like to believe that in the last twenty-five years, the competition between Student Affairs and Academic Affairs, between the Schools or Colleges, and between departments and programs has decreased; unfortunately, in many, if not most institutions, it has not. Still, it is important to define some ways to nurture good relationships across all those lines. It will not be surprising to any administrator at any level that relationships can be nurtured through *access, communication, respect, influence,* and *credibility.*

Access is perhaps the most simple and the most complicated element in assuring relationships, because knowledge is power, and lack of knowledge makes it difficult to do one's job. It is important for the program and its director to have formal or informal access to people responsible for the following functions, so that all of them can support the operation of experiential programs. From our experience, this would include access to representatives of the following offices:

-Those responsible for overall curricular concerns, such as the curriculum committee.
-Department chairs and deans, so that academic department matters, such as new courses and
    programs being planned, and instructional development and evaluation, can be identified
    and influenced.
-The registrar's staff, because of all the data and information they oversee, including how
    transcripts are shaped and made available.
-Career development and placement staff, so that experiential programs can be included in
    Majors Days, Employment Fairs, student workshops, etc.
-Staff responsible for community service programs, such as Greek community activities,
    alternative spring breaks, residence halls, campus ministry, etc.
-Financial aid and student employment staff, so that Federal or state funds that might be used for
    internships or other experiential learning opportunities are not missed.
-Institutional planning and research staff and committees, so opportunities for new affiliations
    and organizational structures can be considered.
-Admissions staff, so that experiential learning can be used as a selling point for prospective
    students.
-Alumni affairs staff, so that alumni events can be used to increase possibilities for student
    participation in experiential learning.
-Public relations staff, for spreading the good news.
-Development staff, so that new funding sources can be sought and so the needs of experiential
    learning won't be ignored.

In addition to access, *communication* is critical. It is essential for experiential educators to learn how to speak in the language and understand the time-frame of the above stakeholders so that they don't come up a day late and a dollar short. If experiential educators want others to fully understand their goals, concerns, and operating styles, they, too, must understand others' goals, concerns, and operating styles. *Respect* on both sides is earned when everyone attempts to communicate and understand the perspective of the other party.

Of course, it is necessary to keep a relationship with students and employers as well. Tom Little, an original author, "talked about how people tend to leave out the students and the employers completely from the tasks--and that these players could systematically be given more responsibility."

Access, communication, and *respect* usually lead to a better understanding of our colleagues' goals. This helps program administrators create or provide win-win situations with these stakeholders in such a way that the others involved benefit in some fashion. If, for example, it is important for alumni affairs staff to cultivate potential donors, an experiential educator who creates opportunities for bright, energetic students to be helpful to potential donors in their business or organizational lives will encourage them to think kindly of the college which continues to educate such students.

After all, the ultimate goal is to increase the *influence* of the experiential office so that other units consult with them on ways to improve their own activities. At this point, experiential educators will be seen as having *credibility, competence,* and *capability.*

Leadership and Strategies for Changing Your Administrative Structure to Support Experiential Learning

The list of goals and relationships for the director of experiential learning programs is long. However, if we consider the most important role of the director of experiential learning, it's **leadership,** professionally both in the field and on campus. "Sometimes you just have to be bold. If you don't figure out what structure makes the most sense and then help others see the reasons, you can be sure someone else will decide it. If you are in a good position to see what is needed, you've got to speak up," noted Nancy Gansneder, who was at the time Director of the Undergraduate Internship Program at the University of Virginia.

If it seems that leadership belongs somewhere else, or to someone else, such as the president of the university, it's important to remember that leaders and change agents are everywhere. A mentor of mine, Dr. Paul Miller, once reminded me that I didn't have to be in any particular position at my university, or indeed to be "important" in order to be a change agent. In fact, collaborating to make change takes the power of one and multiplies it exponentially [see Chapters 3 and 7]. Following are a few ideas to help create the kind of organization of which you want to be a part.

Know What Needs Changing. Walter Sikes, author of *Renewing Higher Education From Within,* quoted Jack Lindquist about change agents: "A change agent must have a sound, internalized understanding not only of the 'facts' but also the feelings important to the change process. Thus, data collection and feedback are essential to initiating either personal or organizational change. A thorough understanding of the particular dynamics of a system that is to be changed will allow one to tailor the innovation to the specific situation--and greatly increase the chances for success. Plan for adaptation, not adoption (Sikes, 1985, p. 5)."

Involve The Faculty and Others Who Are Likely to Be Affected by the Change, Including One's Immediate or Prospective Supervisor. This is based on two general theories about change. First, people tend to support those changes which will lead to benefits for themselves and their units. Thus, if central coordination would reduce faculty load without taking away faculty teaching prerogative, faculty will most likely be receptive. If collaborative work with faculty would raise the general status of student affairs, then the student affairs dean may not feel as territorially protective. The key is to create win-win conditions. Second, persons who are expected to implement the change must be involved in the decision process leading to the change. Such involvement allows the participants to feel a sense of contribution and ownership, which in turn reduces resistance to change and encourages active advocacy for change.

Assert Leadership. Change implies the need for movement, and someone has to get the action started. John Duley observed, "We tend to get stuck in boxes. We are where we are because that's where we happen to be. So, how do we get out of it?" It may sound too simple, but the answer may well be "Do something!" Louis Sullivan, the great American architect, told us "Form follows function." American architectural practice was transformed when form began to follow function. Unfortunately, most of us in higher education seem to be stuck with the idea that the function follows the form. We say we are in a particular form. We came into a position that was already in that form, or our form depends on who we happen to report to. There's nothing wrong with where you are if the form matches the function. But where it is no match, where there is an incongruence between your structure and your functions, then it's up to you to take action.

Illustration and Conclusion

Every campus has its own characteristics and dynamics, created by the people involved--faculty, students, and staff--plus outsiders. To find a place in this environment, a program, course, or individual must be able to contribute to the welfare of the environment and to be in harmony with the environment. These characteristics and dynamics often make change difficult. However, we believe that experiential educators can meet the challenge of helping their universities by articulating the values of experiential education within the framework of their institutions and by being effective change agents, rocking the boat gently so that the people on it can actually enjoy the ride.

Elon University, one of the original institutions for which we consulted, reveals many of the lessons we learned about the effective administration of experiential learning programs. The brief case study was written by Pam Brumbaugh, Director of Experiential Learning at Elon University, a position she has held for over 25 years. She was the original director who applied for our consultation services and she remains an effective advocate for experiential learning. Although she gives a great deal of credit to numerous people at Elon for the growth and development of experiential programs, she neglects to give herself a pat on the back. She deserves one, for her longevity, her determined commitment to the goals of experiential learning, and her charm, which has kept faculty and administrators moving in the direction of institutionalizing good policy and good practices for over a quarter century. One of the pleasures of our consultation project was meeting people like Pam, who continue to work quietly and effectively all over the country.

In the mid-eighties, the Elon Career Center moved to the academic side of the house and hired a Director of Experiential Education, expanding the previous co-op position into a broader role to encompass internships and co-ops. In fall 1986 a team of NSEE consultants visited campus to review the experiential program and offer advice for future growth – most notably to involve and reward faculty efforts. As per the advice, a faculty advisory committee formed to develop policies, procedures and guidelines. Remuneration policies were studied and by 1991 a universal remuneration policy was in place to reward faculty internship activities.

Elon Experiential Education took a leap forward when the General Studies program was changed in 1994 to include an Experiential Learning Requirement (ELR) for graduation. The Career Center played a central role in the writing of the ELR guidelines. In the 1990s, the ELR expanded from internship, co-ops, and study abroad to include leadership (1990), service-learning (1994), and undergraduate research (1998), with staff and resources for each area. Several notable features characterized the Elon ELR: while mandatory for graduation, it offered a broad range of choices; it combined efforts of both Academic and Student Affairs; all options required academic rigor guided and monitored by faculty and staff.

Infrastructures were developed to support each option – advisory boards were developed, program materials were refined. An oversight committee met each semester to study common ground, develop protocols, and host an academic summit. Quality growth in experiential programs was a major thrust, as evidenced by its inclusion in 3 important documents. First, the Strategic Plan focused on academic excellence which included experiential programming. Second, the University Mission Statement changed to reflect the ELR: "We integrate learning across the disciplines and put knowledge into practice, thus preparing the students to be global citizens and informed leaders motivated by concern for the common good." Third, a SACS accreditation self-study focused on "Experiential Education: Connecting Knowledge & Experience." Additionally, Elon used NSSE (National Survey of Student Engagement) as a benchmark for engaged learning on campus.

The School of Communications hired its own internship coordinator and moved toward an internship requirement for all majors by 2007. The School of Business followed suit with its own coordinator in 2003 and mandatory internship requirement. A Center for Teaching & Learning evolved to support experiential pedagogy in the classroom. A University campaign, "Transforming Lives: the Campaign for Engaged learning," focused on transforming the educational experience of students and firmly established Elon as a national model of engaged learning. The first decade of the 21st century saw Elon emerge as a national leader in experiential learning, with awards and accolades attributed to its stature as a place of engaged learning.

In retrospect, much credit goes to the sage advice of the NSEE consulting team and the strong grassroots effort of the faculty in the early 1990s to put an experiential learning requirement in place with the new general studies curriculum revision. Strengthening the experiential programs was enhanced also through the vision and strategic support of top administrators who guided and funded the experiential efforts to ensure ample staffing and professional development. Their vision included a view that the entire campus was involved in learning, which required a seamless effort from both academic and student affairs. This proved to be effective in producing a culture of engagement on our campus. Additionally, the university was masterful at spreading the word about Elon as an "engaged" campus.

The future promises more growth. Our new Strategic Plan suggests that Elon have a Center for Engaged Learning and be a leader in national conversations about engaged learning. Elon continues its sustaining membership in NSEE. Our journey continues toward becoming a learning paradigm university.

(Pam Brumbaugh, Director of Experiential Education, October, 2011)

It is not at all surprising that when we look back at 25 years, we see enormous progress, but if we had looked at 1986-87, we might have been frustrated at just how little happened. Institutional change always needs to be seen as a long-term process. Unfortunately, with changes in staffs and administrations, the history sometimes gets lost. It's important to look back into those files, interview people who have changed positions and/or retired, and treasure those, like Pam Brumbaugh, who have committed themselves to guiding generations of faculty and staff into ever-more sophisticated and complex understandings of experiential learning.

References

Agor, W. H. (1984). *Intuitive management: Integrating left and right brain management skills.* Englewood Cliffs: New Jersey: Prentice-Hall.

From a study of over 2,000 managers in a variety of organizational settings, the author concludes that the use of intuition along with "other brain skills" are critical to effective management and leadership. The settings where the use of integrated left and right brain management skills are most effective are similar to the environments of experiential education programs in higher education. Further, the author relates some of his theories and findings to the personality types described by the Myers Briggs Type Indicator.

Bonoma, T. and Zaltman, G. (1981). *Psychology for management.* Boston: Kent Publishing.

Of particular interest is the synthesis model of the "organizational adoption process" which is helpful in guiding managers in designing and implementing change.

Hersey, P. and Blanchard, K. *Management of organizational behavior: Utilizing human resources,* 4th Ed. (1982). Englewood Cliffs, NJ: Prentice-Hall.

This book describes the use of situational leadership in managing organizational behavior and change. In the formulation of appropriate leadership styles for change, the theory takes into consideration the characteristics of the people involved and affected by the change as well as the setting in which the change takes place.

Kotter, J. and Schlesinger, L. (1979). Choosing strategies for change. *Harvard Business Review,* March-April.

This article suggests four "most common" reasons for resisting change, six strategies to overcome resistance, and four "situational factors" to consider in choosing the right strategy.

Myers, I. (1980). *Introduction to type indicator.* Palo Alto, CA: Consulting Psychologists Press.

Myers, I. (1962). *The Myers Briggs type indicator: Manual.* Palo Alto, CA: Consulting Psychologists Press.

These two publications introduce various personality types based on a modified version of the Jungian theory of personality. Four major variables are considered: judgment-perception, thinking-feeling, sensation-intuition, and extroversion-introversion. It is believed that certain types function more effectively in certain environments. Consequently, certain personality types may be more compatible with the characteristics needed to be an effective change agent.

Sikes, W. (1985). Some principles of personal and organizational change." *NTL Connections.* Arlington, Virginia.

Jack Lindquist, as quoted by Walter Sikes, "Some Principles of Personal and Organizational Change," NTL Connections, NTL Institute, Ar-lington, Virginia, March 1985, p. 5.

Author

SHARON RUBIN PhD, Professor Emerita of American Studies, Ramapo College of New Jersey, was Vice President for Academic Affairs from 1993-2000. While a faculty member, she directed the Honors Program at the College. From 1987-1993, she was Dean of the Fulton School of Liberal Arts at Salisbury University. During her extensive career in experiential learning, she was Director of Experiential Learning Programs at the University of Maryland College Park from 1978-1984. As a participant in the Wingspread invitational conference, she helped draft "Principles of Good Practice for Combining Service and Learning," later published by the Johnson Foundation, 1989. She was president of what was then called the National Society for Internships and Experiential Education, 1989-1991; Vice-President, 1987-1989; Member, Board of Directors, 1986-1994; and Chair of the Executive Director Search Committee, 1990-1991. As a member of the consultant team, Fund for the Improvement of Postsecondary Education grant to the National Society for Internships and Experiential Education, "Project to Promote Institutionalization of Experiential Learning Programs," 1983 -1985, and the follow-up grant, 1986-1988, she was an on-campus consultant to many colleges, including University of Colorado at Boulder, Hartwick College, Skidmore College, the University of Virginia, Bradford College, Manhattan College, the University of New Hampshire, Illinois State University, Vassar College, Elon College, Greensboro College, Mary Washington College, the University of Massachusetts, and San Diego State University. She also consulted for Augsburg College, Allegheny College, Chatham College, Manhattan College, Binghamton University, De Paul University, New Jersey Institute of Technology, and the University of Minnesota. Dr. Rubin was one of the original authors of *Strengthening Experiential Learning Within Your Institution*, 1986. She contributed chapters to *Involving Commuter Students in Learning, The Practice of Service-Learning in Higher Education, Community Service as Values Education, and Liberal Education*, Volume 76, Number 3. From 1991-1993, she was a member of the Maryland Governor's Advisory Board on Service and Citizenship. She has written and spoken extensively about experiential learning, service learning, and liberal education. Among her awards was a grant for study in Japan and Korea from the Fulbright International Education Program and a W.K. Kellogg Foundation National Fellowship, as well as the Pioneer Award from NSEE in 2004

Chapter 6

INTEGRATING EXPERIENTIAL EDUCATION INTO THE FINANCIAL FRAMEWORK OF THE INSTITUTION: CHALLENGES AND STRATEGIES

Susan Shumer & Evelyn Rolloff
Metropolitan State University, Minnesota

Abstract & Outline: What this chapter will offer

The goal of this chapter is to assist you with the financial institutionalization of experiential education at your institution. This chapter addresses financial challenges, ideas for generating financial resources, and examples of successful programs. In many ways, this revised chapter integrates emerging realities of higher education with the realities of one particular institution (Appendix 1). This illustrates, we think, the need to balance basic principles with the particularities of any given institution. Topics covered in the chapter are:

- **Integrating Experiential Education into the Framework of the Institution: Challenges and Strategies**
- **Effective Practices for Generating Revenue**
- **Economic Benefits and Delivery of Experiential Education Efficiently and Effectively**
- **Experiential Education Campus Audits**
- **External Funding Sources**
- **An Optimistic Conclusion**

When consultants visit a campus to review and assist the institution with experiential education programs, the program administrators invariably report that financial resources are a challenge. In addition, some faculty members who sponsor students often contend that they are inadequately compensated for their work. These two patterns reveal *two critical problems in integrating experiential education into the economic framework of the institution:*

1. **Like much of the higher education enterprise, experiential education is faced with securing financial support in the context of competition from other programs within the institution.**

As in all programs in higher education, there is constant competition for institutional resources. The changing demographics of the student population are influencing higher education in powerful ways. Virtually all of the nation's current growth in college enrollments is among adult learners, students of color, and students seeking a non-traditional, convenient, and affordable education. In states with declining traditional student populations, institutions are faced with economic retrenchment. Consequently, it is difficult to secure resources for instructional innovations, such as experiential education, when there is pressure within the college to maintain existing programs. When there are increasing student enrollments without corresponding funding expansion, resources are often insufficient for what are considered basic educational programs. Hence, it is difficult to secure resources for alternatives when traditional programs are not being adequately supported.

In addition, higher education is being scrutinized more closely at both the national and state levels, and the assessment is mixed. On the one hand, graduates are often cited as lacking some basic competencies that are needed for specific professions, with many voices insisting that higher education needs to "attend to the basics and be more productive". On the other hand, the AAC&U LEAP Initiative (Liberal Education and America's Promise, www.aacu.org/leap), underscores and outlines many challenges for reform. These are spelled out in a recent report from the Harvard Graduate School of Education, *Pathways to Prosperity: Meeting the Challenge of Preparing Young Americans for the 21st Century* (2011). The report suggests that education, including higher education, needs to be reformed so that programs are more responsive to business and industry needs, as well as citizen responsibilities. These reports stress "high impact" pedagogies such as apprenticeships, work-based and experiential learning that is needed to prepare students for work and the kinds of interdisciplinary, integrative leadership and problem solving that are increasingly needed.

Thus, there would appear to be an emerging consensus that experiential education is not peripheral to the educational enterprise; it is exactly what is called for in the foreseeable future (Kuh, 2008).

2. **Whatever support might be available for experiential education can be difficult to access because many systems for allocating financial resources within an institution were not developed with experiential education in mind.**

One challenge facing a current generation of experiential educators derives from earlier financial systems that are not sustainable. For example, in the 1980s and 1990s Cooperative Education programs were funded from sources in the Department of Education. Millions of dollars became available, usually on a five year decreasing basis, for initiating or expanding work-related, experiential education programs. Institutions were expected to absorb the decreasing federal funding into their budgets and institutionalize those programs. But for a host of reasons, this rarely occurred, resulting in the disappearance of many co-op programs as the sources from the federal government declined. Colleges that followed some of the suggestions we offer in this chapter created internal funding streams and converted Cooperative Education to "hard money." A similar challenge is currently facing service-learning and civic engagement programs that must also institutionalize their funding sources.

Fortunately, many colleges throughout the country, often with the assistance of the NSEE – FIPSE peer consultants, institutionalized experiential education by creating campus units with institutional budget line items, supporting dedicated staff, to provide administrative and programmatic elements. Directors of these units at many institutions included faculty positions, often supported from teaching responsibilities on a rotating basis each academic year. Programs are often housed in Academic Affairs and positioned as a normal part of the academic program of the institution (see the chapter on Administrative Structures). Other models, like at

Metropolitan State University, Twin Cities, Minnesota, include hybrid designs. At Metro State there is an administrative director of the Institute for Community Engagement and Scholarship working closely with a faculty work group composed of one faculty member from each college within the university. This model has resulted in institutionalizing experiential education within the institution.

Even though experiential education is increasingly viewed as a critical part of "high impact" approaches to effective learning, most campuses have not yet incorporated its funding into the ongoing budgetary system of their campuses. Hence, one short and long-term strategy is make the funding a part of faculty compensation and the promotion system. This takes into account that EE generates credits toward a degree and produces its own income stream through tuition and the overall funding streams devoted to teaching and learning.

Thoughtful Strategies to Begin With—

So what can you do? Start with these basic tasks:

- Appreciate fully the unique characteristics of universities and colleges as organizations and the implications of these characteristics for making experiential education programs economically viable.

- Design experiential education programs and courses that are consistent with the dominant model for allocating your institution's instructional resources.

- Examine and publicize the financial benefits of experiential education programs by doing a cost benefit analysis (return on investment).

- Institutionalize experiential education into the curriculum by working with faculty who have an interest in integrating experiential education into existing courses.

- Institutionalize policies for compensating faculty for sponsoring students on independent study, internships, service-learning and community-based learning.

- Ensure that tenure and promotion policies include all experiential learning initiatives throughout the institution, making use of newer Carnegie Foundation and AAC&U recommendations to support and legitimize your efforts.

Realistic Models for Experiential Education

As noted earlier, each college and university has unique organizational characteristics which influence the process and rules by which resources are distributed. Consequently, thoughtful and locally relevant organizational designs enhance your chance of securing and maintaining institutional resources.

One of the major challenges of experiential education is the organizational segmentation of higher education. Experiential education is inescapably linked to many segments of the academy. For example, experiential education certainly contributes to the educational mission (academic affairs). In addition, it enhances admissions and retention, career development and personal growth (student affairs). These multiple functions of experiential education certainly add to its value and importance to the institution, but it also makes it very difficult for the institution to reward each function or department financially due to higher education's segmented style of budgeting.

On the other hand, *the fact that experiential education contributes to the goals of several units within the institution can also be a tremendous advantage.* Because of this dispersion, experiential education can draw on the economic resources and support of Academic Affairs, Student Affairs, and Public/Community Affairs because it crosses the lines that typically separate these functions. For example, an academic department at UCLA reported that "it took us eight years to realize that the Instructional Development Center is a source we could tap for faculty who sponsor students on field experience." In other words, make lemonade out of the lemons through collaboration and shared resources.

Our thesis is this:
Once you embrace and appreciate the unique organizational characteristics of higher education and of its implications for experiential learning, it becomes more feasible to design (or re-design) experiential education in a way that is consistent with the dominant model for allocating instructional resources within your own institution. In other words, alternatives to classroom-based instruction such as experiential education have to seek positive accommodations within the current system for allocating resources. Experiential education programs and courses that follow the principles described below can often successfully meet this challenge because they emphasize the unit currency—faculty work load in terms of credit courses taught—and make minimum claims on other types of institutional resources.

Effective Practices for Generating Revenue

We suggest, based on our experience and research:

Experiential education programs and courses should be credit bearing. Public institutions received state allocations according to the number of instructional hours provided for academic credit courses. In private institutions, where student tuition provides much of the instructional budget, academic credit for experiential education is usually critical.

Experiential education should provide academic credits which have real value to students. Students are usually not as attracted to experiential programs which do not provide academic credits toward degree requirements. Programs which provide academic credits for experiential education in the academic major are the most attractive because students increasingly concentrate on the major for improving their chances for employability or graduate school admission. The more you can include experiential courses in required sequences helps to insure better class enrollment and better utility from the student perspective in actually taking the course resulting in an income stream for your program.

The amount of academic credit from experiential education should accurately reflect the learning achieved. Except in applied programs where experiential education is traditional, until recently there has been a tendency is to treat experience-based learning as an inefficient learning mode, deserving only minimum academic credit. Research has clearly called this into question, underscored by the current emphasis on "high impact" pedagogy across higher education. Sometimes such courses require additional hours for the same number of credits as found in classroom based instruction. Research and current theories of learning and research by Ewell, Giles, Eyler, Shumer, et al suggest that complete, effective learning requires an experiential component. Consequently, experiential education should receive fuller recognition in terms of academic credit and have equivalent hours compared to all academic instruction.

Experiential education should emphasize and document student learning in areas which are seen as academically important and consistent with the institution's mission. It is unrealistic for experiential education to expect instructional resources for other outcomes such as student career development, which have minimum academic standing. For this reason, wherever possible it is preferred to have experiential education integrated into the academic content of courses and departmental requirements, thus allowing the student to earn credit in an academic application, not a generic course description such as Cooperative Education, or Service-Learning.

Experiential education is best recognized within the institution when it is considered a course. In other words, create budgets that reflect the minimum number of students that are required by the institution for learning under the supervision of one instructor, and during a specified academic term. It should be understood, however, that the work tasks of the instructor in experiential courses will differ greatly from those of a classroom lecturer.

Faculty involvement in experiential education is best recognized in terms of teaching responsibility for a course. A course taught experientially should have the same standing in determining faculty work load as one taught in a classroom.

Whenever possible, support services for experiential education should come from existing institutional resources. Collaboration can and should result in greater effectiveness and efficiency in the ways we support our students in their learning. Such cooperation requires an understanding of the goals of experiential education by all stakeholders and an institutional commitment to a carefully coordinated effort. For example, experiential education programs and courses can use the capacities of career service centers to teach job search skills. Placement, internship, service-learning and student employment centers can provide connections to the community.

A separate administrative support unit for experiential education should concentrate its efforts on coordinating resources and assisting other parties, such as faculty and students, who are responsible for various aspects of experiential learning. The administrative support unit should not assume responsibility for a program task that can be done by another unit already on campus. If the experiential education office tries to do all the tasks itself, the staffing required will be so great that the office will provide an attractive target for institutional budget cutters. In addition, too much centralizing will undercut the goal of integrating experiential education throughout the institution, particularly the goal of integrating experiential education into course, departmental and institution-wide designated learning objectives.

The location of any administrative support unit for experiential education should be consistent with the school's system for managing other educational resources. At most institutions, this means experiential education is best located within academic affairs, and at large institutions it often means within academic divisions or schools.

Economic Benefits: Delivering Experiential Education Efficiently and Effectively

Institution financial support is only one condition needed for experiential education to be economically viable. It is important to use whatever resources are provided in the most cost-efficient manner possible. Without cost-efficient program operations, the resources available will never seem sufficient; with cost-efficient operations, limited resources will be more likely to be adequate, and the program will enhance its reputation for financial stewardship. Experiential education, like higher education generally, has given very little attention to the economic benefit of instructional resources. Relatively few studies on the economics of experiential education have focused exclusively on its cost-effectiveness. Such studies could bolster the claim that the educational and economic benefits of this mode of learning are of such magnitude that its cost, however great, is justified. One advantage of experiential education is the direct impact on community. A claim of outstanding community benefits is seldom persuasive in a contest for institutional resources. As discussed earlier, we find that the allocation of resources in higher education is rarely based on the relative educational merits of different instructional strategies. While we should never stop documenting and validating the learning from experiential education, a more realistic strategy may be to pattern one's efforts according to the dominant "cost benefit" assessment that is practiced in your institution. Then seek your fair share by being an informed and assertive participant.

Securing Budgetary Resources Based on Tasks Required for Effective, "High Impact" Learning

The first step in becoming more cost-efficient is to consider intentionally the different tasks required in providing any experiential learning opportunity for students. There are other tasks involved in a sound experiential education program such as faculty development, and policy development and implementation. The following are eight distinct tasks that NSEE suggest for the actual delivery of experiential education to students and are discussed in further detail in the chapter on "Ensuring Quality in EE":

1. *Establish educational goals for the course or program,*
2. *Develop work or service sites for experiential learning,*
3. *Help students establish appropriate educational objectives,*
4. *Recruit, select and communicate service sites to students,*
5. *Prepare students through intentional orientation and training,*
6. *Support students during the learning experience,*
7. *Evaluate and assess the learning achieved, and*
8. *Report the learning (transcripts and student records).*

With these tasks identified, the next step is to *specify who of the several players is responsible for each task.* The principal players include the student, the work supervisor, the faculty sponsor, and the institutional administrator, and may include the internship program director, service-learning coordinator, cooperative education program director, or other program administrator. In specifying roles, responsibilities are usually shared by the several players with one person having primary responsibility and others having secondary or tertiary responsibility. *In reality, practically none of the eight tasks is done by only one party.* In specifying primary responsibility for the various program tasks, there is no universal set of appropriate role definitions. Instead, there are many possible configurations. Specifying responsibilities is a matter for each institution to determine, as noted in other chapters as well.

One way to enhance efficiency and effectiveness is to give more thought and involvement by two critical players whose roles are not always taken seriously, namely site supervisors and the students themselves. The role of **work supervisors** is usually limited to directing the work of the students. Supervisors typically have not been seen by administrators and faculty as having an important role in assisting the student with educational goals. In today's complex and technologically advanced society, those who direct the work of others are likely to have advanced degrees. In their areas of professional expertise, student site supervisors often have more current and specialized knowledge than the faculty sponsors on campus. To fail to recognize and take advantage of the expertise of these professionals in the instruction of students is a waste of valuable resources. Although many higher education institutions across the country continue offering experiential education in the manner described above, Metropolitan State University has a different model that we recommend highly, although it does add to the cost of delivery of experiential education. The site supervisor's expertise in the field is highly valued and they are compensated for supervision *and* evaluation of student learning. This practice results in a long history of "community faculty" at Metro State University.

Students at many institutions are also an under-utilized resource in experiential education. In many programs and courses, students have minimal roles in planning and managing their own learning. The passive role of the student in the classroom is often transferred to a similar role in off-campus, experiential learning. This abrogates the basic educational goal of any experiential program, namely to aid the transition from passivity to self-directedness and personal responsibility for one's own learning. Examples of this educational paternalism abound in many programs. Students are literally "assigned" to work positions in a community which faculty or administrators have developed with little or no student involvement.

While it is always a work in progress, let us illustrate how Metro State University has endeavored to expand and support student responsibility for each of the eight tasks listed above. With guidance from staff at the Institute for Community Engagement and Scholarship, students are primarily responsible for developing their own work or service positions including researching possibilities, establishing contacts with the organization and potential site supervisors. This includes arranging and having interviews, as well as establishing the conditions of the arrangement. Students are further encouraged to learn the elements of developing a learning plan by defining the work activities, establishing learning objectives for each activity, identifying the resources needed to support their learning, and negotiating with work supervisors and faculty sponsors the procedures for assessment of both work performance and learning.

For the other program tasks, students can also be important partners. With handouts and computer assisted guidance, they can help prepare themselves for the work experience using a variety of written guides and self-paced instructional programs. They can take primary responsibility for learning at the work site through reading, interviews with working professionals, taking advantage of in-service training provided for employees, and having thoughtful conversations with clients and other students. In the assessment task, students should have primary responsibility for providing the evidence of their learning for faculty to evaluate relative to the learning objectives which the student should have actively co-designed at the beginning of the placement.

Some experiential educators make the mistake of equating individualized instruction with personalized instruction. Each student, work activity, and work environment is unique. The beauty of experiential education is that it allows, indeed expects, each individual student to pursue particular interests through work and service responsibilities in an infinitely rich environment. However, one should not mistake the unique opportunity for individualized instruction with a requirement for personalized program administration. Evidence of this personalization of experiential education programs abounds. For example, we often spend hours counseling students to determine their career interests when there are a number of interest inventories and computer-assisted guidance systems which are both more effective and cost efficient. We often monitor students' progress and support their learning with visits to the work site when written reports from students and telephone conversations with work supervisors can often provide more information and a more accurate reflection of the actual learning. This does not mean that site visits are always unnecessary, but they are a time-consuming way to monitor and assess learning. See Sharon Rubin's "soapbox" position for further discussion of the trap behind trying to personalize each task (Appendix 2).

A corollary of the emphasis on personalized program administration is the tendency to work individually with students rather than in **groups**. Working on program tasks in groups is both cost-efficient and educationally effective. One basic task that lends itself easily to groups is simply providing information on the program itself. In many programs this is done individually, with a faculty member or program administrator talking with a single student. A more cost-efficient method that also enhances student learning is group orientation and training meetings for student participants. Many higher education institutions, for example, hold an introductory meeting for all eligible/interested students. In addition, some schools or divisions often hold their own orientation meetings for experiential education.

The task of supporting the student during the experience is also ideal for group work. Increasingly, research and practice is revealing that the collective experiences of, and reflection together, by several students reported in a **seminar** provide a much richer basis for learning than the experience of a single student as reported to a faculty member in an office interview or journal entry. Even the task of assessing and evaluating learning need not be through a one-on-one relationship of student and professor. A group approach to analysis, synthesis, and the demonstration of particular competencies can be most effective. Making meaning is definitely aided by the give and take of Socratic inquiry. Demonstrating key interpersonal skills requires a group setting. How can competence in leadership be shown except as a member of a group? The University of Virginia, Rhode Island College, UCLA, Augsburg College and Metropolitan State University are examples of schools that developed seminars for student interns that are concurrent with their field experiences.

Clearly there are many different ways that staff, faculty, students and supervisors can attend to these with distinct and overlapping tasks. What we are suggesting is that there are usually more efficient cost-effective strategies that also enhance student learning and can be more effective overall.

Experiential Education Campus Audits

Increasingly, Experiential Education continues to move from a position of having little or no economic standing in the allocation of institutional resources toward a position of economic equity. The principles for realistic models for experiential education suggest useful strategies for securing equity position (see above and the chapter on Administrative Structures). For example, if one characteristic of economically viable experiential programs is that they award academic credit consistent with the learning achieved, then the strategy needed is to document the learning achieved, compare the result with that expected from a classroom course, and make a case for equivalent academic credit and the commensurate budgetary allocation.

The most critical element of economic equity is the time of your faculty. The desired position of economic equity is to recognize faculty time in experiential courses in a way that is congruent with classroom teaching. The following strategies may assist you in ensuring economic equity on your campus:

1. Make an assessment of the extent of experiential education at your institution. This assessment will very likely document the contribution that faculty are making to the institution in terms of academic credits. In 2003, Metropolitan State University conducted a university-wide audit to create an inventory of experiential education programs. The reader can find an example at
   http://www.metrostate.edu/msweb/community/ices/ecampus/audit_survey.html

   In addition, you will find the "Inventory of Experiential Education Programs and Courses" in Chapter Two of this book. Such an inventory provides a baseline for the scale of experiential education that is already occurring. Then, if it is not already in place, the institution can develop responsible work load policies that acknowledge the extent of this learning. Important questions about quality can also begin to be addressed. When experiential education is recognized in the economic system of the institution, then it is more likely that the faculty can be held responsible for quality standards as well.

2. Share the results of the inventory with academic administrators, the curriculum and work load committees, and the faculty governance structures, including the faculty union if your faculty members are represented in collective bargaining.

3. If you are an administrator for an experiential education program in which faculty have an official role, make an annual report of the extent of faculty involvement. This would include the number of academic credits generated, the amount of tuition income to the institution, the number of faculty participants, and how many academic credits each generated.

4. Encourage faculty to include involvement in experiential education in their annual reports to their department or division chairpersons. At many institutions, this a regular part of faculty members annual reports to the department chair or the dean.

5. Encourage faculty to include involvement in experiential education in their requests for academic promotion and tenure. If there are written guidelines for what faculty should include in their promotion and tenure folders, be sure that sponsorship of students in experiential education is included. At Metropolitan State University, for example, the Director of the Institute for Community Engagement and Scholarship often writes letters to tenure and promotion committees for faculty who have actively used experiential learning.

6. Assist faculty in documenting the value to the institution of their involvement in experiential education. Work with faculty to create surveys that document the service provided to the community by students in experiential education, as well as the learning that results. There are many examples currently being used in the field and available through NSEE and its members.

7. As is discussed below, small grants and outside funding can be a helpful supplement or catalyst to initiate or improve your program. So, consider applying for outside grant funds for special purposes, but be careful that you do not undermine your long-range goal of strengthening the institution's central commitment to experiential education.

External Funding Sources

We at Metro State, like many other colleges and universities, have sought to clearly identify key internal faculty and staff, critical external community partners, along with shared goals and objectives, all in concert with and support from academic affairs leadership. When, and only when that consensus and clarity are well established, it may be time to meet with your institution's development/ fundraising department or division. Educating our development office about our plans and programs, stressing the broad support we have, has been the key to our seeking and receiving outside funds that have supported start-up initiatives and sustaining programs for several years.

Once internal faculty and staff, and external community partners have been identified, along with clearly defined shared goals, and you have the support of your academic affairs leadership, it is time to meet with your institution's development (fundraising) department. Educating your development office about your plans and programs is key to seeking and receiving outside funds that can support start-up initiatives and potentially sustain programs for several years.

With Campus Compact's permission, we have borrowed one of the best general sources on this topic of external funding, authored by Barbara Holland and Mark Langseth. "Leveraging Financial Support for Service-Learning: Relevance, Relationships, Results, Resources" is chapter 9 in *Looking In, Reaching Out,* in the section on "External Sources, Strategies and Allies" (Holland and Langseth, 2010, pp. 199-204). *We recommend the entire book for your bookshelf and frequent use as a complement to this revision and the original version of Strengthening EE.* Although "service-learning" is the language used in this book and excerpt, the concepts and suggestions are relevant to all of experiential learning.

External Sources, Strategies, and Allies

As mentioned earlier, external sources of financial support are generally not sustainable over the long term. Such sources, however, are often important to campus service programs in three ways:
1. External sources are quite often necessary to launch a service-learning program on campus. In tight budget climates, it is common for a new program to be launched with external sources (often called "soft funding").
2. External sources commonly sustain a program in the short term. Many service-learning programs depend on external funding for their first three to five years or sometimes longer, as they concurrently work to build the internal support necessary to transition, at least partly, into the campus budget.
3. Even programs that receive their core funding from internal sources often rely on external sources to help fuel innovation or growth in their program's scope or impact.

External sources can be divided into government, corporations and foundations, professional associations, and individuals (non-alumni).

Awareness of and investment in service-learning programs has risen significantly among all four groups over the past two decades, largely because of the belief that service-learning helps produce job-ready graduates and better citizens, and that it addresses important community issues. The box on this page offers other benefits of service-learning as a resource-generating strategy.

Government

The most common government sources are federal and state funding, but local and county governments are also possible sources. At the federal level, the Learn and Serve America program of the U.S. Corporation for National and Community Service (CNCS) provides millions of dollars each year to support K-12 and postsecondary service-learning programs. Learn and Serve America Higher Education funds are distributed directly to campuses and to state consortia, which then make competitive sub-grants to campuses in their states. Historically, state Campus Compacts have been the most common recipients of state consortia funding.

CNCS, founded in the early 1990s, has evolved into the federal government's largest hub of citizen service funding, including the national AmeriCorps and VISTA volunteer programs, and the national Senior Corps program, which aims to mobilize older Americans to serve their communities. In addition to tens of millions of dollars distributed to campuses via Learn and Serve America, CNCS human resources-in the form of full- or part-time AmeriCorps or VISTA volunteers-have also been secured by many campuses to assist with service-learning program development and implementation. Many state Campus Compact offices administer VISTA programs.

Another major federal supporter of campus partnerships is the Community Outreach Partnership Center (COPC) program, a program of the Office of University Partnerships at the U.S. Department of Housing and Urban Development. This program targets community development-oriented partnerships between campuses and their surrounding communities.

Though these partnerships most often emphasize institutional engagement on specific community issues (e.g., economic development, job training, educational improvement, youth development, neighborhood improvement, public safety), many also involve service-learning because the grant requires student involvement in the partnership. COPC grants are awarded annually through a rigorous, competitive, peer-reviewed process. The availability of funds for new grants is uncertain from year to year because the program depends on annual appropriations from Congress. (Information on the Office of University Partnerships is offered in the resources section at the end of this chapter. Note that in 2009 an effort was launched to increase COPC funds.)

More and more state legislatures are taking an interest in service-learning, as reflected by their investment of state dollars in postsecondary service-learning. For example, the Minnesota state legislature has appropriated an average of $200,000 per biennium since 1989 for a postsecondary service-learning grant program. Public and private campuses can apply for small grants to create or expand service-learning through this program. In California, the state legislature has allocated millions to the California State University System to support expansion of service-learning through this program. The Kentucky state legislature provides base funding to its regional public universities to support a specified agenda of public service and outreach programs, some of which include service-learning. (Contact Campus Compact for more information about which states have similar programs.)

Other government funding is available at both the federal and state levels, depending on the specific topic or issue. Often, faculty members involved in service-learning activities are aware of government agencies that may offer support in their particular discipline or topic of interest. In general, funds may be available through competitive grant programs (you can monitor opportunities on www.grants.gov, which also has advice on preparing successful proposals) or through earmarks or other special appropriations made specifically to your institution for a particular purpose, You may also find that some of your community partners are eligible for certain kinds of support and may be willing to collaborate with you in seeking those funds; you should return the favor by being alert to opportunities to include partners as co-applicants. In either case, collaborative fundraising activity requires detailed written agreements about responsibilities, roles, and the distribution and uses of funds.

Whether seeking a competitive grant or a special fund, begin by talking with your supervisor, your advancement or development office, the office for research, and the government-relations office. The solicitation of state, federal, county, local government support can be politically complex and sensitive, and you will need the expert guidance and leadership of those appointed to these tasks for your institution. Pursuing governmental support on your own without their approval and assistance is perilous and unwise.

Consider exploring local or county public officials. (Portland State University, for example, has received county support for its service-learning efforts.) Again, consult with your Government-relations office on campus before personally contacting local and county officials, as it can help determine whether such sources might be worth exploring.

Corporation and foundations

On most campuses, the advancement or development office knows of all corporate and foundation sources in your area. Moreover, the office is likely charged with coordinating approaches to these sources in order to avoid competing proposals being submitted to the same funding source. Most advancement or development offices take this coordination role quite seriously. You want to work closely with your advancement or development office in determining possible sources and the timing of conversations and proposals. Corporations and foundations generally do not look kindly on uncoordinated proposals or on random conversations with their representatives about potential funding.

Most corporations and foundations focus much of their giving on communities near their headquarters. Typically, only medium-sized and large corporations and foundations make several annual gifts of $100,000 or more. You should carefully consider their corresponding budgets and patterns of giving as you assess which corporations or foundations might be promising prospects. Again, we recommend strongly that you work with key development or advancement staff and to identify your best possible sources. Doing some research on possible prospects before you meet with advancement or development officers can help them see you as a serious partner in fundraising. Look for foundations that align with your project idea, have a history of funding academic institutions, and serve your community or region. Learn about the application process and calendar, and put together some basic proposal ideas before approaching the development staff for assistance.

Professional Associations

Professional associations that either focus specifically on service-learning or have special initiatives related to service-learning often provide financial support to service-learning through competitive grant processes. Campus Compact, both at the state and national levels, is perhaps the largest, most consistent provider of such support. The American Association of Community Colleges support community colleges. Many other associations, such as the Council for Advancement of Private Higher Education and American Association of State Colleges and Universities, have created special service or civic learning initiatives that support campuses either financially or with other services to help advance service-learning. Faculty in specific disciplines may know of special service-learning initiatives in their disciplinary associations, and other allies on campus might also be aware of opportunities via their professional associations. Due to the rapid growth in service-learning over the past 20 years, more and more associations have developed service-learning initiatives, so consider them as possible financial supporters for establishing, growing, or sustaining your program.

Individuals (non-alumni)

Though individual alumni might be motivated to give because of loyalty to their alma mater, non-alumni must be motivated to give on the basis of your cause and their trust in your operation to advance it. Typically, these people are wealthy members of the community who feel a special bond with a particular community issue or educational agenda and believe that your institution is committed to it. They may have special interest in children, the environment, or another community concern. Or they may be deep believers in alternative approaches to education, such as service-learning. Or they may be concerned about nurturing the next generation of active citizens and philanthropists. Regardless, they must come to believe that your program is important for advancing their priorities. The advancement or development staff knows which wealthy individuals are interested in which causes, and they are charged with coordinating approaches to them. Work closely with your advancement office as you consider pursuing individual donors.

Wherever you seek external support, be sure to consider the donor's financial and program reporting requirements. Sometimes these can be a burden or require expertise not easily available to you. Part of successful fundraising is being prepared to be a successful gift manager. Your reputation as a gift recipient will be shaped not only by the quality of your program but also by your ability to adhere to reporting requirements and meet deadlines. You should also consider how your resource provider wants to be recognized and involved in the program so there are no surprises or complications in the relationship (Holland and Langseth, 2010, pp. 199-204).

An Optimistic Conclusion

As seen in recent AAC&U and Carnegie legitimation, experiential education has achieved good standing at colleges and universities as a valued means for teaching and learning. Consistent with this recognition is the movement for experiential education to a balance between a focus on the institution and on individual academic departments. Departmental commitment provides the key to securing institutional financial support for experiential education. With this perspective, this chapter can be summarized in terms of five principles:

1. *Put your efforts into securing economic recognition for faculty participation in experiential education.* Because the primary commodity of a college or university is the time of its faculty, this is the best way to ensure financial support for experiential education.

2. *Pursue economic recognition for faculty participation in experiential education in the traditional terms of the "coin of the realm"* for courses taught, students enrolled, and academic credits generated in the departments.

3. *A Centralized-Decentralized experiential education program seems to us, to be the best means of securing faculty participation and institutional support.* Institutional support is more easily aggregated from a wide range of faculty engagements and participation with a single university-wide administrative unit providing administrative management which supports and sustains experiential education. Some functions of coordination, faculty development, and policy discussions can benefit from centralized leadership, but the departments or divisions must feel the ownership of (and, therefore, the commitment to) experiential education as a valid process for teaching and learning in their own fields (See revised and original chapter 5).

4. *Provide for program administrative support by expanding the role of non-faculty personnel.* Students are a particularly valuable resource. Greater participation by students is not only educationally valid, but can provide the deficit financing needed for economic viability of most programs. Work supervisors and existing student services such as career services staff also have significant resources and expertise to contribute.

5. *Reduce costs through appropriate technology and greater use of group processes.* Work directly with your IT department to utilize free social media and other technology supporting experiential education at your institution, e.g. assessment and career exploration programs.

References

Holland, Barbara & Langseth, Mark N. (2010). Leveraging financial support for service-learning: Relevance, relationships, results, resources. In *Looking in, reaching out: A reflective Guide for Community Service-Learning Professionals* (pp. 185-210). Boston, MA: Campus Compact.

Kelshaw, Todd, Lazarus, Freyda, Minier, Judy, and associates. (2009). *Partnership for service-learning, impacts on communities and students* (1st edition). San Francisco, CA: Jossey-Bass.

Kendall, Jane C., Duley, John S., Little, Thomas C., Permaul, Jane S., and Rubin, Sharon G. (1986). Supporting experiential education in the financial structure of your institution. In *Strengthening experiential education within your institution.* National Society for Experiential Education (pp. 105-119).

Kuh, G.D. (2008). Excerpts from high-impact educational practices: What they are, who has access to them, and why they matter. American Association of Colleges and Universities. Retrieved August 30, 2011, from http://www.aacu.org/leap/hip.cfm

Root, Susan; Callahan, Jane; & Billig, Shelley H. (2005). *Improving service-learning practice: Research on models to enhance impacts.* Greenwich, Connecticut: Information Age Publishing.

Wagner, Jon. (1983). Cost-Effective design of sponsored experiential education. In Thomas C. Little, New Directions for Experiential Learning, No. 20 (Eds.), *Making sponsored experiential learning standard practice* (pp. 83-97). San Francisco, CA: Jossey-Bass.

Appendix 1: A Metropolitan State University Case Study

This chapter, overall, represents a "case study" of how we have approached the institutionalization of experiential education overall and financing in particular. From its inception, Metropolitan State University has had a commitment to community involvement. Many initiatives, along with dedicated faculty and staff, laid the ground work for institutionalizing experiential education. In 1996, using principles outlined earlier in this chapter (Best Practices for Experiential Education), the university's community partnership and internship programs merged creating the university-wide Center for Community-Based Learning, which, in July, 2012, was renamed the Institute for Community Engagement and Scholarship (ICES), housed in Academic Affairs. The reader may find a "Critical Incident Report" on our website. They document, on an annual basis, the best practices used to attain an engaged campus through experiential education:
http://www.metrostate.edu/msweb/community/ices/home_local_nav/history.html

Today, university leaders support the centrality of community engagement through strong financial support (annual budget of $440,000) and human resources. Metro State's ICES is the largest and most active unit of its kind within the Minnesota State College and Universities (MnSCU) system. The ICES supports students, faculty and staff in being responsible citizens and community partners through high quality academic internships, applied research projects, service-learning, co-curricular activities, community events and university-community partnerships.

 The Institute for Community Engagement and Scholarship (ICES) frames its work in the context of a *Circle of Engagement"* that was developed over a period of three years (2003 - 2005) stressing "where life and learning meet".

198

A sample of an Institution's Measurement of Experiential Education
Circle of Engagement
Metropolitan State University
"Where Life and Learning Meet"

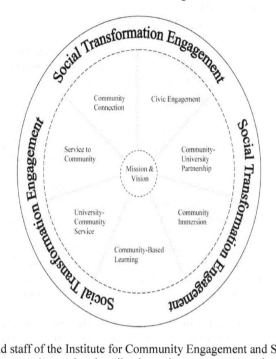

Faculty members and staff of the Institute for Community Engagement and Scholarship developed a list of concepts/terms that describe the various components of community experiential connections at Metropolitan State. Gathering this information helps us better understand the connection between courses and the prevalence of experiential learning instructional strategies, such as service-learning, internships, field studies, and the like, at the university. The list of terms with definitions was created through a process that included input from faculty, administration, community members, and students. Once the categories and definitions were carefully selected they were presented to the university community at a university-wide dialogue. The Institute for Community Engagement and Scholarship Work Group, comprised of faculty liaisons from each academic unit, is responsible for promoting experiential learning and encouraging faculty to use the criteria from the Circle of Engagement for Promotion and Tenure. The items included are:

- **Civic Engagement:** active involvement in exercising the power of citizens in public life and learning. This requires developing a combination of knowledge, skills, values, and reflection to promote one or more of the following activities:

    - Socially responsible daily behavior
    - Direct service

- Community or economic development
- Voting or other formal political activities
- Direct action strategies
- Grass-roots political activity or public policy work
- Community building
- Advocacy through community education

- **Community-Based Learning:** university-wide approach of teaching, research, or experiential learning that combines authentic community or public service activity with academic instruction, focusing on critical, reflective thinking as well as evidence of civic responsibility and/or personal growth

- **Community Connection:** relationship with one or more community organization(s) and one or more department(s) or program(s) within the university to accomplish a shared objective on a short term basis which may or may not include academic learning

- **Community Immersion:** a university course or program that involves significant student immersion in a community-based project, program, organization or governmental unit with a primary focus on reflective learning that supports or enhances classroom learning

- **Community-University Partnership** a mutually defined relationship, between at least one university department or program and one or more community-based organization(s), of sufficient scale and duration to significantly benefit the community organization(s) while providing important learning opportunities and reflection for university students

- **Service to Community:** one or more university department(s), program(s) or course(s) are committed to regular opportunities for students and faculty to assist community organizations with their objectives, which may or may not include academic learning.

- **University-Community Service:** a university department, program or course and a community partner are committed to the mutual sharing of objectives in this reciprocal relationship which may or may not include an academic component.

- **Social Transformation Engagement**: a long-term unified commitment by the University and larger community to alter social disparities by working towards social change and justice.

Appendix 2: A Soapbox Platform

The Counseling Model: Is It Harmful To Our Health?
Sharon Rubin, when she was Assistant Dean for Undergraduate Studies University of Maryland

"It's not surprising that most of the experiential education programs I've visited use the counseling model as the basis for student-program interactions. After all, most experiential education programs started from the interest of a particular faculty or staff person, rather than from a considered administrative decision about educational alternatives. Because many internship programs began on a small scale, a career counselor or academic advisor could easily arrange a few excellent placement sites with friends in the community, counsel the few interested students, and cajole a few good-hearted faculty to grant academic credit. But when hundreds of students are going through elaborate placement processes with the same committed but exhausted person, we need to ask some hard questions about why the model hasn't changed to meet new circumstances.

"Experiential educators' resistance to adopting a less personal model is *fierce*. First, many have come out of counseling backgrounds. We have the kinds of personalities that led us to the field in the first place, and we get lots of positive reinforcement from the gratitude of students we've helped to succeed. Second, we feel we are holding our fingers in the dikes of individualized education. We're afraid that any minute our cozy *gemeinschaft* operation is going to be overwhelmed by the *gesellschaft* education system, where students will be treated identically, and possibly inhumanely. Third, we see ourselves as guardians of the quality. With our fail-safe systems of forms, interviews, careful planning and double checks, we can prevent students from taking unnecessary risks as they mismatch themselves with the wrong organizations. Finally-we keep ourselves busy. If anybody doubts how hard we work, we have the student contact to show that we're indispensable to our schools.

"The other side of the coin is that we're burned out. Often at the busiest time of the semester we feel harassed or even overwhelmed. We can hardly believe our exhaustion, and every time we go through the placement process, it's harder to do it with efficiency, attention to detail, and sensitivity to individual differences.

"The counseling model keeps us from institutionalizing our programs. We haven't the time to do the kind of research that will provide compelling evidence of the educational value of internships, or even that will provide evidence that we need more staff. We don't have time to get to know our institutions inside out, to understand which committees can be used to support our purposes, or which faculty can help us develop strategies for institutional change.

"We sometimes see ourselves as defenders of students against the institution rather than as integral parts of the institution. Our intense contact with students makes us forget that faculty and administrators are our peers.

"We sometimes forget that our final goal is to help students become self-directed learners. In putting such a high value on minimizing student risk, we also sometimes minimize student responsibility. In trying to protect quality, we make students very cynical about paperwork as a substitute for educational meaning. In trying to be supportive, we can stifle initiative and infantilize the very students we hope to help make independent.

"If we cling to a counseling model without considering many other alternatives for sharing our work, our responsibilities, and our many pleasures with other administrators, faculty, and students themselves, we embrace a burden that may prove fatal."

-Reprinted from *Experiential Education NSIEE* (newsletter), May-June 1985

Appendix 3: If You Think a Grant is the Answer...

Many institutions approach NSEE with questions like "Should we apply for soft money?" or "What foundations give grants for experiential education programs?" and often the query is more like "How are we going to sustain our programs beyond the life of the grant?" If you expect grants or outside contracts to fund basic, ongoing program functions indefinitely, think again and consider the following:

- Grants can be an excellent way to provide seed money for something new, to leverage other sources from the institution on a matching basis, or to give the extra push needed at the beginning of a project or program expansion. Such funds can motivate people to participate.

- Grants or outside contracts are not meant to fund basic, ongoing program functions indefinitely.

- Be very cautious about seeking any grant funds for student or faculty stipends. Once you, the students, the departments, or the students' work supervisors get used to a model that involves soft money for stipends or release time, it is very hard to get the same participants to continue their involvement using their own organizational or individual resources.

- If you do seek outside funds for program operations, get funds that can be continued on a relatively long-term basis (at least 3-4 years). At one time, for example, the University of Virginia had so many interns in the human service sector that the institution was able to get United Way funding because the school was providing staff to service agencies.

- If a grant pays for any faculty or staff time, pay for small portions of several people's time rather than paying for two or three full-time salaries. It is much easier to get several departments to pick up small pieces of salaries later than to try to get new institutional funds for full-time positions.

- Do not try to do it alone. Work with the Development Office at your institution and only approach funding sources that have demonstrated serious interest in related efforts. Each grant application or funding source that you approach will require 500% more time than you expect.

Authors

SUSAN SHUMER (susan.shumer@metrostate.edu) is the founding director of the Institute for Community Engagement and Scholarship at Metropolitan State University. She received her B.A. in English from St. Ambrose University and her M.S. in Education with a focus on Experiential and Service-Learning, from Minnesota State University, Mankato. She has successfully secured and administered federal, state and foundation grants focusing on university-community collaborations. Ms. Shumer has twenty-five years of experience working with community engagement in higher education and community-based organizations creating, implementing and directing programs. Her commitment to community partnerships has been published within *Partnerships for Service-Learning: Impacts on Communities and Students.*

EVELYN ROLLOFF (evelyn.rolloff@metrostate.edu) received her B.A. in Training and Development and a M.S. in Technical Communication from Metropolitan State University. She has worked at Metropolitan State for 18 years, currently serving as the Associate Director for the Institute for Community Engagement and Scholarship. Ms. Rolloff has secured public and foundation grants primarily in the areas of school and youth (k-12), family and library programs and partnerships. She has 20+ years of budget management experience through the university, union activities, serving on non-profit Boards, and through volunteer fundraising activities with local and national youth organizations.

Chapter 7

STRATEGIES FOR INSTITUTIONAL CHANGE

Joanne A. Dreher
Lesley University

Abstract

This chapter builds on suggestions that were presented in the original version to advance experiential learning and achieve successful organizational change. In this revised edition, those ideas have been expanded upon using recent research and new approaches to strengthening experiential education programs. Synthesizing what we know about effective experiential approaches to learning, the chapter integrates institutional examples to illustrate the work of practitioners engaged in various forms of experiential application. The chapter is organized around four guiding principles that emphasize organizational and individual responsibilities for change initiatives to be effective and sustained: basic principles of personal and organizational change; general conditions for change to occur; institutional and member resistance to change; and, organizational responsiveness to change.

Introduction

The term *institutional change* is often thought to be sweeping, scary and difficult. For purposes of this publication the term is used on two levels. The *first* level is that of systemic or structural change, which is infinitely complex and has far-reaching outcomes for institutions. On this level, for example, degree requirements are changed or expectations for faculty use of experiential learning are developed; new forms of experiential education such as international programs of study and service-learning are implemented; and assessment models are identified and tested. Change on this level takes time, requires participation from constituents across the organization, and asks that administrators in key leadership positions understand the implications of the change process. On this level, change challenges multiple dimensions of the organization, including institutional mission, the type of academic programs offered, faculty work expectations, student demographics, tools for assessment, governance structures, cross-functional relationships, and institutional resources. These factors are among many that inform and contribute to the process of organizational change.

Within the domain of experiential educators, however, often the most frequent and salient orientation to change acknowledges that significant modifications are not achieved through an identifiable or even planned process, but rather through a series of small incremental adjustments and strategic responses to opportunities and challenges. The *second* level of change is one that captures most of the institution's attention to strengthen experiential learning, with each step contributing to the larger process of *institutionalization*. If the goal is simply to start or improve a field experience program, the process would be much more straightforward. However, in college and university environments the very nature of change and particularly the broader goal of institutionalization is a slow and organic process. Morgan (1997) points out that successful change hinges on the close alignment of variables to meet the challenges proffered by the unique environments in which these organizations operate. Morgan contends that the intricate metaphors and images that often define and influence how the organization's members think about their work may prevent achievement of new frameworks or models for decision-making. It is this complexity of institutional factors that appears to impact not only how members view their own work but also how these characteristics influence the potential for new and enriched dimensions.

This revised edition of *Strengthening Experiential Education* expands on the original version, which focused on the experiences of the NSIEE/FIPSE pilot institutions as they engaged in planned change to strengthen experiential modalities of learning. This edition challenges institutions to develop both long-range vision and the small steps necessary to strengthen their experiential programs. The goal is to increase the institution's capacity to fulfill the multiple missions that identify higher education in the 21st Century. This chapter recognizes an expanded body of literature on organizational change in general and in colleges and universities more specifically that has evolved since publication of the original edition. Understanding the important findings in the research and acknowledging the experiences of practitioners who have been deeply involved in the process of planned change both at a programmatic level and more broadly on a systemic level can advance experiential education more quickly and to a greater degree of effectiveness.

To begin the campaign to strengthen experiential education, an interview with a change maker introduces the reader to strategies and important realities that can guide campuses in the change process. The interview, which appeared in the original version, contextualizes the diversity of institutional processes for expanding experiential pedagogy and is included for its relevance today as when it was first published.

I.   An Interview with a Catalyst for Change

Jim Heffernan, who was Vice President for Student Affairs at the SUNY College of Forestry and Environmental Sciences, conducted this interview with Mary Jo White, then the Assistant Director of Career Services for the Cooperative Education and Internship Program at the University of Colorado, during a national workshop for the NSIEE/FIPSE pilot schools, June, 1985. As this author reflects on the personal experience of overseeing experiential education program development and listens to the experiences of other colleagues, Ms. White's insights continue to resonate for those seeking to be change agents in the educational domain.

Jim Heffernan: What principles of institutional change have you experienced as you participated in this process at your university? You evidently manifested lots of leadership, and it's had an impact.

Mary Jo White: I didn't know that much about the principles of institutional change. What I've experienced in this whole process is just that there is a process, and there are certain steps that you have to go through if you want to change anything in a large institution. I never knew before how the committee on courses works. I never knew that the different colleges are so autonomous in deciding what degree requirements their students will have. I always thought that the President or the Vice Chancellor of Academic Affairs sets the policy, but that's not the way it happens. What I learned about this process is that we need support at every level. First of all, it's *got* to come from faculty because it's *got* to be their initiative that introduces a new process like experiential education. Then you've got to have support from the Committee on Courses or in this case, the Curriculum Committee. You need the support of the dean, first the Associate Dean and then the Dean of the College, because they are the ones who are going to "yea" or "nay" what the committee has to say. Then as you pass things on up the ranks you need support at every single level – the Associate Vice Chancellor, the Vice Chancellor, and then the Chancellor.

JH: And they each have a totally different agenda, and you have to know what these are. You've been a good map maker to have worked through that.

MJW: I was very fortunate in that I had a number of mentors, people in various stages and at different levels of responsibility within the University. On one level I would be introduced to a Vice Chancellor and have to learn how to deal with the Vice Chancellor. On another level I'd be introduced to faculty and I'd have to deal with faculty. And I found that in putting this whole thing together, I had to work on every single layer simultaneously. The only way the changes could happen this quickly was to work on every single layer simultaneously.

JH: So, there's a formal structure, and there are informal policies. It sounds like you've got to be a student of both.

MJW: And ask a lot of questions and do it in a meaningful way and ask people for assistance and make sure what you're asking for is realistic. For example, after Associate Dean Charles Middleton of the College of Arts and Sciences and I came back from a visit to the Washington Center, I said, "Okay, now how can we get the University of Colorado to waive the tuition charge to senior students so that they only have to pay tuition for the fall term?" But then I heard, "Wait a minute, wait a minute. We can't do that. First of all we've got to get them to recognize that experiential education is even important and valid." So I had mentors, people who said, "Stop. We have to go back here." And that whole thing was very interesting, very informative, and very frustrating for me at times because I like to see things happen quickly. And I found out more than once that I needed to back up and start over again and cover this base before I could go on further. On the question, "What did I learn about my leadership style?" I learned that I am a persistent person. If there's something that I feel is worthwhile and that I believe in and that I want to make happen, then I'll do what it takes.

JH: It sounds like a good rule, to back out of a blind alley and not just quit. That persistence really seems to have paid off. We're talking about a lot of progress in two and a half years.

MJW: The other thing I find is that if you really want to win people's respect and their cooperation, then you have to do things. It's one thing when you ask for something, and they say "Fine." And it's another thing for them to say, "Okay, fine, now you do this and get back to me by next Wednesday with such and such" knowing that you're going to do it. So you have to be able to follow through and produce results. And you have to do it to their specifications. So you have to play by other people's rules.

JH: And people will tell you their rules?

MJW: Yes, if you ask. Often I will ask what their criteria are, what their standards are, and what they really want to know. How do you want this written? Those kinds of things. You have to learn not to make assumptions because then people are more comfortable dealing with you. In a political model, it's often thought to be out of place to ask what the rules are because "One is supposed to know." Well, if you *don't* know, you'll never get anywhere if you don't ask for help. I found people are very willing to give me guidelines once we have established a personal relationship. I found in this whole process that first of all I had to convince people that I was qualified, that I was somebody who was committed to this cause and that I had some idea of how to go about doing things. It's almost like you have to win them on yourself personally before they're going to listen to your ideas. By establishing that working relationship first, it became very easy to ask questions.

JH: What would you say to someone from another selective, comprehensive research institution who is two years behind you if that person wanted to make the same kind of progress?

MJW: I would start off by saying to make sure you're very clear on what your objectives are. What kind of program do you really want to have? Do you want a program that just focuses on career development and that has the right faculty support, then I would house that program in the academic affairs side of things. I would say to scrutinize the design of your program. Decide whether or not you want a centralized program or a decentralized one. Who's going to run it? Really think of all the administrative structures that will enable you to set up efficient, effective procedures.

The other advice I would give is to know who your supporters are. And make sure you have support at every level where you need it. You don't want to be out talking to a dean about how wonderful this program is and the concept is and how viable it is for them if your own staff is not already sold on the idea. And also, qualify your support. Does that support mean that somebody says, "Yes, yes, yes, you do a great job," or does the support mean, "Here, I'm going to give you $2000 for this part of the work"? Is it just verbal support, or is it actual participation?

JH: What would you do differently if you could start over?

MJW: I would tie the program closely to Academic Affairs, and I would start with a rather broad definition of experiential education rather than just one model. As I said, we started with cooperative education. So if I could start from scratch, I'd start with a broader definition of my program. What I think is key to our program is faculty support. Now faculty are going to support something that they have a partial interest in. What we do get in being part of career services is the interaction with people who are very well connected to employers. We do need to have a strong employer base in order to offer these field opportunities. Being connected with career services and student services give us that advantage. There are trade-offs.

Before plunging more deeply into strategies to strengthen experiential education, it is important to consider fundamental principles for organizational change that can guide institutional leaders and practitioners in processes to advance experiential learning. Individuals engaged in motivating organizations toward change in past generations report similar conclusions about approaches that have been successful and methods that have proven ineffective.

II.   Principles for Change in Organizations

Four principles relating to change in educational institutions were identified in the original version of this chapter and have remained constant over time. These principles emphasize both organizational and individual levels of responsibility that must be considered for effective and sustained change to occur.

A. *Recognize the basic principles of personal and organizational change.*

Seven principles associated with personal and organizational change were identified in the earlier edition (Sykes, 1985). These principles designate key concepts that can inform and support faculty and academic administrators in the change process.

- *Know what you want to change before you try to change it.* Essential data must be collected and feedback must be considered before initiating either personal or organizational change. Plan for adaptation rather than adoption, understanding which of the particular dynamics in the system are targeted for change.

- *Recognize that change in one part of the system affects the whole system and that one isolated element cannot be changed without impacting other factors.* It is important to recognize the total impact of proposed changes in order to reduce the chances of unwanted and unpredicted side effects.

208

- *Understand that people resist change and that individuals tend to consider alterations to a known and accepted system as a form of punishment.* Those who are impacted by change use extra energy to adapt to new situations and in their acceptance of new approaches to achieving identified goals. Therefore, it is important to make clear the value of newly identified goals and why extra effort and adaptation are important. Creating transparency is important to the change process.

- *Recognize the reluctance of members of the organization to undergo discomfort in the present for gains in the future.* When the prospects of future benefits are uncertain, there is a tendency to hang on to familiar ways of doing things. Those entering a change effort must be provided with support and motivation during the *painful* early stages. Early rewards for participants can be helpful to move change forward and can be an effective strategy to attract others to initiatives.

- *Understand that change generates stress.* Studies about the sources of stress have found that any kind of change can produce disequilibrium as the system responds to new conditions. The most stressful form of change is feeling a loss of control. Those impacted by change must be made part of the process and be provided with the necessary resources that will support them as they transition to new situations.

- *Respect the importance of participation in the change process and how the involvement of others can reduce resistance.* A key principle of social psychology to gain buy in and acceptance of new ideas is to encourage involvement in goal setting and devising strategies for achieving those goals. Initiators of change need to recognize that participation in any new initiative involves consultation time, effective communication, and common purposes and values that allow fruitful exchanges to occur. Those individuals or groups that are most affected by change initiatives must be willing to invest time and energy. Those who hold the most power must be willing to share some of that power to ensure that goals are met.

- *Acknowledge that behavioral change usually is achieved in small, incremental steps.* Few individuals or organizations are willing or able to make broad sweeping changes quickly. Individuals affected by change need time to make behavioral adjustments. Realistically, abrupt changes in behavior are rare and probably unhealthy, both for the individuals who are affected and for the organization as a whole. It is crucial to allow adequate time for change to be successful.

B. Understand the general conditions necessary for change to occur in educational practices.

First, colleges and universities must be responsive to both internal and external forces to maintain stability and balance. Changes in either internal or external needs can initiate modification in the organization. The external environment, however, will always be a strong factor for higher education due to institutional dependence on external resources. Perceptions, whether internal or external, that an institution is not performing a particular function well is enough to cause instability in the organization. Such instability or perception of need often becomes the first general condition to initiate change.

Second, advocates for change are needed. Advocacy usually needs to be from within the institution. External advocates can have tremendous power in initiating change or creating the level of stability needed for change. It is critical to be responsive to the economic, political and social indicators from outside the organization that influence the internal work environment. However, for change to be sustained and institutionalized, strong internal advocacy is required.

The third general condition necessary for implementing change is associated with an adequate level of resources. This does not necessarily mean additional funding. Building forms of experiential learning into the way students are taught and being clear about the targeted outcomes of the curriculum may only require adjustments in the use of existing resources rather than in the generation of new funds.

Five specific conditions necessary for colleges and universities to implement change in their educational practices are noted in the original edition (Evans, 1968):

- Proposed initiatives must be more effective or efficient than current practices in meeting an accepted goal.
- Proposed initiatives must be consistent with existing values and with what is currently being done in pursuit of these values.
- Proposed initiatives cannot be perceived as *too* difficult to implement.
- Proposed initiatives must be able to be divided into separate components that are introduced over time rather than attempted to be fully implemented at one time.
- Proposed initiatives must identify both a mechanism and a language for communicating the benefits of the new practices and their integration into the change process.

C. Respect the reasons that institutions and their members resist change.

The summary of principles for personal and organizational change identified by Sykes (1985) and previously cited suggests several of the most important and valid reasons that people and organizations resist change. According to Mecca (2004) "… change sponsors and agents should try to systematically anticipate participants' perceptions and identify who might resist the change and why" (p. 6). Mecca suggests that people resist change because they fear that they (and the organization) are losing something of value; they misunderstand the kind of change being proposed and its effect on current practices; they believe the proposed change doesn't make sense for the organization; and, for many, they have a low tolerance for change. The value of the proposed change may be discounted due to lack of trust in the change agent, which may result from the position the initiator holds in the institution and an unclear rationale about the purpose of the proposed initiative. When this situation presents itself, the most effective counter-strategy is to identify additional advocates who can envision and translate the potential richness, value and opportunity of the ideas being proposed.

In higher education, administrators and professional personnel almost always must work through others, particularly if they want to influence faculty. As a group, faculty are often resistant to change due to environmental pressures and perceptions of institutional roles that shape faculty organizational culture. These factors influence how faculty approach their work. Rubin (1983) points out that particularly long training in the habits of academe and observations of other academicians contribute to the especially persistent assumptions and habits of faculty. The challenge is to clarify how faculty, administrators and professional staff can co-exist independently from each other yet engage with each other collaboratively to support institutional goals and the core tenets that drive the mission of the organization (Dreher, 2008). While it is important to acknowledge independence, it is essential that interdependent and collaborative work among constituents be promoted, adding value to the unique characteristics that distinguish the organization and its programs.

D. *Expect that people and different parts of the organization will react differently to change.*

The organization's operational mechanisms and the people within the various divisions by their very nature influence and respond to change in different ways. Rogers (1962/1995) outlines five categories of individuals and their respective characteristics and responses to innovation and change:

- Innovators: venturesome, risk-takers (2.5%).
- Early adopters: respected, regarded by others in the social system as models, (13.5%).
- Early majority: deliberate, willing to consider innovation only after peer adoption of change initiatives (68%).
- Late majority: skeptical, willing to consider innovation only before adoption occurs (13.5%).
- Laggards: tradition-bound and oriented to the past (2.5%).

More recent research emphasizes the importance of the ability to respond to changing organizational patterns of behavior. Bolman and Deal (1997) contend that when organizational leaders work toward reframing existing realities, the experience itself enriches and broadens organizational effectiveness. Whether they are administrators, professional staff or faculty, the process helps senior leaders to be creative as they respond to the complex issues they encounter. Using new and diverse perspectives, leaders can be challenged to see organizational realities through new eyes. In this process, they acquire the ability to motivate member engagement in new initiatives, promote greater involvement by others from across the organization, becoming catalysts for change.

The work of social psychologist Kurt Lewin emphasizes the importance of understanding "…that successful change results in 'unfreezing' an established equilibrium…removing the resisting forces, and then 'refreezing' in a new equilibrium state" (Morgan, 1997, p. 294). Reframing experiential learning using a lens that reflects change in the organizational environment can minimize negative factors while enriching and retaining the desirable elements of the initiative. In Morgan's view, creating new contexts, developing new understandings, and

211

reframing key contradictions can reshape how members approach the change process. One example of this to note is the shift in the higher education environment as represented in AAC&U's LEAP Initiative, which fully embraces experiential education and the high impact pedagogies identified by George Kuh (2008).

In addition, Becher (1984) observes that in college and university environments the long road to institutionalizing experiential education will be the only road to sustained improvements. In Becher's view, the pluralistic character of higher education organizations initially can be assumed to be a disadvantage. Yet, it is this pluralistic feature that helps to ensure that wide and open discussions take place before decisions are made. Despite the tendency to reject centrally devised plans, the collegial tradition generally helps to support consensus-building, resulting in policies and perspectives that are more likely to reflect the views of practitioners.

In the original version of this publication, leaders at the NSIEE/FIPSE pilot schools identified various strategies that were shaped by the guiding principles just presented to institutionalize experiential education on their campuses. New approaches that have been identified since the initial publication are included in this revised edition. Depending on individual institutional characteristics and perspectives about program development, some strategies may work better than others. This next section identifies and synthesizes organizational methods that have proven to be effective and conditions under which they appear to be most successful. These strategies have been organized into two categories: first, to address conceptual ideas and member responses to change and second, to identify characteristics of organizational structure that influence the change process.

III.   Strategies for Organizational Change

A. Strategies to strengthen experiential education that focus on conceptual approaches and member behaviors in response to change.

1. Be clear about goals and what you want to change.

The importance of spending time to conduct a thorough assessment of current activities and needs cannot be stressed enough. Individuals may have strong feelings about needed change on the campus, but a clear consensus of current strengths and weaknesses is important to develop a realistic strategy for strengthening experiential education. The organization's purpose to initiate change is contingent on how ready its members are to understand the value of change and the need for a fiscal structure to provide the resources necessary to support new initiatives. Curry (1992) and Kanter (1983) point out that support systems must be connected to the change process and that linkages within the organization must be identified to successfully integrate initiatives.

The following reference to worksheets and guidelines presented in the *original version* can help with the assessment of initiatives:

- Values of My Institution, Chapter 1, Parts 1 and 2, pp. 14-15

- Values of Experiential Education, Chapter 1, p. 16
- Identifying Student-Centeredness in Learning, Chapter 1, p. 18
- Assessing the Value of the Experiential Educator to the Department or Institution, Chapter 1, p. 20
- Inventory of Experiential Education Programs and Courses, Chapter 2, pp. 33-37
- Assessing Faculty Involvement on Your Campus, Chapter 3, pp. 55-56
- Principles of Good Practice, Chapter 4, pp. 71-74
- Assessing Your Institution's Administrative Models, Chapter 5, Parts 1 and 2, pp. 83-87
- Responsibilities for Primary Functions of Experiential Education within Your Institution, Chapter 5, pp. 88-89

2. *Plan incremental, not sweeping changes.*

"Many academics are unwilling to make a five-year plan either on the grounds that nothing will change in five years or that they have no power over circumstances. However, in the course of five years it is possible to introduce a great many changes, a small number at a time, in well-planned stages" (Rubin, 1983, p. 52). According to Curry (1992), three levels of change (structural, behavioral, and cultural adaptation) evolve sequentially and are essential for embedding change into organizational operations. Curry outlines a sequence in the change process that begins with member commitment to the norms and values expressed in new initiatives. New practices then become representative of a revised set of institutional assumptions and are reflected in the social structure of the organization. Schein (1992) and Curry (1992) posit that new practices create meaning as members of the organization engage in a process to adopt new norms and values. Ironically, many in higher education adhere more closely than almost any other social institution to Cornford's (1953) claim that "nothing should be done for the first time" (p. 15). Rudolph (1962/1990) further emphasizes this point: "Experimentation, which was the life of the university and innovation, which was its gift to society were seldom tried upon colleges and universities themselves" (p. 492). As we can all attest, time is necessary to implement initiatives, and time is needed for the review and assessment of outcomes, as is a renewed openness to change itself.

3. *"Use paper-mâché instead of concrete" (Rubin, 1983).*

Avoid the tendency to try to anticipate every possible problem in the program or policy by setting rules to address each one. Doing so may restrict progress by erecting unnecessary barriers that block the ability to move forward. A new approach can sink of its own weight if it is loaded down with too much structure before getting started. Instead, experiment with one department for a limited time and develop a model that can be replicated in other areas of the institution. Develop policies as they are needed rather than artificially imposing limitations at the beginning. A trial approach or *pilot* can be revised during and after the initial period so that the best model emerges. Looking to other models and identifying the factors that have contributed to their successes can be an effective approach to advance singular forms of experiential education. The planning and growth trajectory for service-learning is a case worth noting. Small, incremental steps over time with good feedback mechanisms help faculty and others buy-in and commit themselves to this new approach to teaching and learning (Dreher, 2008).

4. Introduce doubt.

Introducing doubt can be critical for disrupting complacency and challenging old forms of behavior. By creating uncertainty, receptiveness to change can be heightened, new insights identified, and new cultural norms adopted. According to Schein (1992) much change is motivated by mechanisms that shift the current norm and allow for key concepts and values to be redefined. Schein describes a change process as one that requires necessary new behaviors and cognitions that reinforce the adoption and stabilization of new assumptions. In addition to psychological conditions, the cultural layering that defines the institutional environment represents a multitude of specific yet similar processes that contribute to change. When new pressures are exerted on organizational structures and internal practices, disequilibrium and uncertainty are created and the change process begins again. In Cameron's (1984) view, the disruption of a comfortable environment can make members of the organization question current practices and become more open to change. However, a *caveat* is to use caution in making generalized assumptions, questioning how much doubt is the catalyst for change and how much doubt encourages people simply to walk away.

5. Expect resistance.

Institutionalizing experiential education would not be a change process without encountering barriers. Almost by definition, change in educational programming anticipates various types of resistance that emerge from many points of view. However, resistance also helps to identify issues and methods for resolution and often is a signal that progress is being made. Leaders of change should consider resistance as an invitation to negotiate. Senior leaders must recognize that negative responses to change encompass myriad emotional phases. These phases represent steps in a process that move members from the initial point of impact through to a point of acceptance. Mecca (2004) identifies these phases, beginning with immobilization and shock to periods of denial and anger. Bargaining and negotiation often become a turning point and the first step toward acceptance as members begin to recognize the benefits of the initiative. Prior to full acceptance, participants often reach that point when they can recognize the new opportunities posed by the change and become productive within its new context.

The strength of resistance measures just how big the proposed change is and what it means to the organization. If the initiative is too big, this is a signal to slow down and break the initiative into smaller steps. If it appears that resistance cannot be overcome and if the proposed change cannot or should not be scaled back, this is a signal to work around that resistance. The original version referenced Rogers' *Diffusion of Innovation* (1962/1995) and the five types of responders to innovation previously cited in this chapter: *innovators, early adopters, early majority, late majority, and laggards.* There will be several of each type on every campus. It is rarely productive to try to convince the laggards of the need for particular changes when greater advancement can result by focusing on the innovators and early adopters first, followed by the "early majority".

6. Share everything.

Look for opportunities to give visibility and shared ownership of new initiatives or policies to those who must implement them. With ownership comes commitment. If new strategies for institutionalizing a particular program are held too closely, the commitment needed from others rarely will be realized. Kanter (1983) found that for change to be institutionalized initiatives cannot be implemented in isolation from those who are impacted. Change must touch other parts of the organization, be understood in terms of the cultural influences that dominate at each level of the process (Schein, 1992), and involve the participation of others if it is to gain permanence. Corresponding changes to the normative climate of the organization also must occur to help initiators lobby for the added value the innovation brings with it (Curry, cited in Colbeck, 2002). Cooperative relationships that support the implementation of change often exist in very clear and intentional ways, growing out of the mission and cultural history of the institution. However, when these relationships do not appear evident it may not be due to a lack of intent to cooperate but rather complications that are created by structural factors that prevent shared ownership of initiatives.

Keeping others in the organization informed is critical for garnering support for change. Mecca (2004) emphasizes the importance of the human element in organizational change, and understanding the emotional and psychological responses of those impacted by new programs. Having a clear understanding of the steps in the change process and sharing information at each stage can have a calming effect on those being challenged and often motivate greater levels of support. This is especially true for those who are beginning to see that while certain characteristics of the current organizational environment may change, the new initiative will add value to their work. It is the responsibility of those leading change to utilize effective methods of communication and, as Mecca stresses, to recognize that good listening generates trust and credibility in the process.

7. Measure what you want to be noticed.

Cameron (1984) suggests that quantifying activities helps to increase their importance and the way they are regarded in the institution. It is important to collect data to support departmental and cross-campus programs under consideration, including assessment of student inquiries and student participation in internships, field research and other experiential courses such as service-learning. Agency requests for students also are important data that can be crucial not only to the acceptance of initiatives but also to emphasize the role of experiential pedagogy in the institution. Assessment data for experiential programs are crucial to gain visibility with senior leaders, to access new funding sources, and to promote experiential modes of learning in the external community where internship and service-learning sites are located.

According to Robert Shumer, contributing author of this revised edition, a major movement and resulting body of literature in K-16 assessment emerged in the 1990s and continue to gain momentum. This movement emphasizes educational mission and values, which drive not only what is chosen for assessment but also methods for implementing assessment practices. Shumer stresses that qualitative evidence broadens assessment and measures outcomes including involvement by program leaders and those who are being assessed. Qualitative data generated by students and their site supervisors, and by those in the institution who oversee student placements, become a form of *storytelling* that illustrates and supports the nature and observable outcomes of each experience. Sharon Rubin, then the Assistant Dean for Undergraduate Studies at the University of Maryland, emphasizes that consistent collection of student reflections on their experiences along with agency and faculty evaluations of student work can reveal the academic qualities inherent in various forms of field-based learning. Student projects with obvious academic quality can help institutions motivate program expansion. However, as programs grow, academic goals need to be re-evaluated. There must be renewed emphasis on the vast array of possibilities associated with student learning outcomes that have emerged in recent years and that are inextricably tied to experiential and applied models of learning, including civic understanding, global perspectives and community leadership.

8. Publicize the progress.

Keep as many members of the organization and relevant external constituents aware of the progress of proposals and changes as they develop. This will minimize the perception that the next step is not a giant leap. This is not meant to imply that every interim report and set of notes be circulated to the broader constituency. On the other hand, there is a need to look for opportunities for broad communication as milestones are reached. The stakeholders of initiatives need a consistent flow of communication about progress being made while minimizing the perception that future steps will be insurmountable. Well planned publication of achievements toward goals will strengthen constituent support. *The challenge is to determine how much information is sufficient without being overwhelming.* Communicating significant achievements, key developments and new opportunities are critical to keep supporters connected to initiatives and to ensure their continued support.

There are numerous methods for publicizing experiential education programs. In *Creating a Climate for Service-learning Success,* published by the American Association of Community Colleges, Jeandron & Robinson (2010) identify successful methods for service learning. These methods can be used to support other forms of experiential learning as well:

- Orientation sessions for faculty and staff, particularly those who are new to the institution or the pedagogy;

- Celebrations that bring students, faculty, staff and community partners together to share the outcomes of their experiences;

- Symposia that include guest speakers, training workshops and community-building activities for students, faculty and community partners;

- Student leaders who serve as ambassadors for experiential programs;

- E-newsletters to broadly disseminate information about current initiatives;

- Newsletters created by students to highlight programs, profile community partners and create a forum for students themselves to reflect publicly on their internship, service-learning, field research and study abroad experiences;

- Logos and materials that promote experiential learning internally and to external constituents;

- Media sites (e.g. YouTube, Facebook, Twitter) to promote the benefits of experiential learning; and

- Inclusion on the President's web page, the Higher Education Community Service Honor Roll, and emphasis in other presidential documents that are shared internally as well as publicly through the institution's website.

Posters, video streaming and photographs located in public areas of the institution can be effective in highlighting experiential learning. Each form contributes to a visual history of program development, learning outcomes, and faculty-student engagement that strengthens current initiatives and identifies new directions.

9. *Use rituals and ceremonies.*

Symbolic affirmations can be critical to ensure future commitment. Special events are a way to celebrate progress by "…fulfill[ing] analogous symbolic functions at the department level" and managing the meanings and interpretations that constitute the groundwork of change (Cameron, 1984). As a milestone is reached, look for ways to recognize that progress through rituals and ceremonies. Publicly recognizing those who are engaged in experiential learning can be an effective and persuasive method for advancing programs in the institution. These might include a luncheon for the first group of field supervisors, a reception for a newly formed advisory board or a special gathering to honor a newly appointed director of a centralized coordinating office for experiential learning programs. The Dean or President can be called upon to present an award to a faculty sponsor for students engaged in experiential learning and to community organizations that provide the sites for those experiences. Events that celebrate students, faculty and institutional progress in experiential learning can be confined internally to departments or organized on a broader scale to include all departments in the organization. Including community partners and local businesses can help to support the growth of programs but also becomes a way to publicize institutional progress to the wider community.

B. *Strategies that emphasize the influence of organizational structures on relationships between experiential education professionals and colleagues and constituencies within and external to the organization.*

1. *Secure bottom-up support.*

Start with input from those individuals who are most directly involved with the initiative. Most colleges and universities have *bottom heavy* power structures that are directly related to academic freedom and the autonomy of academic departments. The general principle of building grassroots support is even more important in deeply hierarchical organizations. All members of the organization who are affected need to participate in the decision process. Faculty-wide discussions about the nature and benefits of experiential education need to take place. On large campuses, these discussions may occur within departments or divisions. In smaller institutions discussions may convene the full faculty from across disciplines, programs and academic units.

2. *Get top level support.*

Support at different levels is needed for different purposes and at different times in the change process. In the academic environment buy-in takes grassroots support from among the faculty. To implement corresponding changes to a policy or an administrative structure, however, also requires top level support. In the doctoral research of this author, it was found that senior leaders of organizations are critically important to the social context that defines the work environment and for providing the organization with the adaptive mechanisms necessary to respond to change (Dreher, 2008). Often, the highest level of administrators and senior academic leaders of the organization are needed to resolve internal issues facing individual departments or school units. In addition, Walsh & Cuba (2009) point out that creativity, patience and persistence are essential attitudes on the part of senior leaders if faculty are to be motivated to support new approaches to experiential learning and engage in change on multiple levels.

At NSIEE's National Conference in 1984, Sharon Rubin, then the Assistant Dean for Undergraduate Studies at the University of Maryland and previously cited, indicated that their experience emphasized the importance of good information, planning, intentional collaboration, and small faculty research grants. The grants may not be very large, but they can provide helpful funding to further motivate the interests of administrators to pursue excellence through experiential education. According to Rubin, it is really important to involve the highest level of administrators, getting their permission for grant proposals, inviting their participation in meetings, and having the President bestow honors and awards to site supervisors and students to honor their achievements. In this way there is a continuing awareness of initiatives, with attention paid to those who are actively involved in leading each step of the process. Many of us would echo the FIPSE participant in the 1980s, Karen Murtaugh, Director of Cooperative Education at Manhattan College. She and others during that period stressed that support for experiential education is essential at the highest administrative level of the college, particularly when establishing the process and resolving issues related to its institutionalization.

3. *Identify essential characteristics of leadership.*

Developing experiential learning initiatives can teach organizational members about their own leadership style and about how colleges work. This includes an understanding and realization that autocratic leadership styles are increasingly ineffective in educational communities as well as in organizations overall. For leaders to be effective, faculty need to be involved. Their participation must be in a free and open process that defines the problem and identifies the solution. Change agents need to acknowledge and build upon a participatory series of actions that engages constituents at all levels of the process. Administrative decisions require input from members of the organization and being sensitive to the concerns of the faculty and others who are affected by the proposed change. There are many examples of situations in which faculty have not been ready to engage in change, creating the perception that organizational leaders are manipulative and controlling. As a reader of this publication, you no doubt can identify such situations in your own institution.

For new initiatives to be successful, leaders must be sensitive to how change is presented. Senge, Scharmer, Jaworski and Flowers (2005) identified incremental stages that can lead faculty and professional staff to consensus, acceptance and active support. Theory U is a theoretical approach that draws on Otto Scharmer's collaborations with Senge et al. and targets the management of organizational learning with three levels of infrastructure, the technical, social and cultural subsystems of the institution. Senge et al. suggest a change process that first determines what members want and then identifies the values to guide and drive the achievement of goals. In this process, empathic and generative listening allows consideration of the complex systemic issues that can erect barriers to organizational progress. Scharmer (2008) points out that understanding and sensitivity on multiple levels are necessary to move the institution from reaction and superficial fixes to a point of renewal and change. Active resistance may appear to defend substantive concerns about initiatives or past experiences with overpowering administrators. By listening carefully to understand the subculture and allow development of a participatory and open process, leaders can be more effective in their positions to strengthen and advance experiential programs.

4. Expect each department or division to react differently.

The autonomous nature of most academic departments or other sub-units in higher education institutions means that each has its own work life, its own cultural characteristics that reflect the values and norms identified with the department, and its own priorities with respect to academic program development and curricular initiatives. Tremendous variability tends to exist between departments, influencing the degree to which faculty are either self-motivated or prompted by their supervisors to engage in experiential education (Dreher, 2008). The dean or department chair can have enormous influence on whether initiatives move forward. Acting as role models, on the one hand, can advance the growth of an academic idea. On the other hand, the dean or chair can potentially slow program momentum. By not supporting programs in their communications with senior administrators, deans and department chairs often lose access to the resources that move initiatives forward. Consequently, it is important to consider departmental characteristics and the power of department leaders (chairs, senior faculty) to influence change in the organization.

Implementing change will always take more time when more than one department or functional unit is involved. Not much has changed since Becher (1984) noted that "…each basic unit has its own particular type of academic challenge, its own style of operations, its own set of professional practices, its own disciplinary culture" (p. 198). These innate differences have consequences. Solutions to emerging problems must be approached by understanding the individual needs of each unit and recognizing that each school or department, while unique in structural and cultural characteristics, does not operate autonomously outside of the institutional context. Solutions to problems must acknowledge the institutional characteristics that distinguish each unit. Implementing change should be left to those who know the most about the effect of particular policies and how to live with the consequences of the changes they initiate. Those who implement change also must acknowledge the power of senior leaders to spawn or inhibit new ideas.

5. Promote internal collaborations between student affairs and faculty leaders.

The dynamic and active processes that define learning suggest that organizational structures and internal campus relationships also must be considered if effective strategies to strengthen experiential education are to be developed and implemented. Experiential learning can strengthen not only traditional classroom pedagogy but also the co- and extra-curricular learning in which students engage beyond those boundaries. Blending the value domains of the academic and co-curriculum invites strengthened relationships between faculty and student affairs professional staff (Schwartzman, 2007) and can help to bridge the structural silos that are historic in college and university environments. Such collaborations advance the goals and outcomes of experiential learning through resource sharing, cross-divisional teamwork, and multiple forms of feedback and assessment (Jacoby, 1999). These collaborations have been found to strengthen retention initiatives, improve graduation rates, and expand opportunities for faculty scholarship (Engstrom, 2003; Jacoby, 1999; Kezar, 2002; Smith, 2005). A host of organizational benefits also have been found to result from collaboration, such as increasing organizational efficiencies in decision-making processes and framing the "...shared rules, norms and structures that often become their first work together "(Kezar, 2006, p. 807). Service-learning, community-based field research and internships are examples of experiential modalities that enhance relationships between student affairs and academic affairs. Support for these and other structured forms of experiential learning have been found to enrich campus work environments, expand community-university relationships, and deepen students' engagement in their campus experience.

6. Take advantage of research and the changing social and educational context.

The outcomes of a college education have become the focus of considerable attention as economies shift, tuitions increase and cultural values raise public concern about the quality of teaching. However, as Ewell documented in 1997, experiential education is in a position to strengthen teaching and learning because it is premised on what is known about how people learn – through experience and the application of knowledge. As a pedagogical form, experiential education helps students use what they know in appropriate contexts, expands their knowledge through application to new situations, and helps to develop their personal, social and economic capacities (Eyler, 2009). It is important that leaders take advantage of a climate of instability (i.e. receptiveness to change) that is created by this and other social and intellectual developments. According to Hefferlin (cited in Little, 1980), changes in the curriculum are positively correlated with shifts in society. His findings continue to show that modifications to the curriculum correlate positively with faculty turnover, institutional growth and changes in departmental leadership. The experiences of several of the NSIEE/FIPSE pilot schools confirmed this finding as did the doctoral research by the author of this revision.

A major contextual shift has occurred since the 1986 publication of this book and chapter. This fundamental "sea change" underscores and validates the role of experiential education in the curriculum and pedagogy. The Association of American Colleges and Universities is currently leading the way with the LEAP Initiative (Liberal Education and America's Promise), which is organized around a robust set of learning outcomes that are deemed essential to prepare students for challenges in the 21st century (AAC&U, 2008). LEAP guidelines are framed under four essential learning outcomes: knowledge of human cultures and the physical and natural world; intellectual and practical skills; personal and social responsibility; and integrative and applied learning. The LEAP Initiative allies its intended outcomes with a thoughtfully planned sequence of high impact pedagogies identified by Kuh (2008), including internships, field research, service-learning, study abroad and senior capstone courses. These particular modalities are structured to prepare students for the world of work as well as entry into graduate school. Integrative and applied learning that synthesize and advance students' accomplishments across general education and their specialized studies in the majors enable students to apply their knowledge, skills and responsibilities more broadly in new settings and in the resolution of complex problems they encounter in social, professional and community contexts. Experiential educators should exploit this new consensus on their own campuses.

7. Use the views of students, alumni and the community.

Students want experiential education integrated into their academic programs because it engages them in the content of their studies on a deeper level, brings theoretical constructs to life and transforms the process of their growth (Ewell, 1997). Students should be encouraged to voice their desire for experiential learning through the many channels available in the institution. According to Hefferlin (1969) and much of the research done by Campus Compact and academic researchers since that time, including that of this author, curriculum change is positively correlated with student participation in educational policy making. Student commitment to experiential learning has been found to rally support with faculty and the administration to ensure that internships and other forms of experiential education are secured in the academic offerings of the institution.

Alumni, like students, often have strong views about the value of experiential learning. Many graduates wish they had had more opportunities in their student years to apply concepts and gain experience to better understand the relationship between theory and practice. Alumni views can be influential to policy makers in the institution and can be critical to garnering support for new initiatives. Alumni roles can include membership on Boards of Trustees and Presidential Advisory Councils, career connections through the office of Career Services, and more informal relationships through the academic departments. Each can provide an important venue for alumni voices. Interested and appropriately trained alumni may be involved in supervisory roles for internships and student teaching placements, may mentor students in their particular field, or be invited back to the campus to share the values of experiential learning in their own career development. Alumni often may provide financial support to endow internship and service-learning centers, expand study abroad initiatives, and underwrite scholarships to encourage greater engagement of students in experiential learning.

The *community* also can be an ally in the institution's efforts to institutionalize experiential education. In structured experiential modalities, students can be partnered with organizations for internships, service-learning and field research, assisting communities in such initiatives as environmental data collection, opinion surveys, marketing campaigns, technology training, and after school tutoring programs. Community-university partnerships have proven invaluable for promoting and strengthening experiential learning both for students and institutions and have been found to provide fodder for faculty engagement in community-based scholarship. Organizations that provide opportunities that cut across the broad spectrum of business models, not-for-profit, social services, the arts and healthcare sectors, to name a few, offer students a wide range of choices that support the academic focus of their studies. All levels of government, as well as policy-focused organizations and social service agencies, can provide important hands on experiences for students interested in pursuing public service careers. Employers, regardless of the sector they represent, can provide feedback and evaluations about the strengths and weaknesses of student interns and of their potential relative to the degree of their professional skills as they move into the workplace. This feedback can inform guidelines for assessing experiential learning and identify skills and core competencies that, when emphasized in the curriculum, improve student learning outcomes, sharpen the goals of academic programs, and strengthen the contributions that students make in community and organizational contexts.

8. *Get others to speak for you.*

Whether the initiative is to change attitudes or program structures, the support of faculty peers is essential. Hudson and Trudeau (1995) noted the primary importance of senior faculty in fostering the institutionalization of experiential forms of learning. Abes, Jackson and Jones (2002) later identified senior faculty involvement as a conscious political strategy that considers how academic programs fit with institutional mission. It is important to note that support from both units, academic affairs and student affairs, can also have important implications for strengthening particular modalities and moving experiential learning forward. Schmeide's (1998) research identified institutional support and building alliances among faculty and administrators. Schmeide found that the strength of experiential forms of teaching and learning are linked both to faculty and the administration and the degree to which experiential education is conceptualized within the institution. An important *caveat*, however, is the understanding that not all institutions interpret pedagogical models in the same way. Universally held guidelines for experiential education do not guarantee success but rather must be addressed within organizational context and the institutional factors that motivate faculty to engage in experiential initiatives.

The doctoral research of this author found that some faculty would prefer to see experiential learning made a central part of the majors across academic departments, becoming a core approach to the way disciplines are taught in the institution. This is true at Lesley University, where internships and other structured forms of experiential learning are required in the majors. However, many faculty have concerns about mandating academic requirements for which students may not be prepared. When embedded as a core requirement in the major, however, students have a real opportunity to understand the integration of theory with practice and what it means to engage in a particular field, albeit on an elementary level at this stage in their lives. For institutions, to embed new academic initiatives into the fabric of the learning environment, it becomes a question of finding the right balance to motivate and support faculty in the process (AAC&U, 2008; Dreher, 2008).

9. Use other colleges and universities as models.

Higher education relies on social comparison and precedent more than most institutions. While models from within the campus are especially powerful, programs and approaches used in peer institutions also are good targets for emulation. When advocating for particular programmatic or policy changes, the key is to recommend good models from institutions that are ranked the same or slightly better in terms of status and academic reputation. Walsh and Cuba (2009) point out that while numerous sets of guidelines and best practices have emerged in the research, every institution embodies its own distinctive learning culture and methods for implementing change. The examples, then, need to be from comparable institutions but also must be recognized within the context of the uniqueness of each institution's pedagogical philosophy and application.

For example, at Lesley University in Cambridge, Massachusetts, first year field courses in the undergraduate curriculum play an important role in Lesley's approach to experiential learning. These courses help prepare students for the required internships they complete at a later point in their academic careers[1]. Field-based learning is at the center of Lesley's educational purpose and has been institutionalized in all programs of study. At Wellesley College, Diana Chapman Walsh, president emerita and Lee Cuba, former dean of the college offer their own experience. The college engaged in a strategy to move from its traditional classroom formats and discipline-based learning to an approach that focused in more problem-based experiential learning and collaborative study. Wellesley found that building alliances across departments helped to facilitate innovation among those faculty inclined to embrace experiential learning. Incremental steps over time enabled the creation of a process for internal debate that encouraged inquiry into understanding how and what students are learning. Questions focused on the intersection of institutional goals with the way students learn; the relationship between classroom learning and experiential opportunities; the sequencing of various experiences such as service-learning, study abroad and internships; and the alignment of student goals with those of the institution (Walsh & Cuba, 2009, p. 37). These two examples are from very different campuses yet, along with case studies in other chapters, can provide readers of this publication with models to catalyze conversations for change in their institutions (see revised chapter 3).

10. Use outside funding to initiate the first steps.

Grants are resources that can stimulate change and offer opportunities for low-risk experimentation. Grants from either external or internal sources provide small amounts of funding that can result in a larger commitment of institutional funds and the allocation of other types of resources. Funding can come from local businesses, foundations, corporations and government agencies. Educational grants in particular can focus on experiential initiatives such as service-learning and study abroad. It often can take very little in the way of new resources to convince an institution to try something new. Outside funding for specific initiatives not only can be solicited from community organizations but also from members of Boards of Trustees and alumni. These funds may be restricted to particular experiential programs or be provided in the form of scholarships to support students' engagement in internships and other unpaid opportunities tied to academic programs. In the dissertation findings of this author, alumni

---

[1] Lesley's first year field courses are discussed in greater detail in Section VI of this chapter.

endowments have advanced service-learning initiatives through the underwriting of service-learning centers, resulting not only in institutionalized service-learning but also in greater levels of collaboration between academic affairs and student affairs (see revised chapter 6).

11. Engage business and community leaders as partners.

As educators we recognize the need to prepare students with the skills and competencies necessary to effectively transition into an increasingly competitive and changing workforce. The importance of industry and community voice to emphasize workplace needs has never been more salient. The relevance of applied learning has never been more critical to prepare students for active and engaged citizenship. AAC&U's Conference on Liberal Education and Effective Practice, which was held at Clark University in March 2009, included not only educators but leaders from corporate and non-profit sectors to identify the importance of integrated learning and public skills. The conference focused on the fundamental question of how well the learning experiences offered in higher education are aligned with the preparation of engaged, effective professionals and, in a broader context, adults who are equipped to contribute to society (Freeland, 2009). Conference participants examined conventional educational practices that appear to be less effective in fostering the application of ideas to authentic settings. Richard Freeland, conference organizer, makes the point that a less than ideal alignment exists between the professed goals of liberal education, the learning experiences that are typically offered, and the concept of intelligence that underscores these programs.

In the view of conference participant George Kuh, experiential education is representative of high impact practices, previously referenced, that can complement conventional classroom pedagogy and "significantly enhance the capacity of undergraduates to translate ideas and values into effective action" (Freeland, 2009, p. 2). Six common elements identify these experiences as high impact (O'Neil, 2010, p. 2):

- Require effort to deepen students' investment in the activity.
- Help students build substantive and meaningful relationships.
- Support students in their engagement across differences and with those who are different from themselves.
- Provide students with rich feedback.
- Help students apply and test their learning in new situations.
- Provide opportunities for students to reflect on the people they are becoming.

Walsh & Cuba (2009) point out that in their experience some modalities such as study abroad fit well within conventional academic structures yet others, such as internships and service-learning, have proven more difficult to institutionalize. By including business and community leaders in conversations about education, internal and external funding targets can be legitimized and made publicly credible. It is important to acknowledge that while we currently are in a tighter economic climate than in previous periods, identifying educational programs that prepare students for their active participation in work force environments can demonstrate greater legitimacy of funding needs and help position experiential education at a higher level in organizational budgets. By engaging business and community leaders with faculty and academic administrators in conversations about workplace needs, experiential modalities can be more clearly located in organizational contexts, made explicit in academic offerings, and tied directly to initiatives that engage students earlier and more deeply in their education.

12. Use a consultant.

Using an educational consultant who is knowledgeable about experiential education *and* about institutionalization issues can provide helpful resources that clarify institutional needs, support development strategies for addressing those needs, and assist in planning next steps to move change initiatives forward. A *caveat*, however, is that bringing experts in from the outside can create the illusion of change while maintaining the status quo (Rubin, 1983). As Rubin points out, it is important to recognize that while consultants or outside experts can make observations and recommendations, it is the institution that must commit to making its own changes. (See section V in this chapter, Principles for Effectively Using a Consultant.)

Another way to seek out expertise is through peer consultants, either by bringing them to your campus or by arranging to go to them. For example, the National Society for Experiential Education (NSEE) was organized to be the national leader in advancing experiential education as a field and a profession (www.nsee.org). The Experiential Education Academy (EEA) was subsequently developed as a training program to support NSEE members and its external constituents. The EEA reflects a key component in NSEE's mission and can be an important resource for campuses for direction in expanding their programs. According to NSEE's website, the EEA was created to support and contribute to the work effectiveness and long-term growth of experiential learning practitioners, regardless of their specific experiential application. Within its operations, the Academy provides a series of workshops facilitated by members who are recognized for their leadership in experiential content areas. Participants who complete the program earn a Certificate of Completion and acquire a base of knowledge and set of competencies for the field of experiential learning through a grounded theory model. The goals of the Academy are to provide practitioner training at all levels for its members, including

- A foundation in standard theory and practice of experiential education;
- Support for practitioners new to experiential education so that their programs will meet the standards of best practices identified by NSEE;
- Facilitation of access to the expertise and knowledge of senior members; and
- Competencies for all members that will lead to the strengthening of experiential education within their institutions (www.nsee.org/eea).

13. Increase your personal and professional effectiveness.

There are two very specific ways to increase the impact and effectiveness of your involvement in the change process: first, by deepening knowledge and the ability to communicate the values and legitimacy of experiential education and, second by expanding each member's grasp of organizational realities in the institution. The way to do this includes broadening your base in the institution by learning more about how the organization operates and how to expand your professional skills and expertise. For example, becoming an academic advisor will put you in touch with student issues and concerns, and provide you with greater understanding of the student decision-making process. Sitting in on policy committee meetings or communicating with and getting to know the staff in the Center for Teaching Excellence or the Office of Institutional Research can provide you with a deeper view of the organization's infrastructure. Looking at enrollment projections and annual fiscal reports can provide you with a holistic view of the organization's financial structure and institutional obligations. Participating actively and collaborating often in committee assignments will help you to learn more about the progress of programs and initiatives. Sharing information and knowledge with colleagues may prove to be useful in their own work. Finding ways to understand your own approach to leadership will help you set examples for others, particularly junior faculty and those new to the institution. And finally, understanding that change involves risk and, as a leader, it is important to learn how to take risks. In the original version, Rubin pointed out that if you have a strong set of beliefs in experiential education, and if you have knowledge about the effective implementation of programs, which is something you can acquire, then it is perfectly acceptable to engage in risky behavior. Rubin's assertion stands today as institutions and practitioners intensify their efforts to strengthen experiential learning within the current educational, political and social environment.

IV.   Assessing Different Strategies

In the original version, four principles for change were suggested and continue to resonate with practitioners who are engaged in program development and institutional change. It is always important to recognize the unique issues within various types of institutional structures, and to consider those differences in advancing change in higher education. One size does not fit all. Those original questions continue to be a good starting point to assess strategies and identify a direction for advancing experiential education. How do you know if a strategy being considered is the best one for the institution? What is correct for one set of problems may not be appropriate for another. A few questions to ask:

1. *Does the strategy fit the culture of the institution?* (Refer to original Chapter 1 for a discussion of institutional values and cultures.)

2. *Does the strategy fit the size of the institution?* For some issues a successful approach in a small institution will be very different from that for a large institution. At large schools the autonomy and strength of the academic departments may dictate a "one at a time" strategy. For example, the presence of graduate programs can present different types of opportunities. Funding and course designations for experiential courses may be more important in a large university than at a small college. Universities are more likely to have precedents for instructional support services that may provide models for centralized support services for experiential education.

3. *Does the strategy fit the problem?* Various problems require specific strategies. For example, strengthening faculty support may require the development of materials to support faculty training. Compensation for faculty engaged in experiential learning may require information about policies at peer institutions. If the issue is the acceptance of experiential education by the administration, face-to-face exposure to a knowledgeable source may be the most useful.

4. *Is the strategy better than the alternative?* The following questions will help to assess proposed strategies:

    a. What is the level of risk involved? Is the institution/members of the organization willing to accept these risks?

    b. What will be the result if the strategy is successful? How great a contribution is this result to the overall effort to strengthen experiential education?

    c. How likely is the strategy to be successful, and does the likelihood of success make it worth the risk?

    d. How much work will this approach involve? For whom? Is this realistic?

    e. How long will it take?

    f. What is the cost in non-personnel resources?

    g. Does the strategy take into account the short-term needs of the institution as well as the long-term needs?

    h. Does the strategy fit the principles of institutional change outlined in this chapter?

For any strategy to be effective the most important challenge is to help faculty and administrators see the benefits of strengthening experiential education across the institution. By understanding how change occurs and developing strategies to implement those small, incremental steps that are necessary to achieving goals, a real contribution can be made to the educational offerings of the institution. The route, as you may expect, will be interesting even if a bit unpredictable.

The following sections present additional ways to think about strengthening experiential education, including the use of an external consultant to help campus leaders develop effective strategies to move programs forward and a case study about collaboration between faculty and student affairs professional staff that has strengthened the first year experience and provided the cornerstone for institutionalizing experiential learning in the institution.

V.   Principles for Effectively Using a Consultant

The original version of *Strengthening Experiential Education in Your Institution* grew out of a FIPSE-NSEE supported consulting corps. The following guidelines for using a consultant grew organically as the consulting proceeded. This framework seems as relevant today as it did in the mid-1980s.

A. *Consultant roles.*

1. *As co-strategist*: to analyze the goals, approaches, obstacles and tasks identified with experiential education to strengthen the strategy for more fully integrating experiential education into the ongoing curriculum, administrative structures, budget, and reward systems for faculty.

2. *As information gatherer*: to provide a unique outside perspective to identify hidden strengths and weaknesses in existing programs.

3. *As source of credibility*: to share information about successful programs at other institutions and about the validity of this educational approach; to verify the credibility of institutional goals. It is essential that the reasons experiential education fit the mission of the institution be articulated clearly and that the consultant helps to do this.

4. *As evaluator*: to assist in the design of evaluation (or assessment) strategies and provide perspectives of experiential education program strengths and weaknesses.

5. *As professional support*: to provide ideas and perspectives in relation to institutional concerns and needs; to provide a forum for ideas relative to professional growth including literature, workshops and professional development activities.

6. *As speaker or trainer*: to provide training when and if appropriate.

7. *As catalyst*: to convene individual/groups within the organization to provide the stimulus for information and idea gathering that will help to conceptualize a project or change in policy.

B. Inappropriate expectations for consultants.

Consultants should *not* be used to influence the administration to get the resources and support that members of the organization should be able to procure on their own. The consultant should *not* be expected to do the work of the organization's members to advance or transform experiential education programs or to ratify current initiatives. Consultants who are engaged to provide support in the strengthening of experiential education initiatives also should *not* be expected to settle internal disputes between departments or to design or reshape existing programs. The consultant should be utilized to initiate a dialogue that will motivate cross-departmental collaboration to support the goals of experiential education programs in the institution.

C. Preparing for the consultant's visit.

Specific materials should be provided to the consultant one month prior to the first visit. These include the institution's catalog, an organizational chart of the school or university, copies of all written materials related to experiential education including policies and procedures, information about past, current and proposed sites, application and evaluation forms, learning contracts, etc. Samples of representative forms and documentation should be provided from both weak and strong students, faculty and site supervisors. Copies of evaluations whether formal or informal, proposals for internal and external funding, program staff resumes/CVs, and identifying information about the faculty that oversee or advise current experiential programs are important for inclusion in consultant materials. Two weeks prior to the visit most, if not all, of the following should be discussed and clarified with the consultant to ensure the success of the campus visit:

1. Identify expectations and goals by priority.

2. Provide a complete personal analysis of the institution's situation to the consultant that may not be able to be put in writing.

3. Determine the consultant's major functions.

4. Organize the schedule and format of the visit to ensure that the consultant's time is most effectively used, including public meetings and forums and those smaller gatherings that include only key individuals. Clarify with whom the consultant will be meeting, the names and positions of each person, and their respective formal and informal roles. Determine the purpose of each meeting so that the consultant knows how to prepare and what materials to bring. Make sure that each individual and group who will have contact with the consultant are consulted in advance to determine what it is that those involved in experiential education want to discuss and learn.

5. Should there be formal presentations? If so, what are the expectations with respect to purpose, audience and its size, length, format, and anticipated questions?

6. What strategies have been tried, what has worked, what has not been successful? What is your assessment as to "why"?

7. What are the personal interests in the institution of those coordinating the consultant visit and how does this work fit into their career paths?

8. If the consultation is about a particular draft policy or materials, provide the consultant with a copy at least one week in advance of the visit.

Although it is important to leave time for relaxed discussions on the campus, be sure and create a tight schedule that will keep the consultant busy. Consider small group discussions with selected faculty and administrators rather than single meetings. The stimulus of a group can increase energy and motivation, the range of ideas, and the likelihood of effective follow-up action. However, as these events are organized they should not be used as a substitute for each person's specific responsibilities for follow-through. It is important that arrangements be made for students to meet with the consultant, especially those who have previously participated in an experiential program. Students who are included should represent different types of experiences and different levels of success. Other concerns to be addressed with the consultant should be identified in advance to maximize the outcomes of the visit.

VI.   The Road to Institutionalization: A Case Study

In the concluding section of this chapter, the experience of an undergraduate college provides an example of internal collaboration to advance experiential education. Structured in three parts, the first provides a context for collaboration between academic affairs and student affairs. The second describes what currently exists that illustrates important building blocks for successfully institutionalizing an experiential program. The final part highlights how the institutionalization of this program portrays many of the principles identified in this chapter and in this edition overall.

A. *Contextualizing collaboration between faculty and student affairs professional staff.*

Strengthened campus relationships that motivate and support sustained change in higher education identify with collaboration between faculty and professional staff in the division of student affairs. According to Smith (2005), collaboration between the two groups that spend the most time with students is critical to institutional effectiveness and the quality of student experiences. However, Kezar (2006) points out that "...in general, institutions are not structured to support collaborative approaches to learning, research, and organizational functioning" (p, 805). Numerous differences characterize the respective work environments of faculty and student affairs staff, including their education and career trajectories, conditions of employment, and expertise in their specific fields. Departmental silos and hierarchical administrative structures unique to higher education emphasize those distinctions creating, in Magolda's (2005) view, multilayered subcultures and historical contexts in each division. Whether it is faculty or student affairs professional staff, each constituency understands student development from the lens of their educational preparation and unique interactions with students. Those differences, while an asset and an advantage to the organization, also may contribute to conditions that prevent collaboration and the positive outcomes that can result from such relationships.

The literature is replete with examples of partnering between faculty and professional staff in student affairs that yield enormous benefits to institutions. Engstrom (2003) defines collaboration as a form of partnership that can build institutional capacity and contribute to transformational learning. The synergies that develop during such partnering draw on individual as well as interdependent work across departments (Bourassa & Kruger, 2002; Engstrom, 2003; Jacoby, 2003; Kezar, 2002), support the institutionalization of new pedagogical practices such as service-learning (Dreher, 2008), and provide opportunities to draw faculty and professional staff into discourse to enhance the academic and social climate of institutions. Students have an important role in this process, often emerging as catalysts for collaboration. Students in their multiple roles as learners, campus leaders and participants in local and global communities are in unique positions to provide feedback about the academic process and how such collaborations impact their campus experience.

Organizational leaders and academic administrators are in critical positions to motivate faculty engagement in collaborative ventures with student affairs. Their support can result in new pedagogical practices such as team teaching and interdisciplinary approaches to curriculum development. Their support also can influence new directions in residence hall programs, institutionalized service-learning, and strengthened affiliations with community organizations to expand sites for internships and field research. Collaborations of this nature can contribute in holistic ways to the development of structured modalities in which experiential learning can take place. In the institutional example that follows, cross-divisional cooperation has been a key contributor for institutionalizing experiential learning on the campus. The highlighted *first year field courses* have emerged to serve two purposes: an essential component of the freshman academic experience and a benchmark course for experiential learning in the majors.

B. Embracing experiential learning in the first year.

Lesley University, a private non-profit institution in Cambridge, Massachusetts, was established in 1909. Since its founding, experiential learning has been a core value in Lesley's educational mission:

"From its beginnings, the college has prided itself on its ability to offer high quality experientially-based education relevant to the needs of students and society...All programs continue to be based on Lesley College's long tradition of creative instruction, connections between the liberal arts and professional preparation, integration of academic and field-based learning, and commitment to excellence." [2]

Lesley's focus in its undergraduate curriculum is in both liberal arts[3] and professional majors[4], with each program of study intersecting through internships and other structured forms of out-of-classroom learning (www.lesley.edu). *Field-based education* defines an important element of the curriculum, with required, credit-bearing internships and student teaching foremost in its programs. Service-learning and study abroad have more recently taken key positions in the array of structured experiential models offered in the University. The addition of these modes of learning has expanded opportunities for students and deepened the learning outcomes of the curriculum. Philosophically and practically, experiential education at Lesley recognizes the high impact nature of these experiences in student learning identified by Kuh (2008), the purpose each type of experience serves in the majors, and the value added to the campus experience through the intersection of experiential learning in both academic and co-curricular contexts.

Beginning in the freshman year, students are introduced to work environments and professions through *first year field courses*. These courses are core requirements in the majors[5] and should not be confused with *transition to college seminars* that are designed to support students' adjustment to college. The first year field courses, which were conceived as an academic component of the freshman experience, are designed by faculty, subject to review of the undergraduate curriculum committee, carry credit, and focus the content on students' explorations of the majors, the world of work and first steps in career planning. According to the Associate Dean, these courses are positioned in the context of a four year degree that embeds experiential learning throughout a student's educational career. "All first year students take an introduction to field experience course in the spring semester. The course is offered in a variety of disciplines and introduces students to experiential learning at Lesley. With this introduction, students are well-prepared to embark on subsequent internships that are required to fulfill their programs of study."

---

[2] Lesley College Academic Catalog, 2011, p, 6.
[3] Art History, Biology, Child Studies, Creative Writing. English (Drama and Literature tracks), Environmental Science, Environmental Studies, Global Studies, History (American and European Studies tracks), History and Literature, Holistic Psychology, Mathematics, Political Science, Psychology and Sociology and Social Change.
[4] Art Therapy, Business Management, Communication, Counseling, Education, Expressive Arts Therapy, and Human Services.
[5] Courses include Foundations and Systems in the Helping Professions; Teaching, Learning and Social Responsibility; Introduction to the Business Experience; Introduction to Communication; Field Studies in the Humanities; and Global Issues and Challenges. Patterns in Nature is an environmentally-focused field course conducted in a neighborhood near the campus.

The faculty who teach the first year field courses work collaboratively with professional staff in the Career Resource Center (CRC) and the academic staff in the Internship and Field Placement Offices[6]. The partnering of faculty with professional staff supports students in their initial explorations of the majors, introduces students to various career paths, and provides students with increased knowledge about themselves as they embark on a journey of inquiry, experience and reflection. This collaboration enables access to resources and expertise, including speakers who are writers, managers, teachers and educational administrators, media specialists and licensed mental health professionals, to name a few examples. Coordinated field trips to community and business organizations and structured workshops conducted by faculty and career professionals in the CRC engage students in examining their values, interests and skills and are understood by faculty and students as essential components of the freshman experience. Students are introduced to professional behavior and ethical conduct in work environments. They are exposed to the roles and responsibilities associated with functional operations in organizations and the necessary skills to work in those settings. Each course emphasizes current literature, group project skills, and reflection activities to encourage deep thinking about social and organizational issues that are introduced in the course. One student who is interested in working in a community agency that provides services to low income families reflected on her experience, "…I don't know much about politics nor do I care – but, well, maybe I need to care, and maybe I need to learn more because of the political influences on the [social services] system."

Moving from the classroom to field assignments and back to the classroom, the first year field courses represent the entry point that formalizes experiential learning in the college. An associate professor of human services has been deeply involved in the development and assessment of the first year field course model and, in particular, those courses that serve the majors in the helping professions. In her view, "…the experiences students have through the structure of the course help them to connect theory with practice [at least on an elementary level, given their freshman status], interact in an introductory way with professionals in social services agencies and engage in the big questions raised in the course." From her perspective, students gain the ability to make informed decisions about which field to pursue. Since the end of freshman year is generally the time when students declare their major at Lesley, students reach that point with particular knowledge about their educational options in the college. For instance, a student who initially thought about preparing to be an art therapist may decide after taking the first year field course that social work or psychology with tracks to graduate school are a better fit academically and with emerging career interests.

From the perspective of this author, who currently holds the position of Director of Academic Advising at Lesley, *the first year field course* conceptually and practically helps students to gain perspective not only about their passions, skills and interests but also about how their personal values influence their academic, co-curricular and career decisions. Students are encouraged to think about how those characteristics fit together to support their acquisition of the theoretical and applied skills associated with the major, and that are needed to serve them in their upper level courses, including internships and senior capstones. I point to the student who enters the college to prepare to be an elementary teacher and decides after taking the education field course, Teaching, Learning and Social Responsibility, which includes a placement in a local

---

[6] The Field Placement Office coordinates placements for students majoring in Education.

public school, that working full time in an elementary classroom is no longer their educational goal. For this student a more optimal choice working with children may be to major in child studies and minor in education. Both programs integrate complementary internships in child-centered environments. A program of study structured this way would prepare this student for professional work in any number of organizations that focus on child advocacy, including day care centers, community arts initiatives, after school tutoring programs, and pediatric hospital environments. It is important to note the connection to the CRC and stress that this relationship is forged early in the college experience through workshops embedded in the course and one-on-one career counseling. This connection is especially helpful to those students, such as the example previously cited, who are shifting their professional direction, motivating more frequent use of the college's career counselors to help students identify a new or modified career path. Institutionally, the CRC connection emphasizes collaboration across divisions and the importance of cross-sector relationships to enhance and support students' academic experience and their early career decisions.

Once students move beyond freshman year they embark on more independent work with the Internship and Field Placement Offices to identify appropriate sites for internships. Throughout this period, the CRC staff remain active in their work with students, promoting ongoing use of career services and introducing students to alumni through Lesley's Career Connection. Continuing communications on a broader level among the CRC, the academic divisions, and the Internship/Field Placement Offices provide important opportunities for each department to share information about change in the workplace and demands in the job market.

C. Building bridges to advance experiential learning in the long term.

Since its founding, Lesley University has grown in size and in the depth and breadth of its curriculum. This growth has resulted in a more structurally complex organization, challenged the intersection of vertical and horizontal reporting lines, and motivated collaborative relationships between members of the organization. Faculty and student affairs professional staff have been responsive to each other by using the collegial nature of their work, which focuses on student success, to bridge the silo structures often associated with higher education organizations. However, collaboration did not come easily or without intentional efforts of each constituency to integrate creative methods for working together.

Experiential learning historically has been a driving force in Lesley's undergraduate programs. In Chapter 2 of the original version of this publication, John Duley, Professor Emeritus at Michigan State University and then an NSIEE Peer Consultant, indicated that "Courses or programs are included because faculty believe certain knowledge and skills are necessary. They will be convinced to use experiential education if they think it is the most effective and efficient way to learn that knowledge and those skills." From the college's early beginnings, Lesley's faculty have done just this, creating a culture that embraces experience as a core value and identifying the skills, knowledge and practice believed to best prepare students for their success in both their classroom endeavors and in the world of work. The faculty have sought senior level support to move experiential learning forward both in the academic arena as well as in co-curricular initiatives. Internally, this approach has bolstered student and faculty engagement in experiential approaches to learning and strengthened Lesley's academic programs. The spectrum of experiential modalities has expanded, beginning with student teaching in initial licensure programs and expanding to the internships, study abroad, service-learning and field research options now available in all majors.

In the co-curricular environment, the Community Service and Student Activities offices promote experiential activities that connect Lesley's students with the people and organizations in local communities. The Student Activities Office supports the creation of clubs and organizations that range from athletic and recreational groups, performing arts clubs and academically themed initiatives such as the Management Student Organization and the Lesley Public Post (on-line newspaper) to social awareness groups such as Amnesty International, the Environmental Club and Cultivating Healthy Options and Wellness. Examples of initiatives sponsored by the Community Service Office include Alternative Spring Break, REAL Retreat, America Reads, Students for Social Justice and Lesley Delivers, a food delivery program for the homeless in Cambridge. Structured reflection is integrated into each of these experiences for the very reasons it is embedded into academic programs, to emphasize the learning that evolves from the experience and how students change during the process. In a pilot study conducted in 2007/2008 and supported by a Davis Grant, it was found that students were addressing key learning goals in many of these activities, particularly in the areas of social responsibility and leadership (Lesley College Internal Document, 2012). Given the emphasis on experiential learning in co-curricular activities, the college is discussing the development of a co-curricular transcript to document the significance of experiential learning beyond traditional academic requirements. The transcript would be presented to students upon graduation as an accompanying document to the academic transcript.

In a discussion about collaboration between academic affairs and student affairs to advance experiential education, it is important to recognize the teaching and training proficiencies of student affairs professional staff in their respective work with students. Yet Magolda (2005) points out that all too often student affairs professionals are undervalued as experts in their fields. While professional staff do engage with students in the traditionally designated areas of student life (residential life, student activities, new student orientation, community service, academic support services) that engagement is on a different level from that of the faculty. Acknowledged differences between the academic divisions and student affairs highlight the importance of the co-curricular within the broader scope of students' campus experience. Professional staff bring the strength of their expertise in student development not only as they engage with students in their particular roles but also in their interactions with faculty. Professional staff create powerful programs for students as evidenced, for example, by those sponsored by the Community Service Office and cited above, that often include faculty as workshop leaders in residence programs or as facilitators in student leadership training. Lesley's faculty acknowledge that experiences outside the classroom impact student learning in their classes, and bear witness to the ways that students synthesize academic inquiry with their co-curricular commitments.

Looking back on *Strategies for Organizational Change* highlighted in this chapter, the reader can see that Lesley has engaged in many approaches to strengthen and institutionalize experiential education on its campus. For example, in the decades since its founding, Lesley has approached program change in incremental steps, using previous successes as models for future progress and looking beyond institutional boundaries for new directions. Lesley has looked to peer institutions for successful programs to emulate and has used research, organizational consultants and advances in experiential learning identified by NSEE and Campus Compact to bolster new directions for academic programs. National and regional conferences have further provided faculty and professional staff with access to new ideas being explored in higher education. Many of these ideas are referred to in AAC&U's LEAP Initiative. Professional meetings that offer new perspectives to advance experiential learning have helped Lesley's faculty and professional staff gain access to networks of their peers who are engaged in similar work. Clear goals and purposes for change, bottom up support from faculty and professional staff, top level support from senior leaders and the administration, and cross-campus collaborations have proven essential for creating not only the conceptual motivation but also the material resources to institutionalize the internship and education field placement offices. The pilot approach also has demonstrated its importance as a successful tool, particularly to provide a testing ground for integrating experiential learning into the liberal arts. Study abroad, which languished for several years, grew dramatically with funding from a Ford Foundation seed grant. The Study Abroad Office now supports a growing number of students in their preparation for semesters abroad and assists faculty in the development of travel study courses. For some students, study abroad includes credit-bearing internships for their majors and opportunities to engage in international service-learning.

While growing more slowly, service-learning has advanced in certain academic departments with support from the Community Service office. A successful collaboration between an Assistant Professor of Sociology and the Associate Dean for Career and Community Service began with the idea for a course that would explore the emerging discipline of girl studies and the integration of a service-learning component. The course that emerged, *Girlhood, Identity and Girl Culture*, "…focuses on the social and cultural construction of girlhood and how social categories of race, class, ethnicity, education and the media shape girls' lives in contemporary US society. Theoretical understandings of girlhood and girl culture are applied in a seven-week service-learning project for middle school girls in Cambridge."[7] The course, which is now in its third year, is very popular among students who value the collaborative structure of the course and its intellectual and service connections to the local community. However, while recognizing the importance of the course in the curriculum, perhaps the most important outcome institutionally, at least in this author's view, is the demonstrated collaboration between a student affairs administrator and a faculty member in the college with results that span traditional boundaries between divisions, a new platform for connected work between professional staff and faculty, and demonstrated synergy that supports the academic mission of the University.

It is worth noting that peer support and student/alumni voices have been and continue to be important resources to advance experiential learning in the college. The CRC has been particularly effective in engaging alumni with academic programs through the Lesley Career Connection. The CRC is a unit that reports to the Dean of Students and, in its positioning in the organization, provides an important voice to the professional staff who are located in the Division of Student Affairs. Many faculty retain mentoring relationships with alumni from their academic programs, which creates possibilities for on-campus seminars, a speaker's bureau, and events that are tied to new developments in professional arenas such as public education, mental health counseling, and organizational leadership across the diversity of institutional types.

---

[7] Lesley College academic catalog, 2011, p. 249.

Communication and shared information have been key factors to facilitate collaboration. The Experiential Learning Task Force was formed two years ago to focus on consistency of learning goals and outcomes across experiential modalities. The task force was charged with creating a structure for assessing student learning at each level of the four years, giving special attention to mapping goals, assessing sequential development and examining depth of learning. Task force membership[8] comprises representation from academic affairs and student affairs to draw on the expertise of members' various roles and the experiential initiatives each one oversees. The task force has adopted guidelines identified by NSEE, emphasizing that experiential education "…is a triad partnership between students, the college and community partners, with responsibilities of each clearly articulated in pre-defined learning objectives. Facilitated and guided practice, reflection and evaluation are all essential components of this transformative method of learning" (Lesley College Internal Document, 2011). The direction for experiential education proposed by the task force is aligned with that of the general education committee and is consistent with an academically integrated approach for assessment that is focused in Lesley's five learning goals. [9]

- Fundamental base of knowledge
- Critical reasoning
- Social responsibility
- Multiple perspectives
- Lifelong learning

The learning goals provide the standard for developing content in other areas of the curriculum and in shaping the structure for assessing learning outcomes. Beginning with the first year field course and extending to internships, service-learning and other experiential modalities, each stands alone yet is connected to the others through the learning goals that were ratified by the undergraduate faculty.

Lesley students, faculty and student affairs professional staff continue to engage with each other to hone a collaborative campus environment. Softened boundaries between divisions have produced a more open process for faculty and professional staff to convene with each other. Students are invited into the process to inform the academic experience and its intersection with campus life. The results are enriched and diverse experiential learning opportunities for students, and evolving relationships between divisions that embody shared goals, the professional rewards that come with student academic success, and the validation of one's work in that process. Lesley's progress in experiential education resonates with the values espoused in AAC&U's LEAP Initiative and its focus on essential learning outcomes, including high impact educational practices to help students achieve those outcomes, authentic assessments that probe students' application to complex problems and real-world challenges, and excellence in teaching to ensure the benefits of an engaged and practical liberal education (AAC&U, 2008). In its century long history, Lesley's practice in teaching and learning has deeply embedded experiential education into its culture, making it available to students as early as the first year; inclusively, to engage all

---

[8] Experiential Education Task Force membership includes the Associate Dean (chair); Division Director of STEM Programs; Directors of the Internship, Field Placement, Study Abroad and Community Service Offices; Director of the Academic Advising Center; the Associate Dean and Director of Career and Community Service; and the Director of Institutional Research and Assessment.
[9] Lesley College Academic Catalog, 2011, p. 40.

majors over the four years; and authentically, through department structures, formal assessment and coordinated reflection on experience in both academic and co-curricular environments. A common language that resonates in the organization permits *shared meaning* among colleagues and contributes to a fruitful alliance that has moved experiential education beyond a group of individual courses to an institutionalized component of the undergraduate experience.

Conclusion

This revised edition of *Strengthening Experiential Education within your Institution* builds on the first version to provide strategies and new approaches for communicating the benefits of experiential learning to a wide constituency in higher education. The strategies identified in this chapter focus on the change process and build on new realities about change that have been identified in the organizational literature. Ewell (1997) frames such change as 'organizing for learning' and posits that change requires a fundamental shift of perspective that must be systemic, that all members of the organization must rethink *what* they do and *how* they do it.

Organizational change takes many forms and involves complex institutional factors that are particular to higher education. Change can be large and all consuming, leading campuses in broadened institutional directions. Change also can be shaped by small, incremental steps that challenge daily practices while creating the attitudes and structures necessary to support new initiatives at program, department and school levels. Whatever its dimensions, the change process must support those who lead, provide venues for open dialog that invite engagement from across the organization, understand the implications of change at each level of the reporting hierarchy, and respond to the needs of its members as they adjust to uncertainty and the emergence of new normative conditions. For change to be effective, the process must be organic, innovative and cohesive, and clearly connected to institutional mission and the values and beliefs that are central to the social structures and educational context of the campus.

Throughout this revised edition the emphasis has been on relearning roles and assuming new responsibilities, not only in individual campus environments but also holistically across the landscape of higher education. The Lesley case illustrates how changing perspectives of traditional roles can move institutions beyond the narrow boundaries created by departmental structures to create models for cross-sector collaboration. The case further emphasizes how the uniqueness of an institution can frame a model for change that is effective and sustainable over the long term. The traditions and ideals central to Lesley's mission and historic practice reflect many of the values and goals identified in AAC&U's LEAP Initiative, keeping it abreast of change in the wider environment. Institutionally, Lesley has expanded its ability to blend the value domains of academic affairs and student affairs, the two divisions in the organization that are most connected to students.

Consistent leadership, systematic methods to assess outcomes and recognized opportunities are necessary for experiential education to gain new ground and take center stage. Experiential education is a model that motivates new opportunities to achieve productive change as campuses seek ways to prepare students for their responsibilities and evolving roles in a changing world. As we progress further into the 21st century, campus leaderships must continually revisit the precepts that bind experiential pedagogy to organizational mission and

237

earnestly and with intention promote the range of possibilities that experiential applications can provide for future generations of learners in the global community.

References

AAC&U (2008). Liberal Education and America's Promise (LEAP). Association of American Colleges and Universities, Washington, DC: Retrieved April 25, 2011, from http://www.aacu.org/leap/vision.cfm.

Abes, E., Jackson, G., & Jones, S. (2002). Factors that motivate and deter faculty use of service-learning. *Michigan Journal of Community Service Learning, 9*(1), 5-17.

Bailey, F. G., (1977). *Morality and expediency.* Oxford, England: Blackwell Publishers.

Becher, T., (1984, November). Principles and politics: An interpretive framework for university management. *International Journal of Institutional Management in Higher Education. 8*(3), 198.

Bolman, L., and Deal, T. (1997). *Reframing organizations.* 2nd Ed. San Francisco: Jossey Bass.

Bourassa, D., & Kruger, K. (2002, Winter). The national dialogue on academic and student affairs collaboration. In A. Kezar, D. Hirsch & C. Burack (Eds.), *New directions for higher education: Vol. 116. Understanding the role of academic and student affairs collaboration in creating a successful learning environment* (pp. 9-17). San Francisco: Jossey-Bass.

Cameron, K.S., (1984, March/April). Organizational adaptation and higher education. *Journal of Higher Education, 55* (2)

Cornford, F. M., (1953). *Microcosmographia academia: Being a guide for the young academic politician* (5th Ed.). Cambridge, England: Bowers and Bowers

Colbeck, C. (2002, March). Assessing institutionalization of curricular and pedagogical reforms. *Research in Higher Education, 43*(4), 397-421.

Curry, B. (1992). *Institutionalizing enduring innovations: Achieving continuity of change in higher education.* Washington, DC: The George Washington University.

Dreher, J. A., (2008). Collaboration to institutionalize service-learning in higher education organizations: The relationship between the structures of academic and student affairs. Unpublished dissertation, May 2008: University of Massachusetts Boston.

Ewell, P. (1997). Organizing for learning: A new imperative. *AAHE Bulletin* (December), pp.1-6.

Engstrom, C. M. (2003). Developing collaborative student affairs-academic affairs partnerships for service-learning. In B. Jacoby & Associates (Ed.), *Building partnerships for service-learning.* (pp. 65-84). San Francisco: Jossey Bass.

Evans, R. I., (1968). *Resistance to innovation in higher education.* (pp. 16-17). San Francisco: Jossey Bass.

Eyler, J., (Fall 2009). The power of experiential education. *Liberal Education, 24-31.*

Freeland, R., (2010). The Clark/AAC&U Conference on Liberal Education and Effective Practice. *Liberal Education. Vol. 95*(4). Association of American Colleges and Universities. Retrieved 4/28/2011, from http://www.aacu.org/liberaleducation.

Hefferlin, J. B. L., (1969). *Dynamics of academic reform.* San Francisco: Jossey Bass.

Hudson, W., & Trudeau, R. (1995, Fall). An essay for the institutionalization of service-learning: The genesis of the Feinstein Institute for Public Service. *Michigan Journal of Community Service Learning, 1,* 150-158.

Jacoby, B. (1999). Partnership for service-learning. In J. Schuh & E. Whitt (Eds.), *New directions for student services: Vol. 87. Creating successful partnerships between academic and student affairs* (pp. 19-36). San Francisco: Jossey-Bass.

Jacoby, B. (2003). *Building partnerships for service-learning.* San Francisco: Jossey-Bass.

Jeandron, C., & Robinson, G. (2010). Creating a climate for service learning success. Washington, DC: American Association of Community Colleges. Retrieved May 15, 2011, from http://www.aacc/servicelearning/htm.

Kanter, R. (1983). *The changemasters: Innovations for productivity in the American corporation.* New York: Simon & Schuster.

Kezar, A. (2002, Winter). Organizational models and facilitators of change: Providing a framework for student and academic affairs collaboration. In A. Kezar, D. Hirsch & C. Burack (Eds.), *New directions for higher education: Vol. 116. Understanding the role of academic and student affairs collaboration in creating a successful learning environment* (pp. 63-74). San Francisco: Jossey-Bass.

Kezar, A. (2006 September/October). Redesigning for collaboration in learning initiatives: An examination of four highly collaborative campuses. *The Journal of Higher Education. Vol.77* (5), 804-838. The Ohio State University.

Kuh, G. D. (2008). High-impact educational practices. *Liberal Education and America's Promise (LEAP).* Washington, DC: Association of American Colleges and Universities.

Little, T. C., (1983). *Making sponsored experiential learning standard practice.* New Directions. Jossey-Bass.

Magolda, P. (2005, January/February). Proceed with caution: Uncommon wisdom about academic and student affairs partnerships. *About Campus,* 16-21.

Mecca, T. V. (2004, September 25). Basic concepts of organizational change for administrative leaders. Adaptation from papers presented at the Conference of the South Carolina Technical Education Association, 1999 and the NSF Principle Investigators Annual Conference, 2003. Retrieved June 13, 2011, from http://www.pcrest.com/pc/facdev/2010/FI_reading.htm.

Morgan, G. (1997). *Images of Organizations*. Thousand Oaks: Sage Publications.

National Society for Experiential Education, http://www.nsee.org.

O'Neill, N. (2010). Internships as a high-impact practice: Some reflections on quality. *Peer Review, Vol 12(4).* Washington, DC: Association of American Colleges and Universities. Retrieved January 3, 2011 from http://www.aacu.org/peerreview/pr-fa10/pr-fa10_oneill.cfm.

Rogers, E. M., (1962/1995). *Diffusion of innovation* (4th Ed.). New York: Free Press.

Rubin, S. (1983). Overcoming obstacles to institutionalization of experiential learning programs. In T. C. Little (Ed.), *Making sponsored experiential learning standard practice.* (p. 45). San Francisco: Jossey Bass.

Rudolph, F., (1962/1990). *The American college and university.* (p. 492). New York: Random House.

Scharmer, C. Otto. (2008). *Theory U: Leading from the future as it emerges.* Introduction, 1-20. San Francisco: Berrett-Koehler Publishers. Retrieved April 27, 2011, from http://www.bkconnection.com/static/Theory_U_Excerpt.pdf.

Schein, E. (1992). *Organizational culture and leadership* (2nd Ed.). San Francisco: Jossey-Bass.

Schmeide, A. (1998, Fall). Positioning and institutionalizing experiential education in higher education. *Summary report of NSEE member survey.* (pp. 20-26). Raleigh, NC: National Association for Experiential Education.

Senge, P. M., Scharmer, C. Otto, Jaworski, J., & Flowers, B. S. (2005). *Presence: An exploration of profound change in people, organizations and society.* New York: Doubleday.

Schwartzman, R. (2007). Service-learning pathologies and prognoses. Paper presented at the National Communication Association convention, November 2007, Chicago, IL. Retrieved May 2, 2010 from http://www.eric.ed.gov/ERICdocs/data/ericdocs2sq /content_storage.../83.pdf.

Smith, K. (2005). From coexistence to collaboration: A call for partnership between academic and student affairs. *Journal of Cognitive Affective Learning, Vol. 2*(1), 16-20. Retrieved May 25, 2010 from http://jcal.emory.edu/viewarticle.php?id=52&layout=html.

Sykes, W., (1985). Some principles of personal and organizational change. *NTL Connections,* NTL Institute, Arlington, Virginia.

Walsh, D. C., & Cuba, L., (2009, Fall). Liberal arts education and the capacity for effective practice: What's holding us back? *Liberal Education, 32–37.*

Additional Recommended Resources

Bensimon, E. M., & Neumann, A. (1993). *Redesigning Collegiate Leadership: Teams and teamwork in higher education.* Baltimore: The Johns Hopkins University Press.

Bringle, R. & Hatcher, J. (2009, Fall). Innovative practices in service-learning and curricular engagement. In L. Sandmann, C. Thornton, & A. Jaeger (Eds.). *New directions for higher education: No. 147. Institutionalizing community engagement in higher education: The first wave of Carnegie classified institutions* (pp. 37-45). Berkeley: Wiley Periodicals, Inc.

Cantor, J. (1995). *Experiential learning in higher education: Linking classroom and Community.* Washington, DC: The George Washington University.

Eyler, J. (2001). Creating your reflection map. In M. Canada and B. Speck (Eds.), *New directions for higher education. No. 114 (Summer 2001). Developing and implementing service-learning programs* (pp. 35-43). San Francisco: Jossey-Bass.

Eyler, J., & Giles, D. E. (1997). The importance of program quality in service-learning: In A. Waterman (Ed.) *Service-learning Applications from the Research.* (pp. 57 – 76). New Jersey: Lawrence Erlbaum Assoc., Inc.

Furco, A. (2002). Institutionalizing service-learning in higher education. *Journal of Public Affairs, VI* (Supplemental Issue I: Civic Engagement and Higher Education), 39-67.

Gross, E., & Grambsch, P. V., (1968). *University goals and academic power.* Chapter 2. American Council on Education, Washington, D.C.

Halliburton, D. (1997). John Dewey: A voice that still speaks to us. *Change, 29*(1), 24-30.

Havelock, R. G., (1973). *The agent's guide to innovation in education.* Englewood Cliffs, NJ: Educational Technology Publications.

Higgins, P. (2009). Into the big wide world: Sustainable experiential education. *Journal of Experiential Education, 32*(1), 44-60.

Hirsch, D., & Burack, C. (2002, Winter). Finding points of contact for collaborative work. In A. Kezar, D. Hirsch, & C. Burack (Eds.), *New directions for higher education: Vol. 116. Understanding the role of academic and student affairs collaboration in creating a successful learning environment,* (pp. 53-62). San Francisco: Jossey-Bass.

Kuh, G. D., & Hinkle, S. E. (2002). Enhancing student learning through collaboration between academic affairs and student affairs. In R. M. Diamond (Ed.), *Field guide to academic leadership,* (pp. 311-327). San Francisco: Jossey-Bass.

Little, T. C., (1980). Changing Educational Policy, Unpublished paper.

Prentice, M., & Robinson, G. (2010). *Improving student learning outcomes with service learning.* Washington, DC: American Association of Community Colleges.

Serow, R., Calleson, D., Parker, L., & Morgan, L. (1996). Institutional support for service-learning. *Journal of Research and Development, 20*(4), 220-226.

Stebleton, M. J., & Schmidt, L. (2010). Building bridges: Community college practitioners as retention leaders. *Journal of Student Affairs Research and Practice, 47*(1), 78 - 98.

Sweitzer, H., & King, M. (2000, December). Keys to service-learning personal growth and empowerment in internships. *Quarterly Newsletter for the National Organization for Human Service Education, 21*(4), 1-5.

Sweitzer, H., & King, M. (2009). *The successful internship* (3rd Ed.). Belmont, CA: Brooks/Cole

Watson, G. B., & Glaser, E. M., (1965, November). What we have learned about planning for change. *Management Review,* 44-46.

Author

JOANNE A. DREHER, Ed.D. is an Assistant Professor and the Founding Director of the Undergraduate Academic Advising Center at Lesley University, Cambridge, Massachusetts. Joanne has taught for 23 years in the areas of organizational behavior, women's leadership, and experiential education. She organizes peer mentoring initiatives for undergraduate students, and has facilitated mentoring workshops in organizational settings. In her role as Director of Undergraduate Advising, Joanne coordinates both the freshman Transition Seminar and collaborative initiatives between faculty and the Division of Student Affairs to integrate academic inquiry into new student Orientation. She has presented at national and regional conferences including NACADA, the National Academic Advising Association *(Integrated engagement: Faculty do matter),* ASHE, the Association for the Study of Higher Education *(Collaboration to institutionalize service-learning in higher education: The influence of organizational structure),* and New England Regional Campus Compact *(Bridging generations to build campus-community partnerships; Demonstrating the public value of higher education: New research in service-learning).* Joanne Dreher earned a BA in Economics at Framingham State University and a Master of Science in Management at Lesley University. She earned a Doctorate in Education at the University of Massachusetts-Boston under the direction of Dwight E. Giles, Jr. In her dissertation, *Collaboration to Institutionalize Service-learning in Higher Education Organizations: The Relationship between the Structures of Academic and Student Affairs,* Joanne identified six themes that provided a framework for cross-campus comparison to determine the role of collaboration between divisions to institutionalize service-learning pedagogy. Dr. Dreher is the 2009 recipient of the Dissertation of the Year award from the National Society for Experiential Education. She is a member of the Publications Committee of NSEE. Joanne's research interests are focused in experiential education methodology, and in areas related to collaboration between faculty and Student Affairs to create campus structures that advance undergraduate teaching and learning, improve retention, and provide cross-campus fertilization for new academic and co-curricular initiatives. Joanne can be reached at jdreher@lesley.edu.

Chapter 8

EVALUATING AND ASSESSING EXPERIENTIAL LEARNING

Robert Shumer
University of Minnesota

Abstract

Much has occurred in the evaluation field since the original publication of Strengthening Experiential Education within Your Institution (1986). Evaluation has become a field of study, with the American Evaluation Association, the International Association for Research on Service-Learning and Community Engagement, Campus Compact, and NSEE leading the charge. Trends in evaluation of experiential learning have become more participatory and more focused on measuring learning and impact on individuals, institutions, and communities. More tools and frameworks exist for including evaluation and assessment as an integral part of the process of experiential learning. While many things have changed, we have come full circle and moved back to some of the original thinking of the 1980s.

Outline
An Historic Retrospective: A Review of Past Efforts
Moving into the Present and New Collaborators
Evaluation and Assessment in Higher Education
So, What Do We Evaluate?

Introduction

Much has occurred in the evaluation field since the original publication of *Strengthening Experiential Education within Your Institution (1986)*. Evaluation has come into its own as a field of study, with the emergence of the American Evaluation Association and the International Association for Research on Service-Learning and Community Engagement as two of the most productive organizations in the topical area. In addition, much work has been conducted by Campus Compact and the American Association of Colleges and Universities on subjects related to assessment and evaluation. The American Association of Community Colleges has also produced excellent literature on the issues of evaluation and assessment in community colleges.

An Historic Retrospective: A Review of Past Efforts

An historical view suggests many theories and ideologies relating to evaluation and assessment were just beginning to emerge when the NSIEE volume was first published. Debates were developing in the evaluation field between utilization focused study (Patton) and value free evaluation (Scriven), where "use or utility" was the goal for one and "objectivity" and assessing merit were the purposes of the other. Surveys were seen as frequently used instruments for assessment and outside experts developed the systems and processes for evaluation of learning and institutional impact.

In the mid-1980s higher education was beginning to turn its attention to evaluation and assessment just as Campus Compact was entering the scene. As civic engagement emerged larger on the horizon, questions quickly arose about what it was, how it was measured, and what institutions had to do to demonstrate that experiential learning was a credible pedagogy in higher education and in all educational settings.

The late 1980s were marked by a major emphasis on the role of engaging program personnel, even clients, in the evaluation process. This challenged the classical approach that insisted that required "outside experts" and objectivist research methods. Guba and Lincoln (1989) contributed their discussion about the evolution of evaluation in *Fourth Generation Evaluation*, initiating a move toward constructivist theories of learning and assessment. More books about engagement of participants began to surface, notably William Foote Whyte's classic book in 1991, *Participatory Action Research*, focusing organizational studies on the role of engaging program personnel in the evaluation process. Denzin and Lincoln published a large volume, the *Handbook of Qualitative Research* in 1994, and Michael Patton's *Utilization Focused Evaluation* entered its third printing in 1996, with the second edition coming at the same time as the *Strengthening* publication. David Fetterman and colleagues published their first edition of *Empowerment Evaluation* in 1996, and Cousins and Earl published their volume, *Participatory Evaluation in Education: Studies in Evaluation Use and Organizational Learning* a year earlier.

The gates broke open during this period with the rise of phenomenology (Max VanManen, *Researching The Lived Experience*, *1990*) and a flood of critical theories using race, class, and power as areas of focus began to emerge. The classical approaches that insisted on having an outside evaluation expert conducting surveys and other distant methods began to soften. More and more researchers and evaluators were talking about and doing participatory work. At the beginning of the 21st century there would certainly seem to be a sense of parity and established position for qualitative methods of evaluation, including a stress on mixed methods that offered a balanced approach to most assessment questions and issues.

It is important to note that the experiential education community took evaluation and assessment very seriously and made important contributions to the emerging evaluation field. The Council for Adult and Experiential Learning (CAEL) and the National Society for Internships and Experiential Education (NSIEE) partnered with Jossey-Bass, under the CAEL umbrella, to produce over a dozen publications as *New Directions in Experiential Learning.* Long time experts in the field, including Morris Keeton, John Duley, David Kolb, Ronald Fry, Urban Whitaker, Georgine Loaker, Art Chickering, Jane Permaul, Steven Brooks, and many others collaborated extensively. These early NSIEE and CAEL leaders put assessment and evaluation at the heart of the emerging field of experiential education.

NSIEE has kept up the foundational work in areas related to internships and other experiential learning programs. The *NSIEE/NSEE Quarterly* has been publishing articles on assessment and evaluation for decades, focusing more on experiential learning programs, not just service-learning or civic education. More recently NSEE has worked with the Council for the Advancement of Standards in Higher Education (CAS) to develop more than 35 specific standards for high quality experiential learning, focusing on the internship experience. CAS has been working on these issues in higher education since 1979 and has engaged more than 40 organizations to produce standards and guidelines for solid professional practice. There are at least 14 areas of standards development, the last of which (number 14) is assessment and evaluation.

The Council for Adult and Experiential Learning, in collaboration with NSIEE, produced a seminal work on assessing learning, especially prior learning, in Urban Whitaker's book, *Assessing Learning: Standards Principles, and Procedures* (1989). Written as a follow up to Warren Willingham's *Principles in Assessing Experiential Learning* (1977) and the 1988 compilation of assessment information in Susan Simosko's *Assessing Learning: A CAEL Handbook for Faculty*, Whitaker lays out the argument that assessing learning in every context, whether in a classroom or in a field setting, is the same. He sets out 10 principles that cover academic standards and administrative standards. They include topics from "credit should be only awarded for learning, not experience," to "assessment programs should be regularly monitored, reviewed, evaluated and revised as needed to reflect the changes in the needs being served and the state of the assessment arts."

From the outset the early leaders of experiential education, such as Whitaker, insisted that there must always be an assessment process that was both rigorous and flexible, morphing to meet the intended needs of the faculty, students, and institution. He distinguished between "teacher directed, self-directed (but campus monitored….such as internships, service-learning, cooperative education), and undirected learning (prior experiential learning, life and work experience). The book covers principles and procedures for assessing sponsored learning, prior learning, and administrative practices that assure quality assessment. The book was truly a result of years of effort between CAEL and NSIEE leaders and researchers/evaluators to produce a workable document to ensure that assessment was an integral part of every experiential learning program. Whitaker helped with this connection, serving on both the Boards of Directors for CAEL and NSIEE.

Building upon these relationships and this history, NSIEE (in collaboration with the Johnson Foundation, CAEL, and many other higher education organizations) convened a Wingspread Conference on Experiential Learning in 1991. The meeting focused on developing a research agenda for the field and convened more than 40 researchers and practitioners to compile an agenda for future research and evaluation (Giles, Honnet, and Migliore, 1991). The meeting addressed two primary questions: 1) what is the effect of service-learning on intellectual, moral, and citizenship development of participants, and 2) what is the effect of service-learning on the advancement of social institutions and democracy? These two areas of focus led to the development of five areas of importance. They were:

- *The participant:* what are the general effects for the service-learning experience on the individual student?

- *The educational institution:* what is the effect of service-learning on the improvement of the educational system and on specific types of educational institutions?

- *The community:* what is the effect of service-learning on community improvement?

- *Theoretical bases*: how can service-learning research contribute to the development of theories that can further undergird and illuminate service-learning?

- *Program models*: what are the components and outcomes of various models of service-learning?

The framing of these questions and areas of investigation set the tone and focus for research and evaluation not only for service-learning, but experiential education, in general. Almost all of the materials produced in the last twenty years have attempted to address one or more aspects of these critical areas of study.

Moving into the Present and New Collaborators

Organizational activity in the experiential learning world saw Campus Compact and the American Association for Higher Education producing more materials. Under the leadership of Ed Zlotkowski, an NSEE Board member and Chair of the Publication Committee, AAHE published a series of 18 volumes on service-learning in the disciplines, covering some of the most common uses of experiential/service-learning on college campuses. Campus Compact published a *Toolkit on Service-Learning* (2003) and NSEE continued to produce their journal, The *NSEE Quarterly*, with its emphasis on experiential learning, including many pieces on the assessment process. A special issue of *The Michigan Journal on Community Service-Learning* (Howard, Gelmon, and Giles, Fall 2000) was published, focusing exclusively on "strategic directions for service-learning research (and evaluation)." In addition, a later volume of *The Michigan Journal* (2003) published a full issue focused exclusively on Community Based Participatory Research.

A new organization, the International Association for Research on Service-Learning and Community Engagement, was initiated by Andy Furco and Shelley Billig, Furco being a former NSEE Board member and chair of NSEE's Research committee. The group convened first in 2001 in Berkeley and has held successive international meetings ever since. One of the products of these conferences has been a new series on service-learning, *Advances in Service-Learning Research,* edited each year by Shelley Billig from RMC Research and a research colleague from each year's host institution.

During this same period there was a parallel drive by higher education accrediting agencies, state legislatures, and faculty development programs to place evaluation as a central component of quality experiential education programs. Partly guided by new initiatives at the Carnegie Foundation, as well as many agencies charged with accrediting the quality and quantity of civic education offerings, universities were moving to ensure that there were sufficient offerings of experiential learning programs and suitable assessment systems to monitor and guide their progress and impact.

Suffice to say, much has changed in the evaluation world since 1986 with the first volume of *Strengthening*. The remainder of this chapter describes and discusses many of those changes and how institutions are using the new theories and practices to include evaluation and assessment as an integral part of the institutionalization of experiential education in higher education.

Evaluation and Assessment in Higher Education

As indicated above, much has been added to the literature on evaluation in the 25 years since the first volume of *Strengthening* emerged. The last decade has seen the addition of much information and many tools to help guide the evaluation and assessment process. Some of the important work is described below.

In the 1990s a consensus emerged in higher education with the principles proposed in the 1996 American Association of Higher Education [AAHE] Assessment Forum (Appendix A). This document laid out nine principles that would guide the assessment practice in higher education. The principles produced a synthesis between traditional and "social constructivist" assessment. These principles provided an understanding that assessment was a "vehicle for program improvement." Assessment had to be "on-going" and measure outcomes as well as process. Assessment needed to attend to issues of use and important questions necessary for professional conduct of program activities. Lastly, assessment was posited as a necessity in order to meet the responsibilities to students and to the public, ensuring that there was always some measurement and understanding of how and why programs were operated and what impact they had on all involved. The principles cemented the fact that evaluation and assessment were simply integral components of any professional endeavor.

At the end of the 1990s a study was developed, more focused on the K-12 level, to produce a self-assessment system for service-learning. Based on three years of work, the instrument emerged that highlighted and offered important ways to do institutional assessment (Shumer, et al., 2000). The system focused on five important areas of study: *culture and context, philosophy and purpose, policy and parameters, pedagogy and practice, and assessment and accountability.* While focused on school systems, the effort laid a foundation for further examination of the important areas that needed to be addressed in order to determine if service-learning, civic education, and experiential education programs were effective and what impact, if any, they had.

One of the authors of the secondary school self-assessment system, Andy Furco (2002), went on to develop an important self-assessment approach for higher education, called the "Self Assessment Rubric for the Institutionalization of Service-Learning in Higher Education." The rubric is structured around five dimensions, considered key factors for higher education service-learning institutionalization. Each dimension is comprised of several components that characterize that particular area. For each component, a three-stage continuum of development has been established. Progression from *Stage One: Critical Mass Building* to *Stage Three: Sustained Institutionalization* suggests that a campus is moving closer to the full institutionalization of service-learning. The five dimensions included: 1) philosophy and mission of service-learning, 2) faculty support and involvement in service-learning, 3) student support for and involvement in service-learning, 4) community partnerships and participation, and 5) institutional support for service-learning. The reader will see the similarity of these five dimensions to those identified by the original authors of *Strengthening* in 1986.

The field was also guided by an important volume, sponsored by Campus Compact, titled "Assessing Service-Learning and Civic Engagement "(Gelmon, et al., 2001). Contributing to an

248

informed by a shift in emphasis, the authors discuss the movement in higher education from a traditional focus on teaching to a stronger emphasis on learning, as was seen in the 1996 AAHE Principles for Assessing Students Learning. This shift requires all involved to be more actively connected to the assessment process in order to measure learning on all levels. From students, to faculty, to community partnerships and organizations, addressing learning concerns requires assessment become an integral part of both instruction and any effort to measure the impact of the service and/or experiential component of the curriculum. Gelmon and her colleagues suggested that there are five levels of concern when it came to assessing any form of experiential or field-based instruction. These include

- selecting the appropriate person to lead the assessment process,

- conceptualizing what was actually going to be assessed,

- determining who was responsible for conducting the assessment,

- choosing the methods and approaches to be used in the assessment/evaluation process,

- analyzing the findings to determine where and with whom they should be shared.

This seminal work by Gelmon and her colleagues provides a wide range of suggestions that address these five concerns, and describe in detail the kinds of methods used to gather the data for the evaluation process.

Another Campus Compact document, *Introduction to the Service-Learning Toolkit* (2003), summarized what had been written earlier, providing excerpts from the earlier noted volumes. Gelmon asks the critical question: "How do we know our work makes a difference?" Other authors describe the variety of assessment strategies available to the field, reframing the original questions about what is the purpose of the evaluation, who should be involved, how will information be collected, and how will be it shared?

A more detailed study of assessment and evaluation was conducted by the Campus Compact in partnership with the American Association of Community Colleges. In this document, *The Community's College: Indictors of Engagement at Two Year Institutions* (Zlotkowski, et. al., 2004), efforts were made to define and describe the elements necessary for effective evaluation. The thirteen indicators of engagement included these major areas:

- Mission and Purpose

- Administrative and Academic Leadership

- Disciplines, Departments, and Interdisciplinary Work,

- Forums for Fostering Public Dialogue,

- Student Voice.

Each element was an important component that contributed to a civically engaged campus.

Another addition to the literature placed the assessment and evaluation work in a larger context, namely citizen education. In their book examining civic and values education in higher education, *Educating Citizens* (Colby, et al., 2003), the authors study the way higher education contributes to preparing students for lives of moral and civic responsibility. They place the role of assessment and accountability in a central and critical position in the overall function of higher education to implement and measure social and civic action.

As can be seen in the preceding overview, much of the last decade has had an abundance of work on civic and service-learning. Noted earlier, this development has seen a movement from expert evaluator to participatory process. This trend is captured nicely in a 2009 publication on *The Future Of Service-Learning* (Strait and Lima, 2009). In that book Shumer documents the changing trends in research and evaluation, moving from mixed designs, to qualitative/interpretive work, to participatory studies that empower communities and participants, to community-based research. Strand and colleagues (Strand, Marullo, Cutforth, Stoecker, and Donahoe, 2003) emphasize these same qualities when engaging in Community-Based Participatory Research. In all of these endeavors, the members of the community become partners in conceiving, developing, implementing, and interpreting the evaluation outcomes. Evaluation eventually becomes an essential component of all experiential learning programs, and the role of assessment becomes the key activity as the institutions focused more on learning from all involved, rather than just delivering instruction through didactic means.

CAEL continued its collaboration with others and developed other pieces on the importance of assessment for quality assurance in experiential learning. In 2005 they produced a document, *Principles in Practice: Assessing Adult Learner Focused Institutions* (ALFI), which included a series of case studies of institutions that participated in a Lumina Foundation funded effort to explain how to conduct high quality work with adult centered institutions. The effort resulted in the development of the ALFI Toolkit, which is made up of two survey instruments. One deals with institutional issues, the Institutional Self Assessment Survey (ISAS), which addresses issues related to activities, policies, and practices. It covers items addressing the eight principles of Effectiveness for Serving Adult Learners. A second instrument in the toolkit is the Adult Learning Inventory (ALI), which measures satisfaction levels of adult learners with their educational programs.

An important work on internships (Schweitzer and King, 2009) chronicles the lengthy and challenging process of conducting an internship in a college context. The process ends with "culmination" and evaluation, where students undertake a self-assessment by identifying what they have learned and accomplished as part of the experience. Mary King has been a major player in NSEE's work related to Standards and Professional Development in the last decade.

Although there is more that could be elaborated upon, it might be fitting to end with a recent piece by the American Association for Community Colleges designed to help higher education institutionalize service and experiential education. Called *Creating a Climate for Service Learning Success (*Jeadron and Robinson, 2010), the book, in many ways, covers the same issues developed in the first *Strengthening Experiential Education Within Your Institution.* Its focus is on the key components of any good experiential education program offered in any institution at any level, including:

- Campus climate

- Student engagement and leadership

- Faculty development and engagement

- Curricular integration

- Community collaboration

- Administrative involvement and support

- Program development, management, and assessment

- Sustainability and institutionalization

Thus, we have come full circle. Materials published in 2010 are remarkably similar to those developed in 1986. A major focus is ultimately concerned with issues of stability and institutionalization and moving programs from the "margin to the mainstream." Experiential education, in the context of all the developments in the past 25 years, is still focused on some of the basics necessary for any quality experiential learning program. Some of those items are articulated in the next portion of this chapter.

So, What Do We Evaluate?

Based on the recent history and development of the field, those concerned with strengthening experiential education in their institutions need to address a variety of concerns and issues. First, it is clear from the introductory comments that the *change from teaching to learning* shifts the evaluation process to measuring student learning, faculty/departmental learning, institutional learning, and, as Giles and Cruz have determined, community learning. Each of these elements is central to making the case that, in fact, experiential programs meet the critical goal of any education program – they must demonstrate *that those involved are learning something.*

Knowing that learning is happening, it is also important to know whether the *purpose* of *the experiential learning program is being achieved.* Since there are so many reasons/goals for doing experiential learning in higher education, from service, to social justice, to civic engagement, to community empowerment, to career knowledge and skill development, to social transformation, each *reason or goal* serves as a focal point for developing an evaluation effort that determines whether or not these purposes are being achieved.

Along with these purposes is the general notion of *impact.* What kind of impact does the experiential program have on all the *stakeholders* in the process: on the students, on the faculty, on the community, on the organization, etc.? Impacts can vary from attitudes and dispositions, as John Patrick (2000) has identified, to actual changes in health conditions of individuals, reduction in crime, or improvement in reading and math proficiency, etc. Impacts can also be directed at institutional culture and offerings, such as expanding the number of departments that embrace experiential learning approaches, increasing the number of faculty who teach using principles of civic engagement and community involvement (Shumer, 2003), or changing the attitude of college presidents and/or administrations to involve more institutional financial support for community-based, experiential learning programs.

Finally, when all is said and done, strengthening experiential education in your institution requires the *inclusion of evaluation processes at every level of operation and in every activity* that is undertaken. As NSIEE's founding mothers and fathers insisted and spelled out in the original *Strengthening* in 1986, all learning must be documented, including experiential activities, if we truly want to claim that it is learning. Evaluation strategies, like those outlined above, demonstrate and document that learning has occurred and actually contributes to the learning outcomes by making the student a self-conscious participant in the process. In other words, no matter what is done in an institution, experiential education is strengthened when evaluation becomes an integral part of the culture of the organization.

References

Campus Compact (2003). *Introduction to the service-learning toolkit: Readings and resources for faculty.* Providence, RI: Brown University.

Colby, A., Ehrlich, T., Beaumont, E., and Stephens, J. (2003). *Educating citizens: Preparing America's undergraduates for lives of moral and civic responsibility.* San Francisco, CA: Jossey-Bass.

Council for Adult and Experiential Learning (2005). *Principles in practice: assessing adult learning focused institutions.* Chicago, ILL: CAEL.

Cousins, B., and Earl, L. (1995). *Participatory evaluation in education: Studies in evaluation use and organizational learning.* Bristol, PA: The Falmer Press

Denzin, N., and Lincoln, Y. (Eds) (1994). Handbook of qualitative research. Thousand Oaks, CA: Sage.

Fetterman, D., Kaftarian, S., and Wandersman, A. (Eds) (1996). *Empowerment evaluation: Knowledge and tools for self assessment and accountability.* Thousand Oaks, CA: Sage Publications, Inc.

Furco, A. (Revised 2002). Self-assessment rubric for the institutionalization of service-learning in higher education. Service-Learning Research and Development Center, University of California, Berkeley.

Gelmon, S., Holland, B., Driscoll, A., Spring, A., and Kerrigan, S. (2001), *Assessing service-learning and civic engagement: principles and techniques.* Boston, MA: Campus Compact.

Giles, D., Honnet, E. P., and Migliore, S. (1991). *Research agenda for combining service and learning.* Raleigh, NC: National Society for Internships and Experiential Education.

Guba, E. and Lincoln, Y. (1989). *Fourth generation evaluation.* Thousand Oaks, CA: Sage.

Howard, J., Gelmon, S., and Giles, D. (Ed) (2000 Fall). *The Michigan Journal of Community Service Learning.* Special Edition on Research. OCSL Press, University of Michigan Volume 1.

Howard, J. (Ed) (2003). *The Michigan Journal of Community Service Learning.* . OCSL Press, University of Michigan. Volume 9, Issue 3.

Jeandron, C., and Robinson, G. (2010). Creating a climate for service-learning success.

American Association of Community Colleges.

Kendall, J. and Associates (1990). *Combining service and learning.* Raleigh, NC: National Society for Internships and Experiential Learning. Volume I.

Patrick, J. (2000). Introduction to education for civic engagement in democracy. In S. Mann and J. Patrick, (Eds), *Education for Civic Engagement in Democracy: Service-Learning and Other Promising Practices.* ERIC Clearinghouse for Social Studies/Social Science Education. Bloomington, IN.

Patton, M.Q. (1996). *Utilization focused valuation.* Thousand Oaks, CA: Sage Publications, Inc. 3rd Edition.

Schweitzer, H.F. and King, M. (2009). *The successful internship: Transformation and empowerment in experiential learning.* Belmont, CA: Brooks/Cole Cengage Learning.

Shumer, R., Duttweiler, P., Furco, A., Hengel, M., and Willems, G., (2000). Shumer's self-assessment for service-learning. St. Paul, MN: Center for Experiential and Service-Learning, Department of Work, Community, and Family Education, College of Education and Human Development, University of Minnesota.

Shumer, R. (2003). *Civic engagement audit: Metropolitan State University.* St. Paul, MN: Center for Community-Based Learning, Metropolitan State University.

Shumer, R. (2009). "New directions in service-learning research and evaluation: participation and use are key." In J. Strait and M. B. Lima (Eds) *The future of service-learning.* Sterling, VA: Stylus Publishing, Inc., pp.191-205.

Simosko, S., et al. *Assessing learning: a CAEL handbook for faculty.* Columbia, MD: Council for Adult and Experiential Learning.

Strait, J. and Lima, M.B. (Eds) (2009). *The future of service-learning.* Sterling, VA: Stylus Publishing, LLC.

Strand, K., Marullo, S., Cutforth, N., Stoecker, R., and Donahue, P. (2003*). Community based research and higher education.* San Francisco, CA: Jossey-Bass.

Van Manen, M. (1990*). Researching lived experience: Human science for an action sensitive pedagogy.* New York, NY: SUNY Press.

Whitaker, U. (1989). *Assessing learning: standards, principles, and procedures.* Philadelphia, PA: Council for Adult and Experiential Learning.

Zlotkowski, E., Duffy, D., Franco, R., Gelmon, S., Norvell, K., Meeropol, J., and Jones, S. (2004). *The community's college.* Providence, RI: Campus Compact.

Whyte, W. F. (Ed) (1991). *Participatory action research.* Newbury Park, CA: Sage

Willingham, W. (1977*). Principles* of *Good Practice in Assessing Experiential Learning.* Columbia, MD.

APPENDIX A

9 Principles of Good Practice for Assessing Student Learning

Astin AW; Banta TW; Cross KP; El-Khawas E; Ewell PT; Hutchings P; Marchese TJ; McClenney KM; Mentkowski M; Miller MA; Moran ET; Wright BD. 9 principles of good practice for assessing student learning. AAHE Assessment Forum, **July 25, 1996.** http://www.aahe.org/principl.htm

Note: These nine principles, which were created by a panel of assessment experts [identified above] and revised in 1996 and provide a fundamental basis and starting place to assist in the design of an assessment plan for an academic program.

"This document was developed under the auspices of the AAHE Assessment Forum with support from the Fund for the Improvement of Postsecondary Education with additional support for publication and dissemination from the Exxon Education Foundation. Copies may be made without restriction."[5]

1. The assessment of student learning begins with educational values. Assessment is not an end in itself but a vehicle for educational improvement. Its effective practice, then, begins with and enacts a vision of the kinds of learning we most value for students and strive to help them achieve. Educational values should drive not only *what* we choose to assess but also *how* we do so. Where questions about educational mission and values are skipped over, assessment threatens to be an exercise in measuring what's easy, rather than a process of improving what we really care about.

2. Assessment is most effective when it reflects an understanding of learning as multidimensional, integrated, and revealed in performance over time. Learning is a complex process. It entails not only what students know but what they can do with what they know; it involves not only knowledge and abilities but values, attitudes, and habits of mind that affect both academic success and performance beyond the classroom. Assessment should reflect these understandings by employing a diverse array of methods, including those that call for actual performance, using them over time so as to reveal change, growth, and increasing degrees of integration. Such an approach aims for a more complete and accurate picture of learning, and therefore firmer bases for improving our students' educational experience.

3.Assessment works best when the programs it seeks to improve have clear, explicitly stated purposes. Assessment is a goal-oriented process. It entails comparing educational performance with educational purposes and expectations -- those derived from the institution's mission, from faculty intentions in program and course design, and from knowledge of students' own goals. Where program purposes lack specificity or agreement, assessment as a process pushes a campus toward clarity about where to aim and what standards to apply; assessment also prompts attention to where and how program goals will be taught and learned. Clear, shared, implementable goals are the cornerstone for assessment that is focused and useful.

4.Assessment requires attention to outcomes but also and equally to the experiences that lead to those outcomes. Information about outcomes is of high importance; where students "end up" matters greatly. But to improve outcomes, we need to know about student experience along the way -- about the curricula, teaching, and kind of student effort that lead to particular outcomes. Assessment can help us understand which students learn best under what conditions; with such knowledge comes the capacity to improve the whole of their learning.

5. Assessment works best when it is ongoing not episodic. Assessment is a process whose power is cumulative. Though isolated, "one-shot" assessment can be better than none, improvement is best fostered when assessment entails a linked series of activities undertaken over time. This may mean tracking the process of individual students, or of cohorts of students; it may mean collecting the same examples of student performance or using the same instrument semester after semester. The point is to monitor progress toward intended goals in a spirit of continuous improvement. Along the way, the assessment process itself should be evaluated and refined in light of emerging insights.

6. Assessment fosters wider improvement when representatives from across the educational community are involved. Student learning is a campus-wide responsibility, and assessment is a way of enacting that responsibility. Thus, while assessment efforts may start small, the aim over time is to involve people from across the educational community. Faculty play an especially important role, but assessment's questions can't be fully addressed without participation by student-affairs educators, librarians, administrators, and students. Assessment may also involve individuals from beyond the campus (alumni/ae, trustees, employers) whose experience can enrich the sense of appropriate aims and standards for learning. Thus understood, assessment is not a task for small groups of experts but a collaborative activity; its aim is wider, better-informed attention to student learning by all parties with a stake in its improvement.

7. Assessment makes a difference when it begins with issues of use and illuminates questions that people really care about. Assessment recognizes the value of information in the process of improvement. But to be useful, information must be connected to issues or questions that people really care about. This implies assessment approaches that produce evidence that relevant parties will find credible, suggestive, and applicable to decisions that need to be made. It means thinking in advance about how the information will be used, and by whom. The point of assessment is not to gather data and return "results"; it is a process that starts with the questions of decision-makers, that involves them in the gathering and interpreting of data, and that informs and helps guide continuous improvement.

8. Assessment is most likely to lead to improvement when it is part of a larger set of conditions that promote change. Assessment alone changes little. Its greatest contribution comes on campuses where the quality of teaching and learning is visibly valued and worked at. On such campuses, the push to improve educational performance is a visible and primary goal of leadership; improving the quality of undergraduate education is central to the institution's planning, budgeting, and personnel decisions. On such campuses, information about learning outcomes is seen as an integral part of decision making, and avidly sought.

9. Through assessment, educators meet responsibilities to students and to the public. There is a compelling public stake in education. As educators, we have a responsibility to the publics that support or depend on us to provide information about the ways in which our students meet goals and expectations. But that responsibility goes beyond the reporting of such information; our deeper obligation -- to ourselves, our students, and society -- is to improve. Those to whom educators are accountable have a corresponding obligation to support such attempts at improvement.

Author

ROBERT SHUMER PhD has been involved in education for more than 40 years. He has taught from middle school through graduate school. Dr. Shumer is the former Director of Field Studies at UCLA and the past founding Director of the National Service-Learning Clearinghouse and The Center for Experiential Education and Service Learning at the University of Minnesota. He is also the past President of the Minnesota Evaluation Association and current board member of the International Association for Research on Service-Learning and Community Engagement. He currently teaches courses on civic engagement, participatory evaluation, and constructivist curriculum and has conducted more than 25 research/evaluation studies on national service, service-learning, civic engagement, and participatory evaluation. Rob has served on several national organizational boards. He was a member of the National Society for Internships and Experiential Education from 1982-2001 and served as the Chair of the Secondary Education Special Interest Group from 1985-87. He was also a NSIEE Board member from 1985-1988, and served as the Research Committee co-chair from 1988-90.

IS EXPERIENCE THE BEST TEACHER?

David Thornton Moore
New York University, Gallatin School of Individualized Study

A paradox haunts the college internship. On the one hand, students tend to see it as a ticket to a solid career, whether the work is exciting or dull; and some faculty and professional associations promote it as a pedagogical marvel that teaches students about the world, their communities, and themselves.

On the other hand, many faculty, if they think about experiential education at all, regard it with disdain or grudgingly tolerate it because it generates enrollments. Moreover, internship programs tend to be located at the institutional margins, not in the core academic units. So the old adage begs the question: Is experience really the best teacher?

After more than 30 years in the world of experiential learning as both a teacher and a researcher, I am here to say that the internship can be a robust learning experience *when it is done right*. Far too often, however, it is *not* done right, and in that case it is not worth the credit it generates or the energy and resources it demands.

My complaint with the majority of internships is not only that they entail the exploitation of students by employers seeking cheap labor and by schools charging tuition for minimal pedagogical effort–although surely those are serious problems, as Ross Perlin argues in *Intern Nation*. Rather, my discomfort with them is that students too often do not learn the kinds of things higher education should be about.

To be sure, they usually learn *something* by virtue of first-hand experience in a business, a museum, or a community organization–skills that might lead to a career, exposure to an important social issue, or insight into their own strengths and weaknesses. But without rigorous, guided reflection on the experience, they generally don't learn much beyond the kinds of things one gets from a part-time job.

I say that on the basis of having supervised, observed, and interviewed scores of student-interns in work placements ranging from a community newspaper to a veterinary office, from a history museum to a curriculum-development firm. In fact, what they learn most deeply is that fragment of the work process for which they are held responsible. They spend much of their energy figuring out ways to look competent enough to avoid getting yelled at by the boss and to enhance their chances of getting hired when they graduate. They learn the setting's way of doing things, but not alternative practices, or competing theories about social processes. The skills they pick up are often quite local, and they certainly do not learn "all about the industry," as some educators claim. Since their primary motivation tends toward finding a career, they are all right with that.

The theory of situated cognition, that the things we know and the ways we think are particular to the contexts where we encounter them, gives us a handle on the problem. Jerome Bruner, for example, distinguishes between the linear, propositional, and abstract modes of thought that we privilege in schools and the actional and results-oriented modes that we encounter in the world of work. Student-interns, who might learn from exploring the tensions between those forms of thought and action, tend to resist that effort: They prefer to "go native."

Experiential educators claim to engage learners with the real-world versions of things they study in school. But the situationists show that those things do not look the same in the real world as they do in the classroom. Take poverty, for example. Serving dinner in a soup kitchen, as valuable an experience as that might be, simply does not expose a person to the same kinds of information, ideas, or thought processes as does a course on the sociology and politics of homelessness. Interrogating the experience and the theory together can be the strength of the internship–if it happens.

The challenge for experiential educators, then, is to help students explore the intersection between theory and practice. Imagine, for example, a student who is taking a course on organizational sociology and reading Max Weber on bureaucracy; at the same time, she is doing an internship at the New York City Department of Education, surely one of the world's great bureaucracies. How does she examine the relationship between Weber and the DOE? How does one form of knowledge affect the other? And how do her professors support that two-way transfer of learning?

Some programs work hard at producing that intersection between the academic and the practical. Too many, however, leave it to chance, resorting to halfway measures like learning contracts that cannot anticipate all the educational opportunities, or journals that end up sounding like "here's what I did and what I liked about it," or final papers that report intuitive insights without subjecting them to intensive critique. Sadly, some programs do even less than that, essentially awarding credit (and charging tuition!) for the raw experience of work.

The further an internship program slides toward the latter end of the spectrum, the less educational integrity it has. By analogy, imagine a student reading a novel. Think of the novel as the functional equivalent of the work experience, the raw material. The pedagogical question is, would an English professor be satisfied leaving the student to his own devices to make sense of the novel, or would she prefer that he approach it with some understanding of literary theory, critical methods, and history? Higher education is not simply about having an experience–everyone does that. Rather, it is about learning to examine, analyze, and critique that experience, whether reading a novel or managing the samples closet in a fashion house.

Bridging the gap between the academic and pragmatic modes of thought is a worthwhile enterprise, one that engages practical wisdom as well as abstract theory, one that pushes ethical thought and action as well as scholarly inquiry, and one that connects the university to the world in bold, creative ways. But succumbing to student demands for internships on the grounds that they are a necessary step toward careers, and selling credit for them, does not do higher education proud.

Author

DAVID MOORE has been on the faculty of the Gallatin School of Individualized Study at New York University since 1982; he was associate dean for academic affairs for more than five years, and was named Teacher of the Year in 2013. An educational anthropologist with a doctorate from Harvard, he has been doing ethnographic research on high-school and college-level experiential learning for more than 30 years. His articles about internships and service-learning have been published in such journals as *Anthropology and Education Quarterly, Harvard Educational Review, Learning Inquiry, Journal of Experiential Education, Anthropology of Work Review,* and *Michigan Journal of Community Service Learning.* With chapters in seven books on workplace and experiential learning, he is co-author of *Working Knowledge: Work-Based Learning and Education Reform* (RoutledgeFalmer, 2004), and author of *Engaged Learning in the Academy: Challenges and Possibilities* (Palgrave Macmillan, 2013). A long-time member of NSEE, he was a board member from 1986-89 and edited the organization's newsletter, *Experiential Education,* during the same period; in 2004, he was named Researcher of the Year, and in 2011 became a Pioneer in Experiential Learning. An affiliated faculty member of NSEE's Experiential Education Academy, he has conducted workshops in Dubai and Tampa.

CPSIA information can be obtained
at www.ICGtesting.com
Printed in the USA
BVHW040820030320
573937BV00010B/49